E. G. (Edward George) King

The Psalms in three Collections

E. G. (Edward George) King

The Psalms in three Collections

ISBN/EAN: 9783744778763

Printed in Europe, USA, Canada, Australia, Japan

Cover: Foto ©Lupo / pixelio.de

More available books at **www.hansebooks.com**

THE PSALMS

IN THREE COLLECTIONS

TRANSLATED WITH NOTES

BY

E. G. KING D.D.

PART I FIRST COLLECTION (Pss. I—XLI)

WITH PREFACE

BY THE

BISHOP OF DURHAM

CAMBRIDGE
DEIGHTON BELL AND CO.
LONDON GEORGE BELL AND SONS
1898

[All Rights reserved.]

Cambridge:
PRINTED BY J. AND C. F. CLAY,
AT THE UNIVERSITY PRESS.

PREFATORY NOTE.

THE variety and excellence of Commentaries on the Psalter seem to leave little room for fresh illustration of the text; but the Psalter is as inexhaustible as the aspirations of the human soul, and I cannot but think that Dr King has made an original and suggestive contribution to the understanding of it. It was my happiness to hear several expositions of Psalms given by Dr King in sermons at Madingley and Gayton, and I expressed a wish that he would publish, at least in outline, the substance of what he said. The present book is an instalment of the work; and I trust that in due time the remainder will follow.

The notes require careful study, but, if I may speak from my own experience, they will repay it. They are not designed to save the reader from the trouble of thought, but to stimulate him to independent reflection and enquiries which lie within his reach. They constantly remind me of Bengel's pregnant sentences—and I know no higher praise—which point to a conclusion rather than develop it. The scholar indeed if he is to profit by his teacher's words must share his teacher's labour. The memorable saying in which Heraclitus sums up the method of the Delphian king describes the ideal method of the true master: He neither tells nor hides but gives a sign.

In this lies the peculiar merit of the notes. Dr King appears to me, as far as I may presume to judge, to have a natural sympathy with the characteristics of Hebrew thought and of Hebrew poetry. For him, as for the old Hebrew scholars, a single word suggests real if remote associations; and feeling, as they did, that 'all creation was one act at once,' he recognises correspondences between different spheres of the Divine work and working. Under this aspect the relations of the fortunes of the nation to the fortunes of the individual, of the Messianic people to the Messiah, of the vicissitudes of Nature to the vicissitudes of Life (see *e.g.* Pss. xxix., xxx.; xix.) offer fertile subjects for reflection. Even the close analysis of the structure of a Psalm brings out subtle and unexpected lines of thought (see *e.g.* Ps. xv., cxi., cxii.). Difference of opinion will naturally exist as to special applications of the general principles, but the general principles will, I believe, commend themselves if they are fairly weighed; and in all these ways the student is led to consider indications of the harmony which underlies 'the mighty sum of things for ever speaking' in spite of the disorders wrought by the Fall; and the frequent parallels which are drawn from great poets shew how men have striven unweariedly in all ages towards the truth which the voice of the Spirit has revealed to us.

It will be seen from what I have said that the book, while based upon a critical foundation, is specially adapted for meditative and, in the fullest sense of the word, devotional reading. It is this which gives it a peculiar claim on attention at the present time. There is among us far more reading about the Bible than reading of the Bible. Popular interest in questions of pure criticism tends to divert thought from the Scriptures themselves to problems, often insoluble, as to their origin and history. But, however attractive and even important the investigations may be which are thus raised, we are spiritually concerned not with them, but with the meaning of the texts which we have received. We have beyond question the Old Testament as it was read in the apostolic age and accepted by the Lord Himself as the Divine Charter of the hope of Israel. Our first duty therefore is to spare no pains in order to understand its teaching, remembering the necessary canon: *Omnis Scriptura Sacra eo Spiritu debet legi quo facta est*. And in this connexion it may be worth while to notice that with two exceptions, all the primary passages which are quoted in the Epistle to the Hebrews to illustrate the true nature of the Person and Work of Christ are taken from the Psalms. Some of these may perhaps seem to the hasty reader to be far-fetched, but I venture to hope that the course of interpretation which Dr King points out will be found to fully justify the use which is made of them, and that the apostolic usage itself in this respect will open the way to a more intelligent apprehension of the place which the writings of the Old Covenant occupied and still occupy, in the training of the people of God.

It is, then, because I believe that Dr King's notes, which some at first sight may be tempted to think obscure and mystical—a convenient excuse for unwillingness to think—are fitted to encourage and to reward personal study that I heartily commend them to those who hold that the secrets of the LORD are disclosed to such as seek for them with watchfulness and patience in living oracles. Just so far as we are enabled to learn how the Spirit spoke to our fathers in the days of old, we shall come to recognise the messages which He addresses to us to-day in our own language.

B. F. DUNELM.

AUCKLAND CASTLE,
Innocents' Day, 1897.

INTRODUCTION.

THIS book, which is the outcome of some years spent in lecturing on Hebrew in Cambridge followed by many more years in a Country Parish, does not claim to be a complete Commentary on the Psalms. Those who seek for grammatical notes will find them abundantly supplied elsewhere. The task that the writer has set himself has been to shew the leading thought and poetical structure of each Psalm and to do this, as far as possible, by marginal notes and by the arrangement of the text.

The book is intended for the devotional use of the educated English reader and for such of the Clergy as are not afraid of reverent criticism.

The Arrangement of Psalms in the Psalter. It is now generally admitted by competent scholars that the arrangement of the Psalter in Five Books is not the original arrangement. "The *natural* division of the Psalter appears......to be in *three* parts, Ps. i.—xli., Ps. xlii.—lxxxix., Ps. xc.—cl.: the division into *five* parts is generally supposed to have been accomplished later, in imitation of the Pentateuch, Ps. xlii.—lxxxix. being broken into two at Ps. lxxii. the subscription to which would form a natural point of division, and Ps. xc.—cl. being divided at Ps. cvi. where v. 48 was adapted by its contents to mark also the conclusion of a Book" (Dr Driver, *Introduction*, p. 351).

Graetz quotes both the Midrash and Epiphanius in support of his assertion that the Five Books of the Psalms were a Jewish imitation of the Pentateuch. Graetz shews that even the number of the Psalms was determined by this arrangement. The custom of the Synagogue was to read through the Pentateuch once in a three years' cycle. Now, in a three years' cycle, the number of Sabbaths, not coinciding with a Feast-day, will vary from 147 to 150; in order therefore to provide a 'Lesson' for each Sabbath the Pentateuch was divided into 150 sections and was thus read through in the three years. A similar arrangement was adopted for the Psalms which were thus made to vary from 147 (Jerusalem Talmud, *Sabb.* p. 15, quoted by Graetz) to 150. If in the three years' cycle the number of Sabbaths was 147 instead of 150 certain Psalms would be combined and read as one. This will explain the fact that different Congregations had different divisions for the Psalter, *e.g.* the Babylonian Jews read Pss. i. and ii. together, while the Septuagint read Pss. ix., x. as one Psalm and also Pss. cxiv., cxv., while they retained the number 150 by dividing Pss. cxvi. and cxlvii. each into two. To this question we shall have occasion to return; meanwhile the reader is asked never to lose sight of the fact that the present form of the Psalter has been determined by the liturgical use of the Synagogue.

As Dr Driver has said, "the *natural* division of the Psalter" would be in Three Collections rather than in Five Books. The present work will follow this natural division. It is impossible now to restore these Collections to their original form, but the writer feels that something may be done to determine the conditions under which each Collection was made, and that the historical method is the truest and most profitable method of study.

But though we are justified in speaking of the *Three Collections* we do not mean to imply that the form in which they have come down to us exactly corresponds with the form in which each Collection was made. Thus, for example, Pss. i., ii. were added as an Introduction to the whole Psalter; P's. l. was taken from its original position among the 'Asaph' Psalms probably because each of the three cycles would end at the '*Asaph*' or Feast of the Ingathering (cf. Pss. l., c. and cl.). This will appear more clearly when we treat of the 'Asaph' Psalms.

It is, so to speak, an accident that the First Collection coincides with the First Book (Pss. i.—xli.). In this Collection I have however included (pp. 40—66) those alphabetical Psalms which properly belong to the Third Collection. This seemed necessary in order that the whole group of alphabetical Psalms might be studied together and that certain remarkable characteristics which I have pointed out in the alphabetical Psalms of the First Collection might be compared with those of the Third Collection.

Titles and Authorship of Psalms. The Psalms of the First Collection are practically all assigned to David by their titles, but the reader is reminded that the titles *form no part of the original Hebrew text* and consequently that the authorship of any Psalm is known only by tradition. These traditions are most valuable and they are comparatively old since most of them were known to the Septuagint translators (circ. 200 B.C.). But, on the other hand, there are several instances in which the title in the Septuagint differs entirely from that of the Hebrew. Thus they assign Ps. cxxxvii. to Jeremiah, Pss. cxxxviii. cxlvi.—cxlviii. to Haggai and Zachariah. Evidently the titles in the Hebrew were not fully recognized as a binding tradition at the date of this translation, viz. 200 B.C.; but David's date is 1000 B.C., i.e. 800 years earlier. Every candid reader will admit that such traditions of authorship are not to be accepted against strong internal evidence of later date.

There was a growing tendency to ascribe Psalms to David even when

INTRODUCTION. vii

they were anonymous in the Hebrew text; thus the Syriac translators add the name of David to P'ss. xxxiii., xliii., lxxi., xciii., xcix., civ., cxxiii., cxxxvii. (see Graetz, p. 89), and the Septuagint do not hesitate to ascribe to David an apocryphal Psalm cli., which does not occur in the Hebrew text, and even to give the circumstances under which he wrote it!

Who is the speaker in the Psalms? It is difficult for the English reader to realize that "I" in the Psalms can refer to anything except an individual. Still the fact remains that, even in prose, "I" is used of the whole community or nation. Thus Numb. xx. 19, "If we drink of thy water, I and my cattle, then will I give the price thereof: let me only,...pass through on my feet": Judg. i. 3, "And Judah said unto Simeon his brother, Come up with me into my lot" etc. (see many other passages in Driver's *Introduction*, p. 336). Still more frequent was this in poetry, *e.g.* Is. xii. 1, 2, "In that day thou shalt say, I will give thanks unto thee O Lord; for though thou wast angry with me thine anger is turned away" etc. This is virtually a Psalm and the context shews that the words are put on the lips, not of an individual but, of Israel. Jer. x. 19, 20, "Woe is me for my hurt!...my children are gone forth of me" etc. See also Lam. i. 11—16, 18—22 and the whole of Chap. iii. These are but a few instances out of many, but they may suffice to shew that in certain and undoubted cases the Nation or Community of Israel was personified, and that too in a most minute and striking manner quite alien to our Western thought.

If we regard the same question from an historical point of view we note that Revelation came rather through God's dealings with the Nation than with individuals: God was the Father of Israel long before He was recognized as the Father of the individual. The individualism of a modern Christian Hymn would have been quite impossible in Old Testament times.

Since, however, the Psalms were written by individuals, even though they were intended to express the voice of Israel, we should naturally expect that the joys, hopes or sorrows of the time would be moulded in a personal form.

In a letter of Tennyson's, speaking of his poem *In Memoriam*, he says: "'I' is not always the author speaking of himself, but the voice of the human race speaking thro' him" (*Memoir*, p. 305). If it be so in the case of a Poet in an introspective age, how much more shall an Inspired Writer merge his personality in that of the Nation whose future was to mould the whole religion of the world.

The Christian believes that, in Christ, all God's thoughts for Israel have found their completion. If this be so, and if the Psalms are the voice (not of an individual Israelite however great, but) of Israel, then it follows that the Psalms, though not all Messianic, will all become in a certain sense a voice of Christ.

INTRODUCTION.

One great advantage of studying the Psalms in Three Collections rather than in Five Books is that attention is thereby directed to the remarkable interchange of the Divine Names, the First Collection being *Jehovistic*, the Second *Elohistic*, and the Third again *Jehovistic*. If the most holy Name of God had been, in the Second Collection, changed into Elohim through motives of reverence, it is scarcely likely that it would again have appeared in the Third Collection which is of still later date. I must not anticipate the discussion of this point, but when the Three Collections are finished I shall hope to shew the reason for the interchange of the Divine Names. In the translation where the most holy Name occurs I have used the symbol YHVH merely to indicate the letters of the Tetragrammaton. The word Jehovah is, of course, an absolutely impossible form, while the modern pronunciation Yahveh is, in my opinion, incorrect; it has, however, the merit of consisting only of two syllables and the reader may, if he please, give this sound to the letters YHVH.

The Bishop of Durham, at whose suggestion I commenced this work, has very kindly read the proof-sheets as they passed through the Press: while thanking him for his kindness, I wish it to be understood that he is in no way responsible for any opinions I may have expressed.

The labour has been to me a labour of love and of ever-growing interest and delight. Most gladly would I communicate this delight to the reader in the only way in which it is possible—by inciting him also to labour in the same inexhaustible field.

GAYTON RECTORY, BLISWORTH.
The Festival of St Thomas, 1897.

TABLE OF CONTENTS

(WITH LITURGICAL USE OF CERTAIN PSALMS).

N.B. The letters S, W, E, signify the use in the Synagogue, Western Church and English Church respectively.

PSALM		PAGES
I	Easter Day (W). Ps. II Easter Day (E): Christmas (W)	1–4
III, IV	Used as Morning and Evening Hymns (W)	7–9
V	A Psalm of the 'two ways'; v. 8 "*Dirige*..." was the origin of the word *Dirige*	10, 11
VI	Penitential Psalm (Ash-Wednesday (E)); application to Israel and to Christ	12, 13
VII	A Psalm of Divine Judgement. Used for *Purim* (S)	14, 15
VIII	A Pæan of Creation; ignores the Fall: Ascension Day (W, E)	16, 17
IX, X	Partially alphabetical; Introduction to Alphabetical Psalms; the order of the Hebrew alphabet not the same as now	18–25
XXV, XXXIV, XXXVII	Alphabetical Psalms; the use of the Covenant number *ten*; all Alphabetical Psalms of the First Collection are irregular after the same type; reasons for this	26–39
CXI, CXII, CXIX, CXLV	All being Alphabetical Psalms of the *Third* Collection, are introduced here for purposes of comparison	40–66
XI–XIV	Sunday Matins (W)	69–75
XV	Ascension Day (E)	76, 77
XVI	Easter Eve (W)	78–80
XVII, XVIII		80–89
XIX	The Poets' Psalm: Christmas (W, E): Ascension (W)	90–94
XX	For days of tribulation (S): Accession Service (E)	95, 96
XXI	Accession Service (E): Ascension (E)	97–99
XXII	Good Friday (W, E)	100–103
XXIII	At the Handwashing before meals (S); at the distribution of the Bread (Liturgy of St James)	104–107

TABLE OF CONTENTS.

PSALM		PAGES
XXIV	For the first day of the week (*Sept.*): Ascension (E); Easter Eve (W). Talmud (*Rosch haschana* iv. 7; *Berachoth* iv. 1) quotes verse 1 as a reason for Grace before meals; cf. 1 Cor. x. 26, 30.	108-111
XXVI	At the Handwashing in the Mass the Priest repeated v. 6 to end	112-114
XXVII	Another Altar-Psalm: Good Friday and Easter Eve (W)	115-118
XXVIII	v. 10 used in the Suffrages at Morn. and Even. Prayer and in *Te Deum*	118-120
XXIX	For Feast of Tabernacles*: the Seven Voices explained	120-125
XXX	For the Feast of *Hanucca*: Easter Eve (W). Sung by the Levites when the basket of firstfruits was brought into the Temple (T. B. Bikkurim iii. 4)	126-130
XXXI	. . . .	131-135
XXXII	Day of Atonement (S): Ash-Wednesday (E)	135-138
XXXIII	Partakes of the nature of the Alphabetical Psalms	139-141
XXXV	The imprecations compared with those of Jeremiah	142-146
XXXVI	. . . .	147-150
XXXVIII	Good Friday (W): Ash-Wednesday (E)	151-155
XXXIX	Burial Service (E)	155-160
XL	Good Friday (W, E) . . .	160-166
XLI	Used as a Prayer for the Sick (S)	167-170

For the Liturgical use of the Psalms I have chiefly consulted Grünwald, *Ueber den Einfluss der Psalmen, &c.*

---

* Ps. xxix. seems to have been used in the Temple both on the first and last days of Tabernacles; the last verse was also sung at the Evening Sacrifice on New Year's Day (T. B. *Rosch haschana* 30ᵇ, quoted by Graetz).

PSALMS I—II.

A LATE PREFACE TO THE WHOLE PSALTER.

"Ah, poor Man, befooled and slow
    And faint!
Ah, poorest Man, if so
Thou turn thy back on bliss
And choose amiss!
For thou art choosing now:
    Sinner,—or Saint."
(C. ROSSETTI.)

PSALM I.

This is a Psalm of the "two ways"—the way that ends in blessing, and the way that ends in the curse. Ebal and Gerizim (Josh. viii. 33). This thought of the two ways is very widespread and is found in the Zoroastrian religion. "Thus in a fragment of the *Hâdôkht Nask*, which gives an account of the progress after death, we find four steps mentioned in the advance of the soul. The first step of the righteous he places upon good thought, the second upon good word, the third upon good deed, and the fourth and last upon the eternal lights. The account of the contrary progress of the unrighteous soul is lost, except the last clause, 'The soul of the wicked man fourthly advanced with a step he placed on the eternal glooms'" [*Religion of Zoroaster*, R. Brown, Jun.].

Possibly there may be some connexion between the four upward steps of the good man in the Psalm and the four Zoroastrian steps—thus

(a) *Good thought*—not "in the counsel of the wicked."

(b) *Good word*—not "in the way of sinners."

(c) *Good deed*—not "in the company of the scoffers."

(d) *The eternal lights*—"the law of YHVH" (cf. Ps. xix.).

Certainly the "Law of YHVH" does not here signify the Law of Moses but rather that Divine Revelation which fulfils the same part in the world of Spirits as the sun does in the world of nature (see notes on Ps. xix.) and which may therefore be fitly compared with "the eternal lights."

But whether our Psalm has been consciously influenced by the Zoroastrian thought or no it has certainly been influenced by the following passage from Jeremiah:

> "Cursed is the man that trusteth in man and maketh flesh his strength
>   and turneth away his heart from the Lord.
> For he becomes like the heath in the desert,
>   that will not feel it when good comes,
> For it dwells in the parched places of the wilderness,
>   a land not inhabited.
> Blessed is the man that trusteth in the Lord,
>   and the Lord becomes his confidence,

PSALM I.

> And he becomes like a tree established by the waters
> and that spreadeth out its roots by the stream,
> And that will not feel it when heat comes,
> but its leaf becomes green,
> And in the drought of the year it has no care
> nor ceases from yielding fruit." (Jer. xvii. 5—8.)

The picture here is more complete than in the Psalm, since we have the bad tree as well as the good. The bad tree has no root and therefore the very sun that should have brought it life brings death. The good tree is "rooted and grounded," so that it is ever drawing fresh life from the sun.

At first it might seem that in the Psalm the simile of the tree was exchanged in verse 4 for a new simile of the threshing-floor, but if we remember such passages as "their root shall be as rottenness, etc." (Is. v. 24), "their root is dried up, they can yield no fruit" (Hos. ix. 16), we shall, I think, conclude that the Psalmist had in his mind Jeremiah's picture of "the heath in the desert." The whole point of the picture is that the same sun which brings the wealth of the seasons to the good tree dries up the root of the bad. Compare also the last verse, where it is not said that God "*destroys* the way of the wicked" but that "the way of the wicked perishes"—i.e. it is self-destroyed. Thus in our Psalm we find already the germ of that doctrine so often set forth in St John that the real judgement of the world is the incoming of light.

The Way of life.	1 Happy^a is the man who walketh not in the counsel of the wicked, Nor standeth in the way of sinners, Nor sitteth in the company of scoffers: 2 But in the law of YHVH is his delight, And in His law he meditates day and night. 3 So he becomes like a tree established^b by watercourses, That yieldeth its fruit in its season, And whose leaf never falls, And the growth that it makes is all thrifty.
The way of death.	4 Far otherwise with the wicked! For they are but as wind-driven chaff! 5 Therefore the wicked will not arise in the judgement Nor sinners in the congregation of the righteous.
Why life? Why death?	6 For YHVH taketh note^c of the way of the righteous, And the way of the wicked perishes.

PSALM II.

The first and last stanzas should be read together, referring as they do simply to events on earth. "YHVH and His Christ" against whom the nations are rebelling in the first stanza, answer to "YHVH" and "the Son" to whom they are forced to pay homage in the last stanza. The second and third stanzas should then be read together, in which the scene is not on earth but in Heaven; since the rebellion is against "YHVH and His Christ" YHVH speaks in Stanza II. and "His Christ" in Stanza III.

If God can say, "Israel is My son, My firstborn" (Exod. iv. 22, cf. Jer. xxxi. 9), the Christian need not fear to confess that the Messianic Psalms have a relation to Israel as well as to the Christ: indeed the application to Christ will often best be seen by first considering the application to the Messiah-nation.

The rebellion (v. 1 f.) of the "nations, peoples, kings, and rulers" must not be narrowed to the service of any historical allusion. It represents that opposition of earth to earth's God, and therefore to earth's good, which is ever going on and which is "as hopeless as if the stars were to combine to abolish gravitation" [Maclaren]. If a man fall upon any God-laid corner-stone "he is broken" (cf. verse 9), but even that is better than that the corner-stone should fall upon him "and scatter him as dust" (Luke xx. 18, compare v. 12 of our Psalm).

Rebellion against a law of Nature must be futile; and Christ is the central Law of all Nature. The special use of this Psalm for Easter Day is justified by verse 7, "Thou art My Son, It is I that have begotten thee this day." These words mean much the same as Ps. lxxxix. 27, "I too will make him My Firstborn, a Most High to the kings of the earth": the "Day" does not suggest the thought of an eternal generation, but rather that at some signal point of the world's history God had "highly exalted him and given him the Name above every name." This "Day" was the Resurrection, for then he "was declared *to be* the Son of God with power...by the resurrection of the dead" (Rom. i. 4).

St Paul also quotes our Psalm as fulfilled in the Resurrection of Jesus (Acts xiii. 33). Death was the condition on which the Father alone could give him "the nations for his inheritance" (cf. Is. liii. 12, Matt. xxviii. 18). He is "the firstborn from the dead; that in all things he might have the preeminence" (Col. i. 18). It is only as "the firstborn of the dead" that he is "the ruler of the kings of the earth" (Rev. i. 5).

Psalms i. and ii. forming as they do a Preface to the whole Psalter were at one time regarded as one Psalm (see Acts xiii. 33 crit. text). The point of connexion is seen in the first line of Ps. i. and the last line of Ps. ii. Ps. i., like the Old Testament, depicts the happiness that springs from obedience to the Law. Ps. ii., like the New Testament, depicts the happiness of trust in the Christ as the central Law of Creation.

PSALM II.

Israel speaks.

1 Why do the nations rage[a],
And the peoples ponder a vain thing?
2 Earth's kings[b] take their stand,
Rulers take counsel together—
(It is) Against YHVH and against His Christ!

The rebel-powers say

3 "Let us burst their fetters
And let us cast off their bonds!"

Were the heavenly purpose known rebellion would be seen to be futile.

4 The Throned-One of heaven laughs;
The Lord[e] derides them!
5 Then He speaks to them in His anger
And strikes them in fear with His wrath,
6 "It is I that established (?) My King
Upon Zion My Holy Mountain."

The heavenly purpose is revealed on earth in His choice of the Messiah.

7 Let me tell of the decree—
YHVH said unto me, "Thou art My Son[d],
It is I that have begotten thee this day.
8 Ask of Me, I would give thee nations for thine inheritance,
The ends[e] of the earth for thy possession.
9 Thou shalt break[f] them with an iron[g] sceptre,
And shatter them like a potter's vessel."

Therefore let the rebel-powers submit in time.

10 And now O kings be wise;
Be warned ye Judges of Earth;
11 Serve YHVH with reverence,
And tremblingly rejoice.
12 Pay homage to the Son[h] lest He be angry and ye be lost!
For His anger may easily burn!
Happy[i] are all they that take refuge in Him.

[a] Acts iv. 25
[b] Rev. xvi, xix. 19
[c] Adonai
[d] Acts xiii. 11 Heb. i. v. 5
[e] Is. xlix. 6
[f] Aramaic
[g] Rev. ii. 27; xii. xix. 15
[h] Aramaic Prov. xxx Sept. diff
[i] Ps. i. 1

FIRST COLLECTION.

'DAVIDIC' PSALMS.

PSALM III.

Psalms iii. and iv. are usually regarded as a pair; the former being an evening and the latter a morning Hymn. Undoubtedly they are fitted for such use though not originally written for the purpose. The points of similarity vanish on closer examination;—compare "*My Glory*" iii. 3 with iv. 2, where even if the text be correct (see *Sept.*) the word is probably used in another sense. Ps. iii. 5 "I laid me to sleep, I awoke" should rather be compared with Mark iv. 27 than with Ps. iv. 8, since it denotes man's passive "sleeping and rising night and day" as opposed to God's active work of sustentation. The structure of Psalms iii. and iv. is also different.

In Psalm iii. we have four stanzas of two verses each. The Psalm depicts the progress of the soul (or shall we say of Israel?) through four stages to the repose of expectant prayer. In the first stage (Stanza I.) we see nothing but the consciousness of need. In the second stage (Stanza II.) the standpoint is in the unseen world of realities. The soul *knows* that God is its Shield and that, as Luther says, 'a little word can bring Him down' (cf. *v.* 4). But there is a vast difference between knowing a thing and realizing it; hence the soul passes to the third stage (Stanza III.), the stage of experience in which it comes to realize that

> "Man's weakness leaning upon God
> Its end can never miss."

The fourth stage (Stanza IV.) might seem at first sight to be retrograde, since we should scarcely expect petition to follow upon such repose of faith as we have found in Stanza III. The answer to this difficulty is, I think, to be found in the fact that the Psalm depicts the experience of Israel and that Israel is still looking forward to the "far off Divine event" to which every lesser salvation pointed; hence the very triumph of Stanza III. gives birth to the prayer of Stanza IV.

The reader should study the connexion between the verses which are marked (a), (a_1), (a_2), (a_3), and also, in like manner, the verses marked (b), (b_1), (b_2), (b_3).

PSALM III.

What seems
(a) Danger all round.

(b) No help in God.

What is
(a₁) God a Shield all round.

(b₁) God a very present Help.

What I learn by experience
(a₂) When I am weak.

(b₂) Then I am strong.

What will be
(a₃) The unseen God will arise.

(b₃) His salvation will appear.

1 O YHVH, how many are my foes!
   Many are rising against me!
2 Many are saying of my soul
   "There is no salvation for him in God ᵃ."

3 But Thou, YHVH, art a Shield round about me;
   My Glory, and the uplifter of my head.
4 With my voice I but call unto YHVH,
   And He has answered me from His Holy Hill.

5 As for me I laid me to sleep, I awoke—
   But YHVH it is that sustains me.
6 I fear not the myriads of people
   That have set themselves against me round about.

7 Arise, O YHVH, help me O my God,
   Thou hast ᵇ smitten all mine enemies on the cheek ᶜ,
   Thou hast broken the teeth of the ungodly.
8 To YHVH belongeth salvation,
   Upon Thy People be Thy blessing.

ᵃ Is. liii. 4; Matt. xxvii. 43
ᵇ Ps. lxiii. 7
ᶜ Sept. differs

PSALM IV.

The occasion of this Psalm may very possibly have been the Feast of the Ingathering in a disastrous season. Those gifts of the earth had sometimes to be withdrawn because they were attributed to Baal. Thus God complains of Israel, "She did not know that I gave her corn and wine and oil, and multiplied her silver and gold, which they prepared for Baal. Therefore I will return and take away my corn in the time thereof etc." (Hos. ii. 8 f.). But when this was done the sinners still failed to recognize the Giver, "They have not cried unto Me with their heart, when they howl upon their beds; they assemble themselves for the corn and wine and they rebel against Me" (Hos. vii. 14). The point of the Psalm is to shew that man's blessedness consists in the presence of the Giver, not in the possession of the gift.

Israel was "separated" ("singled out") from the nations of the world for this very end that God's Presence should be its all in all. "For wherein shall it be known here that I and Thy people have found grace in Thy sight? is it not that Thou goest with us? so shall we be *separated* (cf. v. 3 of Psalm) I and

PSALM IV.

Thy people, from all the people that are upon the face of the earth" (Ex. xxxiv. 16).

The first verse of our Psalm reads very like a gloss on the last stanza of Ps. iii. In any case the structure of the Psalm is best understood by commencing at verse 2: the Psalm then falls into three stanzas of which the first and last closely correspond. The worldly party in Israel not only craved for temporal goods for their own sake (Stanza I.) but also as a sign of God's favour (Stanza III.). Israel on the other hand feels that his God has "separated" him for Himself (v. 3). This must imply a being "left alone," but yet he is "not alone because the Father is with him" (v. 8).

The application of the Psalm to Christ is obvious.

1 Answer me while I cry, O God of my righteousness!
In straits Thou madest room for me;
O pity me and hear my prayer!

Worldlings crave for temporal goods.	2 Ye worldlings^a, insulting my Glory, How long will ye love the vain, And seek the false?	^a Sons of men
Israel is singled out for God only.	3 Note how YHVH has singled^b me out as His loved one, YHVH hears me while to Him I cry.	^b separated. Ex. xxxiii. 16
Disappointed hopes may lead to sin.	4 Be ye in rage—but sin^c not, Speak with your hearts—on your beds—and be still^d.	^c Eph. iv. 26 ^d resigned
Thanksgiving will lead to God.	5 Offer sacrifices of righteousness And put ye your trust in YHVH.	
Worldlings crave visible signs of God's favour.	6 Many are saying, "Oh for the sight of good times! Display Thou upon us the Light of Thy countenance YHVH."	
Israel's is the greater joy.	7 Thou hast put a joy in my heart Above theirs when their corn and new wine are abounding.	
Alone, yet not alone, with God.	8 In peace altogether I can lay me to sleep^e For thou YHVH in seclusion makest me dwell in safety.	^e Ezek. xxxiv. 25

v. 2. The text is somewhat doubtful. Wellhausen would make it agree with the Septuagint and would read "Ye sons of men:—how long ye slow of heart!—Why will ye love vanity, etc."

v. 6. "*Display Thou.*" If there be any allusion here to the Priestly blessing in Numb. vi. 24 f. the word is purposely changed so as to signify not the "*lifting up*" of God's countenance but the "*displaying it as a sign.*" The words must be taken as those of the unbelievers who are craving for a sign.

v. 8. "*In seclusion.*" The words here translated "in seclusion," "in safety" are almost synonyms, as may be seen from Numb. xxiii. 9; Mic. vii. 14; Deut. xxxiii. 28; Jer. xlix. 31, "His God makes him to dwell free from care, though in seclusion" (Delitzsch). The thought of "seclusion" undoubtedly goes back to v. 3 where Israel was said to be "separated" or "singled out."

PSALM V.

This, like Psalm i, is a Psalm of the 'two ways'; but whereas Psalm i. shewed us the two roads, Psalm v. shews us the two ends, "Either make the tree good, and its fruit good; or make the tree corrupt, and its fruit corrupt" (Matt. xii. 33; cf. Rev. xxii. 11 R.V.).

The general structure of the Psalm will be seen from the marginal notes. It will be convenient to consider first the downward course and its end (verses 4—6 and 9—10). This is founded upon the Nature of God who cannot abide sin (verses 4—6) and the nature of sin which cannot abide God (verses 9—10). Evil, at last, must go to its own place—whatever that may mean.

We now take the upward course which has a *beginning* (verses 1—3), a *middle* (verses 7 and 8) and an *end* (verses 11 and 12).

The *beginning* consists of three prayers followed by three closely related resolves; thus—

PRAYERS.	RESOLVES.
(*a*) 'Give ear to *my words*.'	(a_1) 'In the morning *Thou shalt hear my voice*.'
(*b*) 'Consider my *meditation*.'	(b_1) '......I will *order my thoughts* before Thee.'
(*c*) 'Attend to the *voice of my cry*,' i.e. its *true meaning*, whether I know it myself or not.	(c_1) 'I will stand on my watch,' i.e. to *catch Thy meaning*.

Thus we have a rising order of *word, thought, purpose*.

The prayer that my words may be heard must pass into the resolve of early instant prayer. If I ask God to consider my meditation I must consider it myself, I must order my thoughts as a sacrifice in His presence.

If I ask God further to attend to the purpose of my cry rather than to the words I must myself stand patiently to await His pleasure.

The *word* once was, 'Let this cup pass from Me,' but 'the *voice of the cry*' to which the Father 'attended' was 'not as I will but as Thou wilt.' Those who ask God to attend to the voice of their cry will certainly need to stand, as the prophets did, upon the watch-tower to await and understand His answer.

So much for the *beginning* of the upward course. The *middle* is set forth in verses 7 and 8 which give indeed the central thought of the Psalm, viz. that the good man enters God's presence not through his own righteousness but through God's "*grace abounding*." The reader will notice the contrast between "sins abounding" (*v*. 10) and "*grace abounding*" (*v*. 7).

The *end* of the upward course (verses 11 and 12) is summed up in the joy of two thoughts, *God's Protection* and *God's Presence:* these thoughts will be seen to be a development of verses 7 and 8 but in reverse order.

No higher blessedness can be reached than that of verse 12:

"Thou Thyself dost make the righteous man blessed —
YHVH! Shield-wise with favour dost Thou crown him."

It is the joy of the Beatific Vision.

PSALM V.

Three prayers for
(a) Word.
(b) Thought.
(c) Intention.

Three resolves for
(a_1) Word.
(b_1) Thought.
(c_1) Intention.

God's Presence an
impossibility to evil
negatively

positively.

I, through Grace,
can come into Thy
Presence.
Therefore lead me
with Thy Protection.

They, being evil,
have no part in the
Divine Presence
negatively

positively.

The joy of God's
Protection.

The joy of God's
Presence.

1 O YHVH give ear to my words,
   Consider my meditation,
2 Attend to the voice of my cry, O my King and my God;
        For unto Thee do I pray.
3 In the morning, YHVH, Thou shalt hear my voice;
   In the morning I will order[a] before Thee my thoughts
   And stand on my watch.

4 For Thou art not a God that can find pleasure in sin,
   Evil can be no guest[b] of Thine!
5 Mad-boasters cannot bide Thine eyes,
   Thou hatest all workers[c] of vanity.
6 Those that speak lies Thou destroyest,
   The man of blood and fraud YHVH abhorreth.

7 So I, through Thy grace abounding, can enter Thy House,
   Can worship at Thy holy Temple, in Thy fear.
8 Lead me, YHVH, in Thy righteousness, because of my foes;
   Make Thy way straight before me.

9 For there is in his[d] mouth no steadfastness,
   Their inner being is a yawning-abyss;
   Their throat an open grave, they flatter with their tongue.
10 Shew them as guilty, O God!
   Let them fall through their own counsels!
   Drive them out through their sins abounding!
        For they have rebelled against Thee.

11 So Thy trusting-ones all shall be glad,
   They shall ever joyously sing,
   And Thou wilt protect[e] them;
   Yea those that love Thy Name exult in Thee.
12 For Thou Thyself dost make the righteous blessed—
   YHVH! Shield[f]-wise with favour dost Thou crown him!

[a] Lev. vi. 5; Numb. xxviii. 4

[b] Ps. xv. 1

[c] Matt. vii. 23

[d] their mouths

[e] cover, cf. Ps. xci. 4

[f] Ps. xci. 4

v. 11 f. The pilgrimage to God is often described under the image of Israel's journey to the Land of Promise; as God's guiding Light was then both Light and Shield, so it will be in the future (cf. Is. xi. 16). As God's Presence brooded over His People like the cherubim that "covered" the "mercy-seat," so in the future He will "cover" them: thus protected and guided they will "come unto Zion with joyous songs" (Is. xxxv. 10; li. 11; Jer. xxxi. 12). See also note on Ps. xliii. 3.

PSALM VI.

The first of the seven 'penitential' Psalms (the others being xxxii; xxxviii; li; cii; cxxx; cxli.iii). The language and thought is so similar to that of Jeremiah (see marginal references) as to justify us in asserting that the Sufferer is Israel. Israel was God's 'Servant' whose mission was to make God known to the Gentiles (Is. xlix. 3, 5, 6). This mission involved that "scattering" which seemed like the death of Israel but which was really a "sowing in the earth" (Hos. ii. 23 and cf. St John xii. 24—27). Though Israel may feel "for this cause came I unto this hour" still he prays "Father save me from this hour"—$\dot{\eta}$ $\psi v \chi \dot{\eta}$ $\mu o v$ $\dot{\epsilon} \tau a \rho \dot{a} \chi \theta \eta$ $\sigma \phi \dot{o} \delta \rho a$ (v. 3 Sept.). The sowing of Israel among the heathen was an agony of separation from God (see Stanza i.), but the promised reward was that, in some way dimly understood, the whole world should, through Israel, be separated from evil (see Stanza iii.).

We need not shrink from applying this and other penitential Psalms to Christ; for if He has united Himself, as it were in a Marriage union with our nature, He must feel the *sin* of that nature as if it were His own. The "sowing" of Israel in the earth was a type of that "corn of wheat" which fell into the ground and died that it might not "abide alone."

The Psalm consists of three Stanzas. 1st, The Fear of Sin as *Separation from God*. 2nd, An agony of prayer based on the shortness of opportunity. 3rd, *Separation from evil*. The six lines of Stanza iii. answer exactly to the six lines of Stanza i. Our Lord quotes v. 8 (Matt. vii. 23; xxv. 41; Lk. xiii. 27) with reference to His own final separation from evil men.

If we interpret the whole Psalm of Christ we might say that Stanza i. represents the shrinking fear with which He plunges into the evil of the world and takes the 'nature of sinful flesh' (see especially v. 3 and compare Joh. xii. 27; xiii. 21 and xi. 33). Stanza ii. would represent the "strong crying and tears unto Him that was able to save him from death" (Heb. v. 7); the agony arising from the knowledge that the opportunity for the world was short (cf. Luke xii. 50).

Stanza iii. would then be Christ's triumph-song of victory over the world's evil.

- v. 8. Separation from Sinners (Heb. vii. 26), as contrasted with v. 1 'conviction of sin.'
  The Father hears the voice of His weeping, as contrasted with v. 1 'chastisement in wrath.'
- v. 9. The Father hears His supplication, as contrasted with v. 2 The cry for pity in weakness.
  The Father receives His prayer, as contrasted with v. 2 The cry for healing.
- v. 10. His enemies are troubled, as contrasted with v. 3 His own soul troubled.
  The conviction and conversion in a moment, as contrasted with v. 3 Age-long waiting.

PSALM VI.

The agony of separation from God.

1 YHVH! Convict[a] me not in thine anger,
Neither chastise me in Thy wrath[a].
2 Pity me YHVH for that I am weak;
Heal[b] me YHVH for my bones are troubled;—
3 Yea troubled[c] is my soul exceedingly,
But thou—O YHVH, how long?

[a] Jer. x. 24; xxx. 11; Ps. xxxviii. 1 (2)
[b] Ps. xli. 4 (5)
[c] Sept. ἐταράχθη. Cf. St John xii. 27

The night cometh when no man can work.

4 Return, YHVH, rescue my soul!
O save me for Thy mercy's sake.
5 For not in Death is Thy memorial,
And in Sheôl who can give Thee thanks[d]?
6 I am weary[e] of groaning, each night I water my bed,
I bedew my couch with my tears.
7 My sight is dim[f] through grief,
It is aged through all my foes.

[d] Ps. xxx. 9 (10)
[e] Ps. lxix. 3 (4)
[f] Ps. xxxi. 9 10; Lam. v. 17

The joy of separation from Evil.

8 Depart from me, all ye that work evil,
For YHVH hath heard the voice of my weeping.
9 YHVH hath heard my supplication,
YHVH receives my prayer.
10 All mine enemies will be shamed and troubled exceedingly,
They repent, they are shamed, in a moment.

v. 5. "*For not in Death is Thy memorial*"—i.e. 'in death one cannot memorialize Thy goodness.' The rendering of the E.V. "there is no remembrance of Thee" is far too strong and is not justified either by the context or by the usage of Scripture. Scripture often speaks of the 'memorial' (remembrance) of the wicked perishing (Ex. xvii. 14; Deut. xxv. 19; Job xviii. 17; Pss. ix. 6 (7); xxxiv. 16 (17); cix. 15; Ecc. ix. 5; Is. xxvi. 14). But, on the other hand, God's 'memorial' (remembrance) is "throughout all generations" (Pss. cii. 12 (13); cxxxv. 13; cf. also xxx. 4 (5); xcvii. 12; cxi. 4). The passage must not be used either one way or other in determining the belief of the writer as to the state after death. It merely asserts that the work of life ends with life, and since the work of Israel's life is to "abundantly utter the remembrance (memorial) of God's great goodness" (Ps. cxlv. 7) then, if Israel cease to be, God's 'little human praise' will cease as well.

v. 8. "*Depart from me.*" The meaning may be gathered from the following passages: "Depart I pray you from the tents of these wicked men" (Numb. xvi. 26); "Depart, get you down from among the Amalekites" (1 Sam. xv. 6); "Depart ye, depart ye, go ye out…touch no unclean thing" (Is. lii. 11). In all these passages the *good* are exhorted to separate themselves from the evil so as not to share their fate: but in Lam. iv. 15 the *unclean* are bidden to depart as lepers from those who are, or think themselves, clean. There are two other passages in the Psalms in which the expression occurs, viz. Ps. cxix. 115, "Depart from me, ye evil-doers; for I will keep the commandments of my God"; and cxxxix. 19, "Surely thou wilt slay the wicked, O God: Depart from me therefore, ye men of blood." This is not a sentence of banishment but simply the expression of the necessary separation between good and evil. No doubt in early times the distinction between hating the sin and the sinner was often lost sight of (cf. Ps. cxix. 113; cxxxix. 21), but it should not be so under the New Testament. When then our Lord quotes these words we must interpret them in His spirit.

PSALM VII.

The Seventh Psalm is a Psalm of Judgement, just as the Seventh Month is the Month of Judgement (See my '*Asaph*' *Psalms*, Lect. II.). The editor who arranged the Psalms in their present order was, I believe, guided by this thought both here and in the case of Psalm 1., which is a Jubilee Psalm or a completion of the cycle of seven times seven (see ad loc.). According to the old Semitic religion God took His place for judgement in the Seventh Month and the gods of heaven and earth came humbly round Him bowing down before Him. The destiny of all was then determined (Sayce, *Hib. Lect.* pp. 65, 94 f.). This thought has certainly left its impress on the Jewish observance of 'New Year's Day' (Seventh Month) and has coloured the imagery of the present Psalm (verses 6—10). Israel claims that not Merodach but Elohim the Righteous God is the true Judge who determines the destiny of all (vv. 6, f.). Israel prays to be judged by this Righteous Judge (v. 8); he cannot doubt the result since his own aim is at righteousness (v. 10). On the other hand, because God is Righteous evil must become its own avenger (vv. 9ᵇ, 14—16). Surely this is a somewhat late conception?

Israel unjustly oppressed 'catches at God's skirt and prays.'	1 YHVH, My God, in Thee I take refuge, Save me from all my pursuers and rescue me; 2 Lest he tear my soul like a lion, Rending with none to rescue. 3 YHVH, My God! if I have done this— If iniquity cling to my hands, 4 If I have requited evil to my friend— Then I could exonerate my causeless foe. 5 The enemy might pursue my soul, Might overtake and trample my life to the ground, And lay my glory in the dust.

v. 2. "*Rending with none to rescue.*" If we follow the Septuagint we should read "*None to redeem and none to rescue.*" The word *poråq* signifies to *break* e.g. a yoke (Gen. xxvii. 40), hence to "*redeem*" (Lam. v. 8; Ps. cxxxvi. 24). It is once used of *rending* or breaking claws in pieces (Zech. xi. 16) and might therefore be used of a lion *rending* his prey, but the balance of usage is undoubtedly in favour of the Septuagint. The passage in Lam. v. 8 should specially be noticed since the thought is so similar to that of our Psalm: "Slaves rule over us and *redeemer* there is none from their hand."

v. 3. "*If iniquity cling to my hands.*" Compare also verses 8, 9, 10, 17. Israel as the People of God can claim a holiness which the individual Israelite could not claim. By this very fact Israel becomes a type and a prophecy of the Christ.

v. 4. "*I could exonerate.*" The verb is *subjunctive* or *optative* as is noticed in the Septuagint and Vulgate: this seems to exclude the renderings "*I have spoiled*" or "*I have set free.*" The primary sense of the word is "*to strip*": hence follows the meaning "*to remove*" "*take away*" e.g. stones (Lev. xiv. 40, 43); hence "*to deliver*" "*to free*" out of trouble (Ps. vi. 4 (5); xviii. 19 (20); xxxiv. 7 (8); l. 15; lxxxi. 7 (8); xci. 15; cxix. 153; cxl. 1 (2) &c.). From the sense "*to free*" we might easily get *to exonerate, to free (from blame)*. The LXX read ἀποπέσοιμι ἄρα ἀπὸ τῶν ἐχθρῶν μου κενός· The Vulgate, *decidam merito ab inimicis meis inanis*.

PSALM VII.

The heathen have their fable of a Judgement Day, but the true Judgement is moral, by a Righteous God.

6 YHVH, Arise in Thine anger!
  Lift Thee up against the rage of my foes!
  Yea rouse Thee for me—a judgement Thou hast ordained!
7 The assembly of the Nations comes around Thee,
  Then, above it, do Thou throne Thee on high!
8 YHVH (that) righteth the people,
  Judge thou me, YHVH!
  By my righteousness, by the integrity that is mine.
9 Let the evil of the wicked end itself,
  But uphold Thou the righteous-one.
  The One who trieth hearts and reins
  Is Elohim the Righteous-One!

In that Day of His vengeance Israel will be safe.

10 My shield devolves on Elohim
   Who helpeth the upright of heart.
11 Elohim is a righteous Judge,
   And [a] will not ever be angry [a].   [a] text doubtful
12 Except he repent He whets His sword,
   Bends His bow and makes it ready.
13 For him He prepareth the weapons of death,
   His arrows He maketh burning.

The enemy falls in the Judgement self-destroyed.

14 Behold he is in birth-pangs with iniquity;
   Mischief he conceived and falsehood he brought forth.
15 A pit he dug and scooped it out,
   And fell in the trap of his making.
16 His mischief returns on his own head,
   And on his own crown his violence comes down.
17 I can praise YHVH according to His righteousness,
   And can harp to the Name of YHVH Most High.

v. 6 f. The key-note to the Psalm is to be found in verses 6 and 7 which anticipate a judgement on the nations that are hostile to Israel's God. Just as the stars seem ever to be climbing round the Polestar but it abides changeless on the throne of heaven, so the nations of the world "come round about" the God of Israel but He in calm judgement maintains His throne.

v. 7. The present text reads "*return Thou on high*" but since the change required is only one of the vowel points it is better to read "*sit Thou*," or "*throne Thee*."

v. 10. "*My shield devolves on Elohim*," lit. "*My shield is upon Elohim*." Cf. the similar Psalm of Divine Judgement (Ps. xlvii. 9) "For all the shields of the earth are Elohim's"; also Ps. lxxxiv. 9, "Oh Elohim our shield." Our Psalmist had said (*v.* 1) that he "*took refuge*" as it were under God's wings: he, like Abraham, had given up all for God; therefore to him too God would say "I am thy shield" (Gen. xv. 1). Cf. also on Ps. xviii. 2 (3), 30 (31), 35 (36). Just as in Browning's *Instans Tyrannus* the victim of oppression at last "Stood erect, caught at God's skirts, and prayed!" and then "...from marge to blue marge The whole sky grew his targe." So here God becomes Israel's Shield : indeed it devolves upon Him, cf. 11 Thess. i. 6 f.

v. 11. This verse is very doubtful. Taking the present text we should translate "*Elohim is a righteous Judge*" (or "*Elohim judgeth the righteous*") "*And El is angry every day*." But the Septuagint read *al* "not" instead of *El* "God."

PSALM VIII.

This Psalm is a Pæan of Creation. The episode of the Fall is passed over in the full assurance of God's purpose; for

"what began best can't prove worst,
Nor what God blest once prove accurs't."

The God whose glory fills the heavens has chosen man, of the dust of the earth, as His "stronghold" for self-revelation; the Incarnation, though not yet revealed, was involved in this choice.

We seem in this Psalm to catch an echo of the joy of Him who when on earth rejoiced in the homage of children (Matt. xxi. 16) and in the knowledge that His Father was revealing Himself to babes (Matt. xi. 25, compare 1 Cor. i. 19 ff.).

The Psalm falls naturally into three Parts. In the *first* we have the bold paradox that man's littleness is greater and more glorious and more God-loved than all the galaxy of stars and suns. In the *second* we pass to the difficulty of realizing man's true place when all the stars of night are looking down upon his insignificance. In the *third* we come back to facts:—Man *has* already a growing dominion over the earth. True greatness cannot be measured by a foot-rule. Man's greatness consists in this; that God has chosen him to be the bearer of His Image; all things, at last, will be placed under his feet (cf. Heb. ii. 6—8 in Bishop Westcott's Commentary).

The critic will note that the Psalm is written in the spirit of the Priest-Code (P) not only from the fact that it ignores the Fall but also from the direct allusions to P in verses 3 and 5—8. Is it altogether an accident that the subject of the *Eighth* Psalm should be the *Eighth* Word of Creation, viz. "Let Us make man in Our Image etc."?

1 O YHVH, our Lord,
How glorious is Thy Name in all the earth!

God's wonderful purpose in creating man.

[When Thou didst put]ᵃ Thy Majesty uponᵇ the heavens,
2 From the mouth of babes and sucklings
Thou didst establish a strongholdᶜ;—

v. 1. "*When Thou didst put.*" The text is by no means certain. The translation which I offer provisionally has, on the whole, the authority of Sym. Jer. Syr. and Targum: it is however grammatically difficult. In any case, the general sense of the passage is clear. The Psalmist begins by acknowledging the glory of God's *Name* (i.e. His Self-revelation) in the earth: he then passes to the central thought, viz. the Creation of Man as God's 'stronghold' for Self-revelation to the Worlds. When God created *the heavens*, "the work of His fingers" (*v.* 3), He put upon them something of His own Glory, though it was but physical splendour; but when He created *Man*, in His own Image (*v.* 5), He put upon him the capacity of sharing the joys and sorrows of the Divine Nature and thus becoming Elohim upon earth.

v. 2. "*Thou didst establish a stronghold*"—Lit. 'Thou didst lay a foundation of strength.' By the Creation of the physical Universe, which found its completion in Man, God established His

PSALM VIII.

Because of Thine adversaries;—
To still the enemy^a and the avenger^a.

^a Ps. xliv. 16 (17)

The difficulty of realizing it from the standpoint of earth.

3 When I behold Thy heavens,
  The work of Thy fingers,
  The moon^b and the stars^b which Thou didst establish—
4 What is mortal ^cman that Thou shouldst bear him in mind,
  And the son of man that Thou shouldst so regard^c him?

^b Gen. i. 15 f. (P)
^c Contrast Job vii. 17

Yet man's destiny is foreshadowed in his dominion over the creatures.

5 Yet Thou didst make him little less than Elohim,^d
  And with glory and honour dost crown him.
6 Thou givest him dominion^e over the work of Thy hands—
  All things Thou didst put under his feet—
7 Sheep and oxen, all of them,
  Yea and the beasts of the field,
8 The birds of the air and the fish of the sea,
  Whatever moves through ocean's paths.

^d Sept. *angels*
^e Gen. i. 26 (P)

9 O YHVH, our Lord,
  How glorious is Thy Name in all the earth!

stronghold from whence He might first reveal Himself and finally "gather together all things in One" thus "*stilling the enemy and the avenger*."—The "enemy and the avenger" must denote that proud power which exalts itself against God and which God puts to silence not by violence but by choosing the weak things of earth (1 Cor. i. 19, 27; cf. Jas. ii. 5). If we accept the modern theory of development the argument becomes, not weaker but, stronger.

v. 4. "*Mortal man...the son of man.*" Both these expressions are used to denote man's nature on the side of weakness. The title 'Son of man' always has this meaning in the Old Testament: cf. especially Dan. vii. 13 where the "Son of man" is identified with Israel (compare verses 14 and 18) as an idealized suffering Humanity and contrasted with the other kingdoms of brute violence. In the New Testament our Lord chooses this lowly title to denote not only the reality of His representative Humanity but also to emphasize the fact that His Kingdom was not of this world.

"*That Thou shouldst so regard him*"—Lit. 'shouldst visit him.' 'Visiting' is here used in a good sense, as in Ps. lxv. 9 (10) "Thou visitest the earth and waterest it," Ruth i. 6 "The Lord had visited His people in giving them bread." Compare Luke i. 68 "He hath visited and redeemed His people."

vv. 5, 6. Without pretending that the Hebrew tenses are used with the same accuracy as the Greek we may note here the change of tense. In 5^a and 6^b we have the *past* tense denoting, as it were, the final purpose of God in creating man (the Divine image (5^a) and the Dominion over Creation (6^b) being virtually the same (cf. Gen. i. 26)); whereas the *imperfect* (or *future*) tenses in 5^b and 6^a remind us that the work is still going on and thus justify the argument of the writer to the Hebrews (ii. 6–8) "We see not yet all things put under him."

INTRODUCTION TO THE ALPHABETICAL PSALMS.

Of the Alphabetical Psalms (ix—x, xxv, xxxiv, xxxvii; cxi, cxii, cxix, cxlv) the first four belong to the First Collection and the last four to the Third Collection. For convenience of study we have grouped them together, though in point of time the First Collection is much earlier than the Third.

I shall shew that while the four Alphabetical Psalms of the Third Collection are regular those of the First Collection are all irregular *after a common law*, since in each of them the letter פ probably stood before ע and certainly the ר verses stood before the ק verses. It will also be seen that the alphabet in these Psalms was not used as a mere acrostic, but that it was arranged in two Tables of *ten* letters each with direct reference to the sacred number *ten*, which is the number of the Covenant and which is to the Priest-Code what the number *seven* is to the Prophetic Writers.

The order of the letters in the Hebrew alphabet is supposed to be fixed by the following alphabetical passages: Pss. xxv, xxxiv, xxxvii, cxi, cxii, cxix, cxlv; Lam. i—iv; Prov. xxxi. 10—31. The order, however, is not altogether uniform, for it cannot be an accident that פ comes *before* ע in Lam. ii. 16, 17; iii. 46—51 and iv. 16, 17. If this fact had stood alone it would have justified us in suspecting that, in the time when these Books were written, the order of the alphabet was not altogether fixed as we have it now, and that later editors might possibly rearrange an alphabetical composition making it conform to the order of the alphabet as it is known at present. Thus, for example, out of the four alphabetical chapters in Lamentations we have seen that in three the פ comes before the ע, while in one passage only (ch. i. 16, 17) the order is reversed so as to follow the present alphabet. If any unprejudiced reader will look at the latter passage he will see at once that a much better sense is obtained by transposing verses 16 and 17, i.e. he will conclude that originally the פ verse stood before the ע verse, as it does in the other three chapters of this Book. Now it is an interesting fact that in the Alphabetical Psalms of the First Collection a clearer meaning would in each case be found if we were to transpose the ע and פ verses (see notes pp. 33, 35). But we may go further. Not only was there an uncertainty in the order of the letters ע and פ but also, I believe, in the order of the letters ק and ר. From the alphabetical fragments contained in Psalms ix—x no certain argument can be drawn, but it should be noted that it is on the letter ק that Ps. ix ceases to be alphabetical and on the letter ק that Ps. x begins to be alphabetical, the same words "Arise O YHVH" being found in each place. It is obvious that the *disjecta membra* of two or more alphabetical compositions have been pieced together.

INTRODUCTION TO THE ALPHABETICAL PSALMS. 19

Now let the reader turn to the fragment Ps. x. 11—end and let him transpose the letters ק and ר, i.e. let him read v. 14 after verse 11. Thus:—

- *v.* 11. He says in his heart "God forgets," "He hides His face," "*He never sees.*"
- ר 14. *Thou hast seen*—Thou beholdest violence and vexation.
The poor may leave it all on Thee, placed in Thy hand;
As for the orphan Thou art become his helper.
- ק 12. Arise O YHVH; Lift up Thine hand; forget not the poor!
- 13. Why should the wicked despise God while he saith in his heart "*Thou wilt not require it.*"
- ש 15. Break Thou the arm of the wicked—as for the evil,
Thou wilt require his wickedness till Thou find none.
- [16. YHVH is King for ever and ever; the Nations are perished out of His Land.]
- ת 17. Thou YHVH hast heard the desire of the poor.
&c.   &c.   &c.

The connexion of thought as indicated by the words in italics is thus brought out, whereas it is obscured by the arrangement in the text. I conclude therefore that, in the original text, the ר stood before the ק.

The next alphabetical Psalm is Psalm xxv, and here again we note an irregularity in the letters ק, ר; the ק being omitted altogether and the ר doubled; but, not only so, one of the ר verses (*v.* 18) actually interrupts the sense (see notes) and was probably introduced into the text from some other alphabetical Psalm while the ק verse has been lost. The same transposition must also be made in Ps. xxxiv (see p. 30). In the next alphabetical Psalm (xxxvii) the case is still more clear; If the reader will carefully compare the four Parts, stanza by stanza, he will see that the stanzas which we have printed in parallel columns correspond in a very remarkable way; but when he comes to the letters ק and ר he will observe that it is *absolutely necessary to transpose them* since the ר verse (35) answers to the ג verse (25) and the ק verse (34) to the ס verse (27). Next let him compare Part IV with Part II and he will see that the five stanzas of Part IV exactly correspond with the five stanzas of Part II, *but only on condition of placing the* ר *stanza before the* ק *stanza*. Thus I conclude that in the earliest of the Alphabetical Psalms, the alphabetical order was not altogether fixed as we have it now, or, if fixed, was for some reason or other disregarded in the order of the letters ק and ר. We now proceed to the separate study of these Psalms.

PS. IX* (*First half*).

I can thank God	א 1	I thank YHVH with my whole heart; I tell of all Thy wondrous works;
	א 2	I joy and exult in Thee;
	א	I strike the harp to Thy Name, O Most High!
Because He has heard my prayer.	ב 3	Because mine enemies are turned back, Stumble and perish before Thee:
	4	For Thou hast maintained my right and my cause, Thou art set in the throne a right Judge.
The Nations are fallen.	ג 5	Thou hast rebuked the Nations,—destroyed the wicked— Their name Thou hast wiped out for evermore.

....

They will never rise again.	ה 6	The enemy is ended—an eternal destruction Their cities Thou hast destroyed—their very memory is perished!
Israel is saved at last.	ו 7	And YHVH, seated for ever, hath prepared His throne for judgement.
	ו 8	And He will judge the world with righteousness—and right the Peoples justly.
	ו 9	And YHVH becomes a tower for the oppressed—a tower in seasons of trouble.
	ו 10	And they that know Thy Name will trust in Thee— For never hast Thou deserted them that seek Thee O YHVH.

* For the Introduction to this Psalm and its connexion with Psalm x see page 22.

PSALM IX.

PS. IX (*Second half*).

<small>I can thank God</small>

ז 11 Strike the harp to YHVH who dwelleth in Zion,
Tell among the Peoples His doings,
12 For the Avenger of blood hath remembered them,
For He never forgot the cry of the poor.

<small>Because He heard this prayer of mine.</small>

ח 13 "YHVH be gracious unto me; Look on my poor estate
from my foes,
Thou that upliftest me from the gates of death,
14 That I may tell of all Thy praise in the gates of the
daughter of Zion
And rejoice in Thy salvation."

<small>The Nations are fallen.</small>

ט 15 Sunk are the Nations—in the pitfall they made,
In this net of their hiding their own foot is taken.
16 Known is YHVH—justice He hath done,
Snaring[a] the wicked in the work of his own hands.

<small>They will never rise again.</small>

י 17 Downward to Sheôl the wicked return,
Even all Nations forgetful of God!

<small>Israel is saved at last.</small>

כ 18 For not alway shall the needy be forgotten,
Nor the expectation of the poor perish for ever.

———————

פ 19 Arise, O YHVH! Let not frail man prevail;
Let the Nations be judged in Thy sight.
ש 20 Put them in fear, O YHVH! that the Nations may know
That they are but frail men.

<small>*v.* 17. "*Downward to Sheôl....*" The P. B. version, "The wicked shall be turned into hell &c." is quite impossible. *Sheôl* is not *hell*, and the context clearly proves that the judgement is not one of individuals but of Nations. Keble has unconsciously reproduced the Psalmist's thought in his description of Balaam's vision:</small>

<small>"In outline dim and vast
Their fearful shadows cast
The giant forms of empires on their way
To ruin : one by one
They tower and they are gone."
...................................</small>

<small>So 'the wicked return to Sheôl, Even all Nations that are forgetful of God.'</small>

PSALM IX—X.

The arrangement of Psalms ix—x suggests an interesting problem in Psalm structure. If with the Septuagint we regard them as one Psalm we might suppose that the portion between the letters ר of Ps. ix and ק of Ps. x had accidentally lost its alphabetical arrangement; but against this we have to set the fact that Ps. ix is altogether a ·thanksgiving for victory while Ps. x is a prayer out of the depths of oppression. Again the letter ק is found in both Psalms with the words "Arise O YHVH." Consequently we are led to the conclusion that two or more alphabetical Psalms having much in common have been pieced together possibly for some special effect like music in a major and minor key. The general structure of the alphabetical arrangement would seem to have been two verses to a letter as in Psalm xxxvii. We note however that in Ps. ix the *Aleph* and *Vaw* letters are fourfold, just as in Lam. iii each letter is threefold; these verses which have a different alphabetical structure have no very direct connexion with the sense, possibly they are fragments of a Psalm in which each letter was arranged in *fours*. The reader is asked to suspend his judgement until he shall have studied the whole group of alphabetical Psalms which, for this reason, have been placed together.

It appears to me that the original writer of Ps. ix omitted the letter *Daleth* because his object was to emphasize the number *ten* by using only ten letters of the Alphabet and by so dividing them that the five letters of Part I should answer exactly to the five letters of Part II. Thus *Aleph* corresponds with *Zain*; *Beth* with *Cheth*; *Gimel* with *Teth*; *Heh* with *Yod* (see marginal notes). Then there came an editor who wished to extend the use of the number *ten* by making *ten verses* in each Part. To effect this he makes four verses of the letter *Vaw* instead of two verses and adds verses 19, 20 from another alphabetical Psalm, thus forming also a link of connexion with Psalm x. Psalm ix is from beginning to end a magnificent thanksgiving for victory. It is quite impossible that *vv*. 19, 20 should have been written at the same time. It is interesting to observe that in the alphabetical fragment (*vv*. 19, 20) the letter ש follows immediately after ק. This, so far as it goes, confirms my contention that the original order of the alphabet was ר, ק, ש and not ק, ר, ש as at present.

PSALM X.

This Psalm is at the same time a continuation and a contrast to Ps. ix. A continuation, in that it contains striking similarities of thought, language and alphabetical structure; a contrast, in that the enemy is no longer the Heathen without but the Heathen within; no longer a conquered foe but a foe elated with prosperity and contemptuous alike of God and man. The Psalm must belong to a time when the Godless party in Israel was making common cause with the Heathen.

The writer of Pss. ix, x, or the editor to whom we owe them in their present shape, must have intended, by placing these Psalms side by side, to imply that as the World-powers had perished (ix. 6, 17), so the Heathen party in Israel must perish in spite of its present prosperity. The verse x. 16 interrupts the sense: may not its proper place have been after *v.* 5 of Ps. ix? It is of course quite possible that the unalphabetical verses (2—11) may be due to an editor who wished thus to point a Psalm against apostates which was originally written with reference to other enemies (cf. Cheyne, *Orig. of Psalter*, p. 228).

PS. X (*First half*).

Let the hot pursuer himself be trapped.

1 Why, O YHVH, shouldst Thou stand afar?
  Why hide in seasons^a of trouble? ^a Ps. ix. 9
2 Proudly the wicked hotly pursueth the poor.
  Let them be trapped in the very deeds of their devising^b. ^b Ps. ix. 15

He believes in no retribution.

3 For the wicked boasted of his own self-will,
  And the rapacious hath 'blest'—hath blasphemed YHVH.
4 The wicked, pride-led (thinks) "He will not require it";
  "There is no God" is the sum of his plans.
5 His ways are ever prosperous^c; ^c Targum &c.
  Far above, out of sight, are Thy judgements.
  All foes he laugheth to scorn.
6 He says in his heart "I shall never be moved;
  From age to age I shall come to no ill."

7 His mouth is full of cursing, fraud and wrong;
  Under his tongue is violence and mischief.

v. 2. "*Hotly pursueth* &c." This word is used of *chasing* an enemy in Gen. xxxi. 36; 1 Sam. xvii. 53. It is used of "*burning* lips" (Prov. xxvi. 23), and of "*fiery* arrows" (Ps. vii. 13 (14)), but the *locus classicus* for our Psalm is the alphabetical chapter Lam. iv, where we read (v. 19 f.) "Our persecutors......have *hotly pursued* us upon the mountains, they laid wait for us in the wilderness......the anointed of the Lord was taken in their pits &c."

PSALM X.

PS. X (Second half).

The lion trapped.

8 He lurks in the hamlet thickets;
In secret he slays the innocent;
His eyes are in wait for the helpless.
9 He waits in the secret places, as a lion in his lair;
So he waits to capture the poor.
He will^a [capture the poor]—when He draws him into
His net,   ^a Text uncertain. See Versions
10 He is crushed, brought low and falls^a.........the helpless.

He did not believe in retribution but it is coming.

11 He said in his heart, "God forgets"—
"He hides His face"—"He seeth not."
ר 14 Thou hast seen—Thou beholdest violence and vexation.
The helpless may leave it all on Thee, placed in Thy hand.
As for the orphan Thou art become his Helper.
12 Arise, O YHVH! God, lift up Thine hand; forget not
the poor.
13 Why should the wicked blaspheme God?
While he saith in his heart "Thou wilt not require it."
ש 15 Break Thou the arm of the wicked—as for the evil
Thou wilt require his wickedness till Thou find none.
16 [YHVH is become King for ever and ever:
The Nations are perished out of His Land.]
ת 17 Thou, YHVH, hast heard the desire of the humble,
Thou tunest their heart and lendest Thine ear thereto:
18 Righting the orphan and oppressed that earth-born man
may tyrannize no more.

v. 9 f. This corresponds with *v.* 2. There we read the prayer that the proud pursuer might be trapped, here the lion is trapped. The text in 9^c, 10 is uncertain; the words "capture the poor" may possibly be a repetition from the preceding line. If we might omit them we should read "He waits to capture the poor while He (i.e. God) is drawing him into His net." This, in any case, must be the general meaning of the passage. The translation "He croucheth, he boweth down" is contrary to the use of the words and to the authority of the Versions. The man-eating lion is drawn into God's pitfall and is there crushed. Cf. Ps. ix. 16, 17.

v. 15. " *Thou wilt require his wickedness till Thou find none.*" Wellhausen would alter the text and read " Require Thou his wickedness, forgive (it) not." But there is no need for this. God is the "requirer" of guilt (Ps. ix. 13), though the wicked man is self-blinded to the fact (Ps. x. 4). The judgement will make this manifest. The words "till Thou find none," lit. "till Thou find not," doubtless implied (to the Psalmist) a total extermination of evil men, but the Christian will see in the words the deeper thought of the extermination of evil in itself.

v. 17. " *Thou tunest their heart and lendest Thine ear thereto.*" The human heart is God's harp. Humility is its concert-pitch. The "desire of the humble" is the music of Heaven to which God can listen with delight and lend an attentive ear. The immediate reference is to the cry of the oppressed.

PSALM XXV.

This alphabetical Psalm should be studied first with its twin Psalm (xxxiv) and then with the other pair of twins (Pss. cxi and cxii). In all these cases we shall see that the alphabetical arrangement is subjected to the number *ten*. The number *ten* is the number of the Covenant.

In our present Psalm the close correspondence between the two halves (see marginal notes) makes it all but certain that the purpose of the original writer was to use the alphabet only so far as it fell in with his division of the Psalm into *two parts of ten letters each*; thus, out of the twenty-two letters, two must be omitted; the servile letter *Vav* would be a natural one to omit in the first half, and, since the second half ought to begin with *Mem* as the middle letter of the alphabet, it would follow that *Lamed* would be the other omitted letter. This being so, the original Psalm would have consisted of two equal parts of ten verses each, viz. verses 1—10 and verses 12—21. A later writer, wishing to maintain the structure of the Psalm and yet to make its *verses* correspond in number with the twenty-two letters of the alphabet, may have added verse 11 at the end of the first half and verse 22 at the end of the second half. This suspicion becomes well-nigh a certainty when we find that it also explains the formation of Psalm xxxiv.

The question now arises—The number *ten* denoting, as it does, the Covenant, what are we to understand by the *two* tens? Do they represent the two Tables, i.e. *God* and *Man*? The analogy of Pss. cxi and cxii would certainly point to this (see *ad loc.*). We observe also that in our present Psalm the first half seems to refer to deliverance from *sin* (*vv.* 7, 8), the second half to deliverance from *outward foes* (*vv.* 15, 17, 19). It is true that in the second half (verse 18) we find the words "forgive me all my sin," but a certain amount of doubt rests upon this verse since it begins with the letter *Resh* instead of the letter *Koph* which ought to stand here. Except for this doubtful verse the whole reference in the second half is to outward afflictions and foes.

In any case it would seem that the author of verses 11 and 22 recognised some such distinction as I have pointed out, since he sums up the first half in the words

v. 11 "For Thy Name's sake, YHVH, *pardon mine iniquity* for it is great,"

and the second half in the words

v. 22 "Redeem Israel, O God, *out of all his distresses*."

If these verses were added by a later writer he certainly entered into the spirit and purpose of the Psalm.

The first half, like the first 'Table' of the Covenant, relates to *God*. The second half, like the second "Table" of the Covenant, relates to *Man*, and, like the second Table, begins with the "promise" to "inherit the Land" (*v.* 13). In the first half the thought is of *God's own Nature* for which the soul longs, whereas in the second half we find ourselves dealing with the *moral law* and relation of *man to man*. This may be exemplified by the following table:

First Half.	Second Half.
v. 1. Unto Thee...I lift up my soul.	*v.* 12. Who is the God-fearing man? (cf. notes on Ps. xxxiv. 12): he has the promise of the life that now is (*v.* 13).
v. 5. Guide me, lead me, teach me.	*vv.* 16—19. Bring me out of the distresses and troubles in which I am entangled.
vv. 6, 7. Look at Thy own Nature, Thy compassions how eternal they are!	*vv.* 19 f. Look at my enemies how many they are!
vv. 8—10. God *is* goodness and rectitude itself, therefore He must impart that goodness as forgiveness, that rectitude as guidance.	*v.* 21. (My own) integrity and rectitude shall keep me, being as they are the faint reflex of Thy Nature.

The contrast between verse 8 and verse 21 should be noted. In *v.* 8 God, being, as He is, *goodness and rectitude*, keeps and guides man, whereas, in *v.* 21, it is not said that man's *goodness* and rectitude keep him but his "*integrity* and rectitude." The word here translated *integrity* is never applied to God: it denotes the *sincerity* of a conscience void of offence both (α) towards *God* (Gen. xx. 5, 6; 1 Kings ix. 4; Job i. 1, 8 &c.) and (β) towards *man* (Ps. lxxviii. 72; Prov. x. 9; xix. 1 &c.). If the assertion seem too strong that a man's own integrity and rectitude should keep him, we must remember the words that follow: "For I have waited for Thee." We may also compare Prov. xx. 28 "Mercy and truth keep the king, and his throne is upheld by mercy," and Prov. xiii. 6 "Righteousness keeps the man of upright way...."

In both these passages it seems clear that the mercy, truth and righteousness which "keep" the man are the mercy, truth and righteousness which he shews in his dealings with others; for "Merit lives from man to man" though "not from man, O Lord, to Thee."

Verse 1 is a line too short, while verse 5 is a line too long, the redundant line beginning with א; the sense is greatly improved if we restore this redundant line which I have placed in brackets to what was doubtless its original position in verse 1.

The reader will observe that I have transposed two ר verses (18 and 19), the doubtful verse 18 being enclosed in brackets. Originally a ק verse would have stood here and I have shewn (p. 18) that in some of the earlier alphabetical arrangements the order was not ק, ר but ר, ק. Compare also these letters in Ps. xxxiv and Ps. xxxvii.

PS. XXV (*First half*).

The Covenant must mean redemption from sin.

א 1 Unto Thee, O YHVH, I lift up my soul.
  [Thyself it is I hope for all the day.]
ב 2 In Thee, my God, I trust; I shall surely not be confounded!
  Nor shall mine enemies triumph over me.
ג 3 Yea, none that hope in Thee shall be confounded.
  Confounded be the wantonly treacherous ones.
ד 4 Thy WAYS, O YHVH, make me to know!
  Thy PATHS, teach me them!

Prayer for this redemption based on my sin.

ה 5 Guide me in Thy truth and teach me,
  For Thou art the God of my salvation.
ו 6 Remember Thy compassions, O YHVH,
  And Thy kindnesses, how eternal they are!
ח 7 My sins of youth and transgressions remember not
  In Thy kindness remember—Thou art mine!
  For the sake of Thy goodness—O YHVH!

Echo of vv. 1—4 with the added assurance of experience.

ט 8 Goodness and rectitude (itself) is YHVH,
  Therefore will He guide sinners in the WAY.
י 9 He will guide the humble aright,
  And teach the humble His WAY.
כ 10 All the PATHS of YHVH are kindness and truth
  To those that keep His covenant and testimonies.

——— —— —

ל 11 For Thy Name's sake, YHVH, pardon mine iniquity
  for it is great.

PS. XXV (*Second half*).

The Covenant must mean redemption from outward evils.

מ ₁₂ Who is the man that feareth YHVH?
  Him should He teach in the way He should choose.
נ ₁₃ His soul should dwell in good,
  And his seed should inherit the Land.
ס ₁₄ The intimate fellowship of YHVH is for those that fear Him,
  And His covenant is for their instruction.
ע ₁₅ Mine eyes are ever towards YHVH;
  He Himself frees my feet from the net.

Prayer for this redemption based on my misfortunes.

פ ₁₆ Turn Thou toward me and pity me,
  For lonely and poor am I.
צ ₁₇ Oh set my heart free from its troubles,
  And bring me out of my deep distress.
ר ₁₉ Behold my enemies how many they are!
  And they hate me with virulent hate.

Echo of vv. 1—4 with the added assurance of experience.

[ר ₁₈ Behold my affliction and misery
  And forgive me all my sin.]
שׁ ₂₀ Keep Thou my soul and deliver me;
  Let me not be confounded for in Thee I trust.
ת ₂₁ Integrity and rectitude shall keep me,
  For I have trusted in Thee.

פ ₂₂ Redeem Israel, O God, out of all his distresses.

PSALM XXXIV.

This alphabetical Psalm when compared with the alphabetical Psalm xxv suggests a most interesting study. Both consist of two closely corresponding halves. Both contain 22 verses, i.e. a verse for each letter of the alphabet. Both omit the letter *Vav*. Both duplicate the letter *Pe*. In both the 11th and 22nd verses (i.e. the letters *Lamed* and *Pe*) are superfluous and destroy to some extent the symmetry of the Psalm. Both therefore suggest an earlier arrangement in which each half of the Psalm consisted of 10 verses, the second half in each case beginning with the letter *Mem* which is the middle letter of the alphabet.

In Ps. xxxiv the two verses which begin with *Pe* (viz. *vv.* 16 and 22) have, I think, been transposed; I have therefore restored them to what I believe to have been their original position. The motive for the transposition would be the well-known Jewish feeling that no Psalm should end in malediction. As restored, Stanza II of the second half answers exactly to Stanza II of the first half, while verse 17 becomes intelligible.

The relation between the three Stanzas of the first half and the three corresponding Stanzas of the second half is very remarkable and should be studied with the marginal notes. It should be observed that the first half deals almost entirely with the relation between *God and an individual speaker* (*v.* 1 "I can bless...," *v.* 2 "My soul exulteth...," *v.* 3 "Magnify YHVH with me...," *v.* 4 "I sought...," *v.* 6 "This sufferer cried, i.e. *I* cried)," whereas the second half applies to *men generally*; compare also Ps. xxv.

We may also trace in the two halves of the Psalm an allusion to the two Tables of the Covenant.

As the second Table begins with "the Commandment of promise" so the second half of our Psalm begins with the "promise of the life that now is." Compare also on Ps. xxv and Pss. cxi and cxii.

I have again transposed the letters ק and ר (*vv.* 18 and 19). We have already seen strong reasons for believing that in other alphabetical Psalms the ר stood originally before the ק (see p. 27). Suffice it here to remark that the transposition suits the context and makes Stanzas II and III of the second half exactly correspond with Stanzas II and III of the first half. There is a direct connexion between "the contrite-hearted...the crushed in spirit (*v.* 18)" and the fact that God "keepeth all his bones, not one of them is broken (*v.* 20)." This connexion is lost if we read with the text

    19 "Many are the misfortunes of the righteous,
       But YHVH frees him out of them all.
    20 He keepeth all his bones,
       Not one of them is broken."

After saying that God frees the righteous out of all his misfortunes it were surely needless to add "He keepeth all his bones &c.," whereas the "nearness of YHVH" is the pledge that the "crushed in spirit" shall not be utterly broken.

Compare 2 Cor. iv. 8 ff. "pressed on every side, yet not straitened; perplexed, yet not unto despair; pursued, yet not left behind; smitten down, yet not destroyed." The words " *Come ye children* " &c. (*v.* 11) are usually taken with the words which follow, but they should, in my opinion, be taken as a summary of those that precede, i.e. of the first half of the Psalm. The "fear of the Lord," i.e. true religion, begins with the Duty to God, not with the Duty to Man. No doubt *v.* 12 begins abruptly but not more so than the 12th verse of the parallel Psalm xxv; indeed we find the same words in each case, "Who is the man...?"

Verse 2 contains two thoughts, (*a*) the personal deliverance of the speaker and (*b*) the fact that other sufferers would find courage from that deliverance. These two thoughts are expanded in verses 4, 5, the relation being seen as follows:

v. 2ᵃ. In YHVH my soul exulteth.   *v.* 4. $\begin{cases}\text{I sought YHVH and He answered me,}\\ \text{And from all my fears He set me free.}\end{cases}$

v. 2ᵇ. Sufferers shall hear and rejoice.   *v.* 5. $\begin{cases}\text{They looked unto Him and were}\\ \text{drawn,}\\ \text{And their faces were not ashamed.}\end{cases}$

Those who "look" are "sufferers" and the One to whom they are "drawn" is either God or' *the* Sufferer: the reason why they are drawn is because (*v.* 6), "This Sufferer cried and YHVH heard." The word which we have translated "drawn" (*v.* 5) occurs only in five other passages, two of which (Is. ii. 2 and Mic. iv. 1) are identical. In all these passages the word is applied to People or Nations which "flow together" as a river, drawn by some overmastering attraction. Thus:

Is. ii. 2 (Mic. iv. 1) "...all nations *shall flow* unto it," i.e. to the uplifted Temple of God.

Jer. xxxi. 12 "And they shall come singing with joy to the height of Zion and shall *flow together* (or *be drawn*) to the goodness of YHVH...."

Jer. li. 44 "And I will visit upon Bel in Babylon and will bring forth from his mouth that which he hath swallowed down, and the nations shall not *flow unto* him (i.e. *be drawn* unto him) any more."

Is. lx. 4, 5 "Lift up thine eyes round about thee, and see; they all gather together and come unto thee; thy sons come from far......then shalt thou fear and *flow together* (or *be drawn*), yea, thy heart shall fear and be enlarged; for the abundance as of a sea shall be turned unto thee, the host of the nations shall come unto thee."

This last passage is not without difficulty, but the general sense is clear. The Daughter of Zion is compared to a river into which tributary streams (the Gentile nations) suddenly pour themselves, so that the River 'fears as it is enlarged' and flows onward to its goal with a volume never felt before.

Thus in every passage in which our word occurs it signifies an overmastering attraction to which the Nations are drawn and in which they are united. In the present Psalm the attraction is by means of a Sufferer. The Christian will read it in the light of St John xii. 32 "I if I be lifted up out of the earth (cf. Is. ii. 2; Mic. iv. 1) will draw all men unto myself."

PS. XXXIV (*First half*).

The Covenant (Duty to God) the key of life.

א 1 I can bless YHVH at all times,
    His praise is continually in my mouth.
ב 2 In YHVH my soul exulteth,
    Sufferers shall hear and rejoice.
ג 3 O magnify YHVH with me
    And let us extol His Name together.
ד 4 I sought YHVH and He answered me,
    And from all my fears He set me free.

It means safety in suffering.

ה 5 They looked unto Him and were drawn,
    And their faces were not ashamed.
ז 6 This sufferer cried and YHVH heard
    And saved him out of all his afflictions.
ח 7 The Angel of YHVH encampeth round them that fear
    Him and delivereth them.

The test of experience.

ט 8 Taste and see that YHVH is good,
    Happy the man that finds refuge in Him.
י 9 Fear YHVH, O ye saints of His,
    For there is no lack to them that fear Him.
כ 10 Young lions may need and may hunger,
    But those that seek YHVH shall never lack one good thing.

[ל 11 Come, ye children, hearken unto me,
    I will teach you the fear of YHVH.]

v. 7. This verse must be read with *v.* 19. The angel host of Mahanaim (Gen. xxxii. 2) is a pledge of Jacob's victory (cf. Gen. xlviii. 16) but not of freedom from "misfortunes." The history of Jacob is the history of Israel.

PS. XXXIV (Second half).

The Covenant (Duty to man) the key of life.

מ 12 Who is the man that delighteth in life,
　　That loveth to see good days?
נ 13 Keep thy tongue from evil,
　　Thy lips from speaking fraud.
ס 14 Turn away from evil and do good,
　　Seek peace and pursue it.
ע 15 The eyes of YHVH are toward the righteous,
　　His ears are toward their cry.

It means safety in suffering.

פ 22 YHVH redeems the souls of His servants,
　　And none that trust in Him shall be held guilty.
צ 17 They cry and YHVH hears,
　　And from all their afflictions He frees them.
ר 19 Many are the misfortunes of the righteous,
　　But YHVH frees him out of them all.

The test of experience.

ק 18 Near is YHVH to the contrite-hearted,
　　He saveth the crushed in spirit.
ש 20 He keepeth all his bones,
　　Not one of them is broken.
ת 21 A misfortune brings death to the wicked,
　　And those that hate the righteous shall be held guilty.

[פ 16 The face of YHVH is against evil-doers,
　　To cut off their remembrance from the earth.]

v. 15 f. If following the alphabetical arrangement of Lamentations, we transpose the verses ע and פ the sense becomes clearer and the parallelism more complete.
v. 21. "*A misfortune brings death to the wicked.*" Contrast *v.* 19 "Many are the misfortunes of the righteous, but YHVH frees him out of them all" (cf. *v.* 7), but one single misfortune may bring destruction upon those whose lives are not stayed upon God, who become "as natural brute beasts made to be taken and destroyed" (2 Pet. ii. 12); cf. the "young lions" of *v.* 10.

K.　　　　　　　　　　　　　　　　　　　　　　5

PSALM XXXVII.

If in this alphabetical Psalm we omit as before the letters *Vav* and *Lamed* (i.e. *vv.* 10, 11 and *vv.* 21, 22) we see at once that the Psalm divides itself into *four* equal parts of *five letters each*, with two verses (originally) to each letter, i.e. we have four tens of verses so arranged that Part I corresponds closely with Part III and Part II with Part IV, as may be seen from the marginal notes. We are further confirmed in the omission of letters *Vav* and *Lamed* when we remember that, in two other alphabetical Psalms (xxv and xxxiv, see notes), these same letters *Vav* and *Lamed* had no place in the original structure. I suggest therefore that, in the present Psalm, the letters Vav (*vv.* 10, 11) and Lamed (*vv.* 21, 22) are due to a later editor who recognized the fact that the Psalm consisted of *four tens* of verses and therefore was obliged, while introducing four new verses, to retain the original number of forty. This he did by making the letters ד, כ, ע and פ consist of one verse each instead of two (see *vv.* 7, 20, 28ʰ and 34); thus, by taking one verse out of each of the four parts, the original number of forty was somewhat violently retained. If the reader will compare the parallel stanzas of Part I and Part II he will see that whereas Part I refers to the Duty to *God*, Part II refers to the Duty to *Man*. 'Blessed are the patient' (toward God), 'Cursed are the violent' (toward Man) is the moral of each.

In like manner it will be seen that Part III refers to *God*, Part IV to *Man*; the moral of Part III being 'Blessed are the righteous' (regarded as imitators of God's mercy; see note on *v.* 26), i.e. 'Blessed are the merciful,' while the moral of Part IV is 'Cursed are the wicked,' i.e. the unmerciful. The number *ten*, which is the number of the Covenant, enters doubly into the structure of this Psalm, for, if we regard the *verses*, each of the four Parts consisted originally of *ten* verses; if, on the other hand, we regard the alphabetical *letters*, of which each Part has five, we see that Parts I and III, which refer to *God*, have *ten* letters, while Parts II and IV, which refer to *Man*, have also ten letters.

Just as the words "inherit the Land" (*vv.* 9, 11, 22, 29, 34) imply all the promises of the Covenant, so the words "cut off" (9, 22, 28ʰ, 34, 38) imply all that is included in being "cut off" from the Covenant (cf. Exod. xii. 15; Lev. xviii. 29 &c.). This technical use of the *Niphal* which is so common in the Priest-code is found nowhere else in the Psalms.

PSALM XXXVII.

I have again transposed the letters ק and ר (i.e. v. 35 f. and v. 34) because the parallelism of the stanzas seems to require it and also because the ר stood before the ק in other alphabetical arrangements.

As to the letters ע, פ I think it probable that the original text of the Psalm followed the order of the alphabetical chapters of Lamentations (see p. 18), and placed פ before ע. The transposition of these verses has caused a confusion between עוֹלִים נִשְׁמְדוּ "the unrighteous are destroyed" (Sept. *Alex.*) and (לְ)עוֹלָם נִשְׁמְרוּ "they are preserved for ever" (E.V.; the P.B.V. combines both readings). If we might transpose the ע and פ verses the sense would be clearer and the correspondence indicated in the margin by the letters d d_1 d_2 d_3; e e_1 e_2 e_3 would become symmetrical.

The parallel texts as printed will shew the relation of Part I to Part II and of Part III to Part IV, but the reader is specially asked to study the still closer relationship between Part I and Part III and between Part II and Part IV.

FIRST COLLECTION, ALPHABETICAL PSALMS

Part I.

(*a*) Patience towards God,

א 1 Fret not thyself about the evil-doers,
Be not jealous about the workers of iniquity.
2 For like grass they shall quickly fade,
And like the green herbage shall wither.

(*b*) being the reflex of His Patience, inherits the promises of the Covenant,

ב 3 Trust in YHVH and do good,
Dwell in the Land,
And feed on (His) Faithfulness.
4 Delight thyself also in YHVH,
And He shall grant thee thy heart's desires.

(*c*) is seen in its end,

ג 5 Cast (the burden of) thy way on YHVH,
Trust in Him and He will act,
6 And will bring forth thy righteousness as light
And thy judgement as the noon-day.

(*d*) The moral of letter ב, i.e. of vv. 3, 4,

ד 7 Hold thou still in YHVH
And wait for Him;
Fret not thyself about one whose way prospers,
About the man who effects his bad designs.

(*e*) The moral of letter א, i.e. of vv. 1, 2,

ה 8 Cease from anger,
And forsake wrath;
Fret not thyself—it merely tends to harm,
9 For evil-doers shall be cut off,
But those that wait for YHVH—
They shall inherit the Land.

Summary of the above,

ו 10 Yet but a little while and the wicked is no more,
Thou mayest ponder over his place—but he is not!
11 But the meek shall inherit the Land
And delight themselves in abounding peace.

v. 3. "*Trust in YHVH*"—here we have man's duty to God (First Table)—"and do good," χρηστότητα, i.e. man's duty to man (Second Table). The reward of the Second Table is "dwell in the Land." The reward of the First Table is "feed (lit. *pasture*) on (God's) faithfulness." The unusual expression brings out the parallelism. Those whose love of God is shewn in "trust" will enjoy His *trustworthiness* (cf. *v.* 5 and 1 Pet. ii. 7) just as those whose love of man is shewn in "doing good" will enjoy the promise of earth. It seems necessary to take the *imperatives* "dwell in the Land &c." as promises, cf. *v.* 27 "...do good and dwell for evermore," but if this be a difficulty in grammar it is no difficulty in Theology.

PART II.

(*a₁*) Violence toward man,

ו 12 The wicked layeth plans for the righteous
 And gnasheth his teeth at him.
 13 The Lord will laugh at him
 For He sees that his day is coming.

(*b₁*) being opposed to Nature, ends in self-destruction,

ח 14 The wicked draw the sword and bend their bow
 To cast down the poor and needy,
 To slaughter those that go right.
 15 Their sword shall pierce their own heart
 And their bows shall be broken.

(*c₁*) is seen in its end.

ט 16 A righteous man's little is better
 Than the abundance of many wicked;
 17 For the arms of the wicked shall be broken,
 While YHVH upholdeth the righteous.

(*d₁*) The moral of letter ח, i.e. of vv. 14, 15.

י 18 YHVH noteth the days of the upright
 And their inheritance shall be for ever.
 19 They shall not be shamed in the time of evil
 And in the days of dearth they shall have enough.

(*e₁*) The moral of letter ו, i.e. of vv. 12, 13.

כ 20 But the wicked perish—
 And the enemies of YHVH,
 Like the beauty of the meadows,
 Are gone as smoke—
 They are gone.

Summary of the above.

ל 21 The wicked borrows—but cannot pay,
 While the righteous is gracious and giving.
 22 For those that are blessed of Him shall inherit the Land,
 And those that are cursed of Him shall be cut off.

---

v. 21. "*The wicked......but cannot pay.*" It is not through his wickedness that he *will not* but through his misfortune that he *cannot* pay. He has no real root (cf. *vv.* 35, 36) and so perishes like the bad tree. Herein he is contrasted with the righteous who being 'rooted and grounded in love' partakes of God's own attribute of mercy (see *v.* 26) and so becomes himself "gracious and giving" out of an endless store.

Part III.

(a₄) Righteousness towards God,

בּ 23 From YHVH it is that the steps of a man are established,
And his way gives Him pleasure.
24 Though he fall he is not cast away,
For YHVH upholds his hand.

(b₃) being the reflex of His Mercy, inherits the promise,

ג 25 I have been young and now am old,
Yet never saw a righteous man forsaken
[So that his seed should beg for bread]ᵃ.
26 He is always merciful and lending
And his seed is for a blessing.

ᵃ Possibly a gloss

(c₂) seen in its end.

ד 27 Turn from evil and do good
And dwell for evermore,
28 For YHVH loveth right
And will not leave His saints.

(c₃) Out of place. Transpose with ב stanza.

ע [The unrighteous are destroyed]
And the seed of the wicked is cut off.
29 Righteous ones inherit the Land
And dwell therein for ever.

(d₃) The moral of letter ג, i.e. of vv. 25, 26.

פ 30 The mouth of a righteous man meditates wisdom
And his tongue will be speaking of judgement.
31 The Lawᵇ of his God is in his heart
So his steps do not falter.

ᵇ Ps. i. 2

---

v. 26. "*He is always merciful and lending.*" It is worthy of note that in the pair of alphabetical Psalms cxi and cxii which compare the character of God with the character of the God-like man it is said of God (cxi. 4) that He is "gracious and merciful," and of the God-like man (cxii. 4) that he is "gracious, merciful and righteous." So here, the good man is "gracious and giving" because his roots touch the springs of God's grace and bounty.

Part IV.

(a_3) Injustice toward man,
   צ 32 The wicked sets watch for the righteous
And seeketh to slay him.
33 YHVH will not leave him in his hand,
Nor condemn him when he is judged.

(b_3) being opposed to Nature, ends in nothingness,
   ר 35 I have seen the wicked tyrannically strong
Outspreading like a verdant native tree.
36 But one passed—and lo he was gone!
I sought him but he was no more!

(c_3) seen in its end.
   ק 34 Wait for YHVH
And keep His way,
And He shall exalt thee to inherit the Land.
Thou shalt see the cutting off of the wicked.

(d_3) The moral of letter ר, i.e. of vv. 35, 36.
   ש 37 Observe the perfect and regard the upright,
That there is a future to the man of peace;
38 While transgressors are utterly destroyed,
The future of the wicked is cut off.

(e_3) The moral of letter צ, i.e. of vv. 32, 33.
   ת 39 The salvation of the righteous is from YHVH,
Their stronghold in time of distress.
40 And YHVH helped them and delivered them—
Will deliver them from the wicked and will save them—
Because they confided in Him.

---

v. 35 f. The contrast between this stanza and the parallel stanza of Part III reminds us of the "two ways" of Psalm i and Jer. xvii. 5–8. The bad man is "like the heath in the desert." Compare also verses 19, 20 in Part II of our Psalm.

v. 37. "*Observe the perfect.*" We are reluctantly compelled to give up the rendering of the P.B.V., "*Keep innocency...*" Both the usage of the language and the parallelism of the thought are against it.

THIRD COLLECTION, ALPHABETICAL PSALMS.

The four Alphabetical Psalms of the Third Collection would seem to have been moulded upon the pattern of the four Alphabetical Psalms of the First Collection. Not only are they alike in number but they begin with the same words, "I thank YHVH with my whole heart" (Ps. ix 1, and Ps. cxi 1), and have several thoughts in common, such as *inheriting the Land* (Ps. xxv 13, xxxvii 11, 22, 29, with Ps. cxii. 2), *The Promise of the Covenant; The Kingship of God on Earth*, etc.

Perhaps it is not altogether an accident that as the Alphabetical Psalms of the First Collection begin with a closely related *pair* (Psalms ix—x) so the Psalms of the Third Collection begin with a closely related *pair* (Psalms cxi—cxii). In the Third Collection there are traces of the same use of the number *ten*, the same allusions to the Covenant, and in one case (Ps. cxi—cxii) we find the same peculiar redundance of the letters ו and ל: but, whereas in the First Collection we have shewn that ר stood before ק, and probably ס before ע, we note that *in the Third Collection the order of the Alphabet was fixed as we have it now*. This is extremely important, tending, as it does, to shew that the order of the Hebrew Alphabet, as we have it now, was fixed between the dates of the First and Third Collections.

In the Psalms of the First Collection the number *ten*, the sacred number of the Priest Code, governs the whole construction, but in the Psalms of the Third Collection (Pss. cxi—cxii excepted) this is no longer the case. Thus Ps. cxix is governed by the number *eight* (see *ad loc.*), while in Ps. cxlv the Holy Name occurs *eight* times, the reference to the Covenant number *ten* is much less clear than in the Psalms of the First Collection.

These later Alphabetical Psalms approach more nearly to the nature of the simple acrostic.

PSALM CXI.

Psalms cxi. and cxii. form a pair and must be studied together. Their structure is identical. Both have 10 verses in 22 alphabetical lines. Each verse consists of two lines with the exception of verses 9 and 10, which have three lines apiece. If we might follow the pattern of earlier Alphabetical Psalms (see p. 34) and omit the letters ו and ל each Psalm would fall naturally into *two parts of* 10 *lines* (*i.e.* 10 *letters*) *each*, the division being at the letter ב, the middle letter of the alphabet. The number *Ten* is as we have seen (p. 26) the number of the Covenant which plays such an important part in the Alphabetical Psalms. In order to preserve the structure I have enclosed the ו and ל lines in square brackets. If the reader will study the parallel texts he will see, especially in the case of the ו line, how easily these lines may have been introduced and how much more complete and symmetrical the parallelism is if we ignore them.

For the purpose of comparison I have printed in parallel columns each Psalm twice; the first table enables us to compare Part I with Part II of each Psalm; the second table shews Psalm cxi. (of the good God) with Psalm cxii. (of the good man).

THIRD COLLECTION, ALPHABETICAL PSALMS.

PS. CXI (PART I).

The good God as He is in Himself.

His blessedness and stability.	א 1 I thank YHVH with my whole heart, ב In the Communion of Saints and Assembly. ג 2 Great are the works of YHVH, ד Exquisite to all desire. cf. *Vulg.*
His liberality.	ה 3 Splendour and Majesty is His work [ו And His Righteousness abideth for ever]. ז 4 He hath made a Memorial-Name for His wonders. ח "Gracious and Merciful is YHVH."
The practical result.	ט 5 He hath given provision to them that fear Him, י He will remember His Covenant for ever. כ 6 The power of His works He declared to His People, ל To give them the heritage of the Gentiles.]

v. 1ª. "*I thank &c.*" This line is identical with the first line of Ps. ix., which is also an alphabetical Psalm. It should also be compared with the first line of the alphabetical Psalm xxxiv, with which our present Psalm has much in common in point of structure. The motive for the thankfulness of line א is found in line ב, "The works of His hands are truth and judgement." The collocation of "truth and judgement" is rare and reminds us of Ps. cxix. 160, "The sum of Thy Word is *truth*, each righteous *judgement* of Thine is eternal." The Hebrew word for *Truth*, consisting as it does of the *first*, *middle* and *last* letters of the Hebrew alphabet, became in later times the sign-manual of God, Who is not only the *Alpha* from which all things proceed and the *Omega* to which they tend but also the Middle Term by which they exist. When then the poet says, "The sum of Thy word is truth" he expresses the thought that "All creation is one act at once—the birth of light."

v. 1ᵇ. "*In the Communion of Saints and Assembly*"—i.e. This joy in God is mine not only in the familiar intercourse of like-minded friends but also in great congregations. When joy in God is shared with others it gains stability—there is a *firmament* in our Heaven. The parallel line (letter ב) gives the outward justification of this inner joy, for "All His precepts are sure."

v. 2ᵇ. "*Exquisite...*"—i.e. 'worthy of searching study':—Vulg. "Exquisita in omnes voluntates ejus." All God's works are exquisitely adapted in all their purposes to His great ends, being (as the parallel line 8ᵇ tells us) "wrought in truth and right." Hence it follows that

"This world's no blot for us,
Nor blank; it means intensely, and means good;"

Thus the other rendering is virtually implied—God's meanings must be "sought out by all them that have pleasure therein." And so we must complete the quotation:—

"To find its meaning is my meat and drink."

v. 3ª. "*Splendour and Majesty.*" These words bespeak the glory of a King, but this glory is shewn in "sending forth Redemption for His People" (see the parallel line 9ª).

"Conquering kings their titles take
From the foes they captive make;
Jesu, by a nobler deed,
From the captives He has freed."

v. 3ᵇ. "*His Righteousness &c.*" Though we do not accept these words as part of the original text we

PS. CXI (PART II).

The good God as He is towards the world.

His blessedness and stability.
- מ 7 The works of His hands are truth and judgement,
- נ All His precepts are sure.
- ס 8 They are stable for ever and ever,
- ע Being wrought in truth and right.

His liberality.
- פ 9 He hath sent forth Redemption for His People,
- צ He hath enjoined His Covenant for ever,
- ק Holy and reverend is His Name.

The practical result.
- ר 10 The fear of YHVH is the foundation of wisdom,
- ש A good intelligence comes to all those that practise them.
- ת His praise abideth for ever.

are bound to interpret them as they stand. When then we take them with the parallel passages in Ps. cxii. 3 and 9, where it is also stated of the good man that "his righteousness abideth for ever," we are compelled to give to the word its *later* significance of *beneficence* [cf. St Paul's quotation of Ps. cxii. 9 in II Cor. ix. 9]. The active beneficence of God is continued through Creation and must be imitated by man: "My Father worketh hitherto, and I work."

v. 4. "*A Memorial-Name for His wonders*"—i.e. *A Memorial-Name* to which all His wonders point. The word translated *Memorial* signifies the revelation of God's nature, e.g. Ex. iii. 15. "This is My Name for ever, and this is My *Memorial* unto all generations" [cf. notes on Pss. xxx. 4 (5); xcvii. 12]. The Memorial-Name which summed up all the Old Testament revelation was that Name revealed to Moses in Exod. xxxiv. 6 "And the Lord passed by before him and proclaimed, The Lord, The Lord God, *merciful and gracious*..." Our Psalm does not quote the whole passage because the object was merely to set forth those attributes of God in which He could be imitated by men; thus in the parallel verse of Ps. cxii. it is said of the good man that "*he is gracious and merciful*."

Without founding any argument on the date of Exodus it is clear that such a revelation of the *attributes of God* had been made in early times, for it is alluded to in Joel ii. 13; Jonah iv. 2 [cf. also Neh. ix. 17, 31; Pss. lxxxvi. 15; ciii. 8; cxvi. 5; cxlv. 8].

This word 'Memorial' which is almost identical with 'Name' is also used of the righteous man in the Companion-Psalm (cxii. 6). "For an eternal Memorial (i.e. name) he is 'Righteous,'" i.e. As God is known by His Name (Character) of "Gracious and Merciful" (Ps. cxi. 4) so the good man is known by the name (character) of "gracious and merciful *and righteous*" (Ps. cxii. 4). This is his name for ever (Ps. cxii. 6) even as it is God's "Name for ever" (Exod. iii. 15). The added term "righteous," cf. *v*. 4, does not, of course, imply that the good man is something *more* than a copy of the good God; it merely qualifies the attributes of 'gracious and merciful' in so far as they can be copied by man on earth. God is the great Almsgiver; man must copy Him in this.

v. 4. "*His wonders*":—The word carries with it the thought of darkness, terror and mystery. God's way was terrible, His footsteps were not known, but through all He was carrying out His purpose of Redemption and revealing His hidden Name of Love. See also note on the parallel verse of the next Psalm. The same thought is repeated in verse 6, "The power of His works He declared to His People, so as to give them the heritage of the Gentiles."

v. 5 f. The parallelism between the lines מ, נ, ס, and the lines ר, ש, ת is not easy to trace. In both cases they sum up the practical result of the two preceding stanzas.

PS. CXII (PART I).

The good man in his inner life.

א 1 Oh happy is the man that feareth YHVH,
ב   In His commandments he finds exceeding joy.
ג 2 Mighty on earth shall his seed become,
ד   The generation of the saints shall be blessed.
ה 3 Wealth and riches are in his house
ו   And his righteousness abideth for ever].
ז 4 There is risen in darkness a light for the saints.
ח   "He is gracious and merciful and righteous."
ט 5 It is well with the man, he is gracious^a and giving,
י   He will maintain his words aright.
כ 6 Everlastingly he remains unmoved.
ל   For an eternal Memorial he is "Righteous."]

^a Prov. xxii. 8; II Cor. ix. 7

PS. CXII. COMPARISON OF PARTS I AND II.

Letters א and ט. The man who fears God need have no other fear. If we apply the Psalm to Christ then His courage in persecution is the best commentary.

ב and י. He delights in doing his Father's will (Matt. xi. 25 f.) and so finds perfect peace and rest of heart (cf. also Is. xxvi. 3, "the *stable* mind Thou wilt keep in perfect peace because it is *stayed* on Thee"). The Midrash, which applies the Psalm to Abraham, gives instances of his ready obedience.

ג and כ. He will not fail nor be discouraged until he sees a seed that shall prolong its days and the purpose of YHVH prospers in his hand. Compare the confidence with which Christ in the presence of death looked forward to the triumph of His work.

ה and ל. He is rich in himself and rich in his bounty, he empties himself, that the poor through his poverty may become rich.

ז and ט. Because he thus pours himself out for others therefore in his darkness the sunrise of a new Day begins, and it is a "Sun of Righteousness." His righteousness (i.e. his *justification before God and man*) shines forth and 'abides for ever.' The shining forth of righteousness like light is also found in the alphabetical Ps. xxxvii. 6, "He will bring forth thy righteousness as light." This is a characteristic of the second Isaiah (see Chap. lxii. 1 f., and compare for the thought of a *revelation* of righteousness, Chaps. lxvi. 1; lxi. 11; xlv. 8; li. 5). We also read of a sowing of righteousness as if it were a seed, e.g. Hos. x. 12, "Sow to yourselves in righteousness, reap in grace;" cf. Prov. xi. 18. The double thought of the springing forth of righteousness like seed and the springing forth of righteousness like light is curiously combined in the prophecies of the 'Branch' (lit. *Outspring*) which becomes in St Luke "The Day-spring from on high." The outspring of the sun out of the darkness and the outspring of seed from the cold earth are closely kindred thoughts; compare the double reading of Ps. xcvii. 11, "Light is sown (*or* risen, like a sunrise) for the righteous." This double thought seems to have been in St Paul's mind when he quotes our present Psalm as an inducement to alms-giving II Cor. ix. 9 f. At first sight when we compare the parallel lines, "There is risen in

PS. CXII (PART II).

The good man in his outer life.

- ט 7 He will not fear because of evil tidings,
- נ His heart is fixed—stayed upon YHVH.
- ס 8 Stable is his heart—he feareth not,
- ע Until he see his desire upon his enemies.
- פ 9 He hath scattered abroad, he hath given to the poor,
- צ His righteousness abideth for ever,
- ק His horn is exalted with honour.
- ר 10 The wicked shall see and be vexed,
- ש He will gnash with his teeth and melt away.
- ת The desire of wicked men perishes.

darkness a light for the saints," and "his righteousness abideth for ever," the connexion does not appear obvious, but when we have studied the texts which speak of the rising of righteousness like a glorious sunrise we see that the connexion is most close and exact. The first denotes the reward that the good man has in himself, the second the reward that he has in the world. Thus if we applied the Psalm to Christ we should say that the 'light that rose' for Him 'in the darkness' was the transfiguring consciousness that He was doing His Father's will, while His 'righteousness abiding for ever' was His victory, with all its fruits in the world.

ח and ק. 'He (i.e. the righteous man) is gracious and merciful and righteous,' i.e. the very Name of God is named upon him, so 'His horn is exalted with honour,' cf. Phil. ii. 9, "Wherefore also God highly exalted Him, and gave unto Him the name which is above every name."

In the three lines which follow, ט, י, ב with ר, ש, ת, we have, not parallelism, but sharp contrast.

The allusion to the wicked man in the three lines ר, ש, ת, should be compared with the three last verses of Ps. i, "Far otherwise with the wicked!" &c. and also with the ת line of Ps. xxxiv.

"A misfortune brings death to the wicked,
And those that hate the righteous shall be held guilty."

The thought of the "two ways" (see notes on Ps. i.) is constantly present to the Psalmist's mind,

PS. CXI (PART I).

The good God as He is in Himself.

[Hallelu-Yah.]

{ א 1 I thank YHVH with my whole heart,
ב In the Communion of Saints and Assembly.
ג 2 Great are the works of YHVH,
ד Exquisite to all desire.

{ ה 3 Splendour and Majesty is His work
ו And His Righteousness abideth for ever].
ז 4 He hath made a Memorial-Name of His wonders.
ח " Gracious and Merciful is YHVH."

{ ט 5 He hath given provision to them that fear Him,
י He will remember His Covenant for ever.
כ 6 The power of His works He declared to His People,
ל To give them the heritage of the Gentiles.]

NOTES ON PS. CXI (PART I) COMPARED WITH PS. CXII (PART I).

cxi. 1 with cxii. 1. I thank God for the Covenant—Happy alone is the man who finds his joy therein.

cxi. 2 with cxii. 2. God's works are mighty and enduring so that man (through the Covenant) shall be mighty and enduring.

cxi. 3ᵃ with cxii. 3ᵃ. His state is kingly—so too the good man's.

cxi. 4 with cxii. 4. The mystery of God's terrible wonders unfolds at last the Divine Name as "Gracious and Merciful." So out of the darkness which seems to beset the good man there rises a Divine Nature: he too is "gracious and merciful and righteous."

cxi. 5 with cxii. 5. As the good God gives food to all so the good man shares His joy in giving.

As the good God abides by His Covenant in spite of all provocation, so of the good man—his word is his bond.

(cxi. 6ᵃ with cxii. 6ᵃ). These words are difficult. They do not mean that God "shewed" i.e. *caused* His People *to see* "the power of His works," for then a different verb would have been used (as in Exod. ix. 16). They must mean that God "declared" or "told," as a revelation to His people, what the whole bearing of His mighty works had meant; thus the line is similar in meaning to verse 4. The relation with cxii. 6ᵃ is not evident, but we notice in both Psalms the same relation between verses 6 and 4.

Psalm cxi. should never be separated from its companion—Psalm cxii. Read together they become a prophecy of the Incarnation. The Latin Church (according to Blunt) appointed Pss. cxi–cxii. for Christmas Day; but our Church, misled by a Patristic interpretation of "*provision*" (in cxi. 5), reads

PS. CXII (PART I).

The good man as he is in himself.

[Hallelu-Yah.]

א 1 Oh happy is the man that feareth YHVH,
ב   In His commandments he finds exceeding joy.
ג 2 Mighty on earth shall his seed become,
ד   The generation of the saints shall be blessed.
ה 3 Wealth and riches are in his house
ו   And his righteousness abideth for ever].
ז 4 There is risen in darkness a light for the saints.
ח   " He is gracious and merciful and righteous."
ט 5 It is well with the man, he is gracious and giving,
י   He will maintain his words aright.
כ 6 Everlastingly he remains unmoved.
ל   For an eternal Memorial he is " Righteous."]

Ps. cxi. as a Proper Psalm for Easter and neglects the connexion with Ps. cxii. The 9th verse of Ps. cxi., "He hath sent forth Redemption for His People.........Holy and reverend is His Name," seems to be alluded to both in the Magnificat and in the Song of Zacharias. Thus,—"Holy is His Name" (Luke i. 49); "He hath visited and *redeemed His people*" (Luke i. 68). But the obvious fitness of the two Psalms for Christmas depends not on these allusions only but on the whole subject-matter. The following outline should be filled in by the meditation of the reader :

Blessedness and stability. The Will of the good God is worthy to be embraced in the hearts of His creatures (cxi. 1 and 7)...One Man there is, a second Abraham, who finds "exceeding joy" in doing to the uttermost this perfect Will of God (cxii. 1 and 7). All God's works in Nature and Grace are stable, i.e. they have a glorious future to which they tend and grow; they are, as it were, the children of God's thought (cxi. 2 and 8). The good Man enters into their purpose, and becomes partaker of their growing future. Like another Abraham his "seed" is "mighty on earth" (cxii. 2 and 8)...

Liberality. All the Glory of God is revealed at last, not in receiving but in giving...All is for the children ! Hence His abiding Name is Love (cxi. 3, 4, and 9). So the good Man, entering into His thought, shews on earth that it is more blessed to give than to receive,...Hence too His Name is one with God's Name (cxii. 3, 4, and 9).

Summary. The good God binds Himself to the Covenant (cxi. 5) and gives His People a perpetual remembrance of it (cxi. 6 note), because the blessings He has in store can only be attained through Reverence (cxi. 10). So the good Man binds himself to his promise (cxii. 5) and becomes an "eternal Memorial" (cxii. 6). The wicked, being destitute of Reverence, cut themselves off from the Covenant and perish (cxii. 10).

PS. CXI (PART II).

The good God as He is towards man.

God's *works* and *thoughts* are stable.

His liberality is
(α) *free*,
(β) *continuous*,
(γ) *and brings him honour.*

See the practical result!

{ פ 7 The works of His hands are truth and judgement,
נ All His precepts are sure.
ס 8 They are stable for ever and ever,
ע Being wrought in truth and right.
פ 9 He hath sent forth Redemption for His People,
צ He hath enjoined His Covenant for ever,
ק Holy and reverend is His Name.
ר 10 The fear of YHVH is the foundation of wisdom,
ש A good intelligence comes to all those that practise them.
ת His praise abideth for ever.

PS. CXII (PART II).

The good man as he is towards man.

The good man's *works* and *thoughts* are stable. His liberality is (α) *free*, (β) *continuous*, (γ) *and brings him honour*. Contrast the wicked man!	מ 7 He will not fear because of evil tidings, נ His heart is fixed—stayed upon YHVH. ס 8 Stable is his heart—he feareth not, ע Until he see his desire upon his enemies. פ 9 He hath scattered abroad, he hath given to the poor, צ His righteousness abideth for ever. ק His horn is exalted with honour. ר 10 The wicked shall see and be vexed, ש He shall gnash his teeth and melt away. ת The desire of wicked men perishes.

K.

50   THIRD COLLECTION, ALPHABETICAL PSALMS.

PSALM CXIX.

"In each verse—so runs the Masoretic note on *v*. 122—*v*. 122 alone excepted, there is found one of the ten expressions (pointing to the ten words of the Law given at Sinai)." (Delitzsch.) The ten expressions are (1) *Oracles*, (2) *Word*, (3) *Testimony*, (4) *Way*, (5) *Judgements*, (6) *Precepts*, (7) *Commandments*, (8) *Law*, (9) *Statutes*, (10) *Faithfulness* (according to another reading *righteousness*).

This Jewish tradition gives us a valuable hint but it is not strictly accurate. The characteristic number of Ps. cxix. is not *ten* but *eight*; each of the twenty-two letters being repeated *eight* times. Thus we are led to expect rather the number *eight* than *ten*. And so we find it.

The Divine Name, YHVH, occurs 22 times and, if we study the above ten expressions we shall find that *eight* of them occur (practically) 22 times each.

Thus *Law*   25 times, i.e. (22 + 3) times,
     Oracles   19 times, i.e. (22 − 3) times,
     Word   22 times,
     Commandments   22 times,
     Judgements   22 times,
     Statutes   22 times,
     Testimonies   23 times, i.e. (22 + 1) times,
     Precepts   21 times, i.e. (22 − 1) times.

Thus, on an average, each of these *eight* terms under which the Law can be described occurs 22 times just as YHVH occurs 22 times, the letters of the alphabet being 22 in number.

Thus I conclude that these eight terms have a special significance and I have printed them in small capitals.

Of the other two expressions suggested by the Jewish tradition, "*faithfulness*" only occurs five times and can scarcely be said to be one of the names of the Law; "*way*" (דרך) occurs 13 times, in six of which, at least, it refers not to God's way but to man's way.

The significance of these eight terms must now be considered.

1. תורה *Thora* "Law," lit. "teaching." Nothing can be more misleading than to confine the word, as is usually done, to the Law of Moses. There is an inwardness in the word which makes it almost identical with *inspiration*. Thus of the priest, through whom it came continuously as a Divine message to men, it is said "The *law* of truth was in his mouth..." (Mal. ii. 6; cf. Jer. ii. 8; viii. 8; Ezek. vii. 26). The true seat of *Thora* is in the heart (Ps. xxvii. 31; xl. 8 (9); Is. li. 7). The

PSALM CXIX.

Law of God is properly the inspiration which proceeds from God just as the "*law of kindness*" (Prov. xxxi. 26) is the inspiration which proceeds from kindness, and "*the law of a mother*" (Prov. vi. 20) is the inspiration of a mother's influence. The *Law* is thus often compared to Light from Light (see notes on Ps. xix.), e.g. Is. li. 4 "a law shall proceed from Me...as a light to the nations." Zion is the centre from which this inspiration shall go forth: "The Law shall go forth from Zion..." (Mic. iv. 2). The prophets felt that the written Law was only a shadow of that Law which must at last be "written in the hearts" of men (see Jer. xxxi. 33). There is no one word in English to express the meaning of *Thora*; if we must use the word *Law* we must read into it the meanings which I have here stated. *Thora* is found 25 times in the 119th Psalm.

2. מִצְוָה "*Commandment*." This word differs from *Thora* as the command of a father differs from the influence of a mother; thus it is said "Observe, my son, the *Commandment* of thy father and forsake not the *Thora* of thy mother" (Prov. vi. 20). Or, to use another illustration, as a *lamp* differs from the *light* of the sun; so it is said (Prov. vi. 23) "the *Commandment* is a lamp and *Thora* is Light." *Commandments* may be many but *Thora* in its essence is one. "*Commandment*" occurs 22 times in Ps. cxix. i.e. as many times as there are letters in the alphabet.

3. מִשְׁפָּט "*Judgement*." This word also occurs 22 times in our Psalm and in almost every passage it must be taken as a synonym for "*law*," as in Ps. lxxxi. 4 (5), where it is translated "a *law* of the God of Jacob" (cf. Exod. xv. 25 &c.). This sense is common in Leviticus, where we often read of the "Statutes and the judgements." The "judgements" of God were the Divine *decisions* on special cases from time to time which came through the medium of the priest. "They shall teach Thy *judgements* to Jacob and Thy *Thora* to Israel" (Deut. xxxiii. 10).

4. חֻקִּים "*statutes*." There is a feeling of permanence in this word: it is used to describe what we should call the 'laws' of the sun, moon and stars (Jer. xxxi. 35; xxxiii. 25; cf. v. 24; Job xxxviii. 33), consequently it is often coupled with the words "for ever," i.e. a "perpetual statute" (Exod. xxix. 28; xxx. 21; Lev. vi. 18 (11), 22 (15); vii. 34; x. 15; xxiv. 9 &c.). It is a favourite thought with Jeremiah that the permanence of the laws of Nature is a type and pledge of the permanence of God's statutes to Israel (Jer. xxxi. 36; cf. v. 22—24). The word "statutes" also occurs 22 times in our Psalm.

5. עֵדָה (עֵדוּת) "*testimony*." This is another name for the Law regarded as that to which God has *borne witness*. A stone upon which the Law was written might be called a "testimony" (Josh. xxiv. 27) or "witness"; so the "two tables" are called the "tables of the testimony" (Exod. xxxi. 18; xxxii. 15; xxxiv. 29), and the Ark which contained them is constantly called the "Ark of the testimony." The word "*testimony*" is found 23 times in our Psalm.

6. אִמְרָה *word, oracles* or *logia*. It generally signifies speech of a more solemn nature than the more common term *dabar*, and it is worthy of note that the

Memra of later Judaism which prepared the way for the doctrine of the *Logos* is derived from this same word.

It is often coupled with the thought of *purity out of a fiery trial*, e.g.:

Prov. xxx. 5 "Every *oracle* of God is purified" (i.e. as by fire).
Ps. cxix. 140 "Thy word (*oracle*) is purified exceedingly and Thy servant loveth it."
Ps. xii. 6 (7) "The *oracles* of YHVH are pure *oracles*, silver purified &c."
Ps. xviii. 30 (31) "The word (*oracle*) of YHVH is purified &c."
Compare also my suggested text in Ps. xix. 10.
Ps. cxix. 103 "How sweet are Thy *oracles* unto my taste—more so than honey to my mouth."
Prov. xvi. 24 "Sweet oracles are (like) dripping honey, sweet to the soul and healing to the bones."
Compare also note on Ps. xix.

Not only is the *word* (*oracle*) of God "tried," "purified" but it is itself the *trier*; it is ζῶν...ἐνεργὴς...κριτικός (Heb. iv. 12): so it is said of Joseph "the *oracle* of God *tried* him" (Ps. cv. 19).

דבר "*Word*." *Davar* differs from *Imra* somewhat as *logos* differs from *logia*. In Psalm cxix. the *Word* points to a written word of Scripture but undoubtedly it must not be confined to the written word.

8. פקודים "*Precepts*." This word, which is used only in the plural, occurs 21 times in Ps. cxix. The only other passages being Pss. xix. 8 (9); ciii. 18; and cxi. 7. It signifies a *sacred deposit*. This root-meaning is not always obvious but it should always be present to the mind of the reader in studying verses 4, 15, 27, 40, 45, 56, 63, 69, 78, 87, 93, 94, 100, 104, 110, 128, 134, 141, 159, 168 and 173 of Ps. cxix.

Though Ps. cxix. appears to be merely a collection of aphorisms arranged under the letters of the Alphabet, I feel sure that there is a deeper meaning if only it could be discovered. The analogy of the other Alphabetical Psalms would lead us to expect a division in, at least, two parts, so that the letter *Mem* should correspond with the letter *Aleph* etc. I have indicated traces of this in my marginal notes.

There are, I believe, three leading thoughts in the Psalm, viz. *Happiness, Guidance, Revelation* (compare the Way, the Truth, the Life) which recur in the following order:

Happiness	א	ד	ז	י	מ	ע	ק
Guidance	ב	ה	ח	כ	נ	פ	ר	ת
Revelation	ג	ו	ט	ל	ס	צ	ש

The vertical line marks the chief division of the Psalm at the letter ל, which the Jews call the middle letter of the alphabet.

The student is specially asked to study the references to Ps. xix.; the reason for this will appear when we come to that Psalm.

PSALM CXIX.

God's Word brings happiness when accepted with a whole heart.

א 1 Happy are they who are heart-and-soul in the way,
  That walk in the LAW of YHVH;
א 2 Happy are they that keep His TESTIMONIES,
  That seek Him with a whole heart;
א 3 Yea they do no unrighteousness,
  In His way do they walk.
א 4 Thou hast ordained Thy PRECEPTS
  For a strict observance.
א 5 Oh that my ways were established
  So as to observe Thy STATUTES.
א 6 Then I should not be put to shame
  When I have respect unto all Thy COMMANDMENTS.
א 7 I will thank Thee with an upright heart
  When I learn Thy righteous JUDGEMENTS.
א 8 Thy STATUTES I will observe;
  Oh forsake me not utterly.

God's Word brings guidance when stored in the heart as the heart's chief treasure.

ב 9 Wherewith shall a young man cleanse his way?
  By observing Thy WORD.
ב 10 With my whole heart[a] have I sought[a] Thee;
  Let me not wander from Thy COMMANDMENTS.
ב 11 I have stored[b] Thy ORACLES in my heart[b],
  That I should not sin against Thee.
ב 12 Blessed art Thou, YHVH,
  O teach me Thy STATUTES.
ב 13 With my lips do I rehearse
  All the JUDGEMENTS of Thy mouth.
ב 14 In the way of Thy TESTIMONIES I delight,
  As it were in all manner of riches.
ב 15 I will meditate on Thy PRECEPTS
  And have regard to Thy ways.
ב 16 I will delight myself in Thy STATUTES,
  And will not forget Thy WORD.

[a] 2 Chr. xxx. 18 f.
[b] Luke ii. 51

---

v. 3. "*In His way*, &c." The P. B. Version "For they who do no wickedness : walk in His ways" reads rather like a truism. The LXX clearly felt the difficulty for they translate, "for they that work wickedness do not walk in His ways." This third verse, as it stands, does not contain one of the eight synonyms for the Law; if however we might venture to change דרכו into דברו i.e. *His way* into *His word* we should gain, I think, a deeper meaning, which would be parallel to that of verse 9, viz. that the walk of life must be guided by the Word of God. The same would apply to the text of v. 37.

God's Word (Revelation) draws back the veil and lets the eye see wonders though apostasy seem to prevail (cf. letter *Samech*).

ג 17 Deal bountifully with Thy servant that I may live,
For I would fain observe Thy WORD.
ג 18 Unveil mine eyes that I may behold
The marvels of Thy LAW.
ג 19 I am but a sojourner[a] on earth;
O hide not Thy COMMANDMENTS from me.
ג 20 My soul is crushed with longing
For Thy JUDGEMENTS at all times.
ג 21 Thou hast rebuked the proud, as accursed,
Who go straying[b] from Thy COMMANDMENTS.
ג 22 Roll away from me reproach and contempt
For I have kept Thy TESTIMONIES.
ג 23 Yea though princes sit and speak against me,
Thy servant will meditate in Thy STATUTES.
ג 24 Thy TESTIMONIES also are my great delights;
They are my counsellors[c].

God's Word the remedy for depression. The soul that cleaves to His testimonies (v. 31) will not long cleave to the dust (v. 25).

ד 25 My soul cleaveth to the dust;
Quicken me according to Thy WORD.
ד 26 I have rehearsed my ways and Thou hast answered me;
Teach me Thy STATUTES.
ד 27 Make me to understand the way of Thy PRECEPTS
That I may meditate in Thy wondrous works.
ד 28 My soul droopeth through heaviness;
Uphold me according to Thy WORD.
ד 29 Put from me the false way,
And be gracious unto me (with) Thy LAW[d].
ד 30 I have chosen the way of faithfulness,
Thy JUDGEMENTS have I set before me.
ד 31 I cleave unto Thy TESTIMONIES,
O YHVH put me not to shame.

v. 21. "*The proud*"—i.e. not in a social but in a religious sense. The word is almost a synonym for a *scorner* (Prov. xxi. 24; Mal. iii. 15; iv. 1 (iii. 19)). In the Psalter it is only found eight times, of which *six* are in our present Ps. (*vv.* 21, 51, 69, 78, 85, 122), *one* in the closely related Ps. xix. 13 (14) (see notes), and *one* in Ps. lxxxvi. 14. In all these passages "*the proud*" denote, I believe, the *freethinkers* in Israel who made common cause with the heathen. Compare also the allusions to the *proud* in the *Psalms of Solomon*.

v. 29. "*And be gracious unto me (with) Thy LAW.*"—In *v.* 58 we read "be gracious unto me according to Thy ORACLES" which gives much more intelligent meaning. May it not be that in the present instance תורתך *Thy Law* has been read by mistake for אמרתך *Thy Oracles*?

We have already seen (p. 50) that LAW occurs three times too often in Ps. cxix. while ORACLES occurs three times too seldom to make up the number of twenty-two.

PSALM CXIX.

ד 32 I will run the way of Thy COMMANDMENTS,
    For Thou dost enlarge my heart.

God's Word the remedy against the lust of the eyes and the pride of life (1 Joh. ii. 16).

ה 33 Teach me, O YHVH, the way of Thy STATUTES;
    And I will keep it unto the end.
ה 34 Give me understanding that I may keep Thy LAW;
    And I will observe it with my whole heart.
ה 35 Make me to go in the path of Thy COMMANDMENTS,
    For therein is my delight.
ה 36 Incline my heart to Thy TESTIMONIES,
    And not to covetousness.
ה 37 Turn away mine eyes from seeing vanity;
    Quicken me in Thy way*.   * ? text
ה 38 Establish Thy ORACLE(S) to Thy servant
    Which tend unto Thy fear.
ה 39 Take away my reproach which I am afraid of;
    For Thy JUDGEMENTS are good.
ה 40 Behold I long for Thy PRECEPTS;
    Quicken me in Thy righteousness.

God's Word gives heart-freedom and boldness.

ו 41 Let Thy lovingkindness come unto me O YHVH,
    Thy salvation according to Thy ORACLE(S).
ו 42 So shall I have a word of answer for my reviler,
    Because I trust in Thy WORD.
ו 43 Take not the word of truth utterly out of my mouth;
    For I hope for Thy JUDGEMENT(S).
ו 44 I would keep Thy LAW continually,
    Even for ever and ever.
ו 45 I shall walk at liberty,
    Because I seek Thy PRECEPTS.

v. 37. "*Quicken me in Thy way.*"—This verse does not contain one of the eight words for God's Law. I suspect that the original text read *word* instead of *way* as in *v.* 3. This would bring it into line with such expressions as "Quicken me according to Thy Word" (*vv.* 25, 107), "Strengthen me according to Thy Word" (*v.* 28). This suggestion is confirmed from a study of the eight other passages in which "quicken me" occurs in the Psalm. Thus:—

v. 25.	"	Quicken me according to Thy word."
v. 40.	"	,,	,, in Thy righteousness."
v. 88.	"	,,	,, according to Thy lovingkindness."
v. 107.	"	,,	,, according to Thy word."
v. 149.	"	,,	,, according to Thy judgement (i.e. Thy wont?)."
v. 154.	"	,,	,, after Thy oracles."
v. 156.	"	,,	,, according to Thy judgements."
v. 159.	"	,,	,, according to Thy lovingkindness."

THIRD COLLECTION, ALPHABETICAL PSALMS.

ו 46 I would speak of Thy TESTIMONIES even before kings,
And would not be ashamed.
ו 47 I delight myself in Thy COMMANDMENTS which I love,
And will lift up my hand to [Thy COMMANDMENTS which I love].
ו 48 And will meditate in Thy STATUTES.

God's Word (Promise) gives hope in dark hours (cf. letter Daleth).

ו 49 Remember the WORD to Thy servant,
Seeing Thou hast caused me to hope.
ו 50 This is my comfort in my affliction:
That Thy ORACLE(S) quicken me.
ו 51 The proud have scoffed at me exceedingly
(Because) I have not swerved from Thy LAW.
ו 52 I remember thy JUDGEMENTS of old time, YHVH,
And I console myself.
ו 53 Indignation seized me because of the wicked,
The forsakers of Thy LAW.
ו 54 Thy STATUTES have been my songs
In my pilgrimage home.
ו 55 I remember Thy Name in the night, YHVH[a],
And observe Thy LAW.
ו 56 This much hath been mine
Because I keep Thy PRECEPTS.

God's Word makes God Himself my portion.

ח 57 My portion is YHVH,
I have promised to observe Thy WORDS.
ח 58 I have sought Thy favour with my whole heart;
Be gracious unto me according to Thy ORACLE(S).
ח 59 I have bethought me of my ways,
And have turned my feet unto Thy TESTIMONIES.
ח 60 I made haste and did not delay
To keep Thy COMMANDMENTS.
ח 61 The cords of the wicked surround me
(Because) I forget not Thy LAW.
ח 62 At midnight I rise to give Thee thanks[b]
Because of Thy righteous JUDGEMENTS.
ח 63 I am a companion of all them that fear Thee,
And of them that observe Thy PRECEPTS.
ח 64 Thy lovingkindness, YHVH, fills the earth;
Teach me Thy STATUTES.

PSALM CXIX. 57

God's Word reveals God as the One who *is Good* and brings *Good*, even out of evil.

ט 65 Thou hast dealt with Thy servant,
O YHVH, according to Thy WORD.
ט 66 Teach me good discernment and knowledge,
For I believe in Thy COMMANDMENTS.
ט 67 Before I was afflicted I went astray,
But now I observe Thy ORACLES.
ט 68 Good art Thou and doest good,
Teach me Thy STATUTES.
ט 69 The proud have forged a lie against me,
I keep Thy PRECEPTS with my whole heart.
ט 70 Their heart is gross as fat!
As for me, Thy LAW is my great delight.
ט 71 It is good for me that I was afflicted,
That I might learn Thy STATUTES.
ט 72 Better to me is the LAW of Thy mouth
Than thousands of gold and silver.

God's Word shews me to be the work of His hands; therefore His hands must still mould me, correct me and complete His work.

' 73 Thy hands have made me and fashioned me,
Give me understanding that I may learn thy COMMANDMENTS.
' 74 They that fear Thee shall see me and be glad,
Because I set my hope on Thy WORD.
' 75 I know O YHVH that Thy JUDGEMENTS are right,
And that in faithfulness Thou hast afflicted me.
' 76 Let Thy lovingkindness be to comfort me
According to Thy ORACLE(S) unto Thy servant.
' 77 Let Thy compassion visit me that I may live,
For Thy LAW is my great delight.
' 78 Let the proud be shamed for that they have falsely wronged me,
Whereas I for my part meditate in Thy PRECEPTS.
' 79 Let those that fear Thee be turned to me,
And they shall* know Thy TESTIMONIES.
' 80 Let my heart be whole in Thy STATUTES,
That I be not put to shame.

* or, *they that know*

God's Word my one stay in utter desertion.

כ 81 My soul longeth for Thy salvation,
In Thy WORD do I hope.
כ 82 Mine eyes long for Thy ORACLES,
Saying "When wilt Thou comfort me?"

K.

THIRD COLLECTION, ALPHABETICAL PSALMS.

כ 83 Though I am become like a bottle^a in the smoke,   ^a i.e. wine-skin
    I have not forgotten Thy STATUTES.
כ 84 How many are the days of Thy servant?
    When wilt Thou execute JUDGEMENT on my persecutors?
כ 85 The proud have dug pitfalls for me,
    (They) who are not in accord with Thy LAW.
כ 86 All Thy COMMANDMENTS are faithfulness,
    Wrongly do they persecute me;—help Thou me!
כ 87 They had well nigh made an end of me in the Land,
    Whereas I had not forsaken Thy PRECEPTS.
כ 88 According to Thy lovingkindness quicken me,
    So would I observe the TESTIMONY of Thy mouth.

God's Word lets me see the stability of Nature as the pledge of a faithful Creator—I trust what He will do.

ל 89 For ever, O YHVH,
    Thy WORD hath its stand in the heavens.
ל 90 From age to age is Thy faithfulness,
    Thou hast founded the earth and it stands.
ל 91 They stand to-day according to Thy JUDGEMENTS,
    For the whole are Thy servants.
ל 92 Except Thy LAW had been my delight,
    I should then have perished in my affliction.
ל 93 Never will I forget Thy PRECEPTS,
    For through them Thou hast quickened me.
ל 94 Thine I am: Oh save me,
    For I enquire into Thy PRECEPTS.
ל 95 The wicked wait for me to destroy me,
    I ponder over Thy TESTIMONIES.
ל 96 To all perfection I see a limit,
    Thy COMMANDMENT is exceeding broad.

God's Word has the promise of the life that now is (cf. letter Aleph).

מ 97 Oh how I love Thy LAW,
    It is my meditation all the day.
מ 98 Thy COMMANDMENTS make me wiser than mine enemies,
    For it^b is ever with me.   ^b i.e. Thy Law

---

v. 90. This verse as it stands does not contain one of the eight synonyms for Law. I cannot doubt but that the original text, instead of אמנתך "*Thy faithfulness*," read אמרתך "Thy ORACLES."
It may also be worth noting that, out of the nineteen verses in this Psalm in which the word ORACLES is found, eight times at least it comes in connexion with WORD in the preceding or following verse (see *vv.* 41, 50, 58, 82, 140, 148, 162, 170). If the readings I have suggested in *vv.* 29, 38 and 90 be adopted, we should have three additional instances of this juxtaposition of WORD and ORACLES.

PSALM CXIX.

מ 99 I have more insight than all my teachers,
    For Thy TESTIMONIES are my meditation.
מ 100 I ponder more than the aged,
    For I keep Thy PRECEPTS.
מ 101 I have refrained my foot from every evil way,
    That I may keep Thy WORD.
מ 102 I have not swerved from thy JUDGEMENTS,
    For it is Thou who teachest me.
מ 103 How sweet to my taste are Thy ORACLES—
    More than honey to my mouth.
מ 104 Through Thy PRECEPTS I have understanding,
    Therefore I hate every false way.

God's Word is a guiding light in this dark world (cf. letter Beth).

נ 105 Thy WORD is a lamp to my feet,
    And a light unto my path.
נ 106 I have sworn, and will make it good,
    To observe Thy righteous JUDGEMENTS.
נ 107 I am humbled exceedingly,
    Quicken me, O YHVH, according to Thy WORD.
נ 108 Graciously[a] accept the freewill-offerings of my mouth, [a] Ps. xix. 14
    O YHVH,
    And teach me Thy JUDGEMENTS.
נ 109 My life is ever in my hand,
    And I do not forget Thy LAW.
נ 110 The wicked have set a snare for me,
    And I stray not from thy PRECEPTS.
נ 111 Thy TESTIMONIES are mine heritage for ever,
    For the very joy of my heart are they!
נ 112 I have inclined my heart to perform Thy STATUTES,
    Eternal is (their) after-gain[b].   [b] cf. v. 33 and Ps. xix. 11 (12); Prov. xxii. 4

God's Word is the stay amid apostasy which prevails (cf. letter Gimel).

ס 113 The double-minded I hate,
    And Thy LAW do I love.
ס 114 My covert and my shield art Thou,
    For Thy WORD I hope.
ס 115 Depart from me ye evil-doers,
    For I would keep the COMMANDMENTS of my God.
ס 116 Uphold me according to Thy ORACLES that I may live,
    And let me not be disappointed of my hope.

THIRD COLLECTION, ALPHABETICAL PSALMS.

ס 117 Hold Thou me up and I shall be safe,
And shall regard Thy STATUTES continually.
ס 118 Thou lightly esteemest all those that err from Thy STATUTES,
For their artifice is but a lie.
ס 119 Thou puttest away as dross all the wicked of earth,
Therefore I love Thy TESTIMONIES.
ס 120 My flesh trembleth for fear of Thee,
And I reverence Thy JUDGEMENTS.

The Eye of the Servant is unto God's Word (cf. Ps. xix. 11 and letter *Daleth*).

ע 121 I have executed JUDGEMENT and righteousness;
Oh leave me not to mine oppressors!
ע 122 Be surety for Thy servant for good;
Let not the proud oppress me!
ע 123 Mine eyes long[a] for Thy salvation,   [a] cf. v. 82
For Thy righteous ORACLE(S).
ע 124 Deal with Thy servant according to Thy lovingkindness,
And teach me Thy STATUTES.
ע 125 I am Thy servant, Oh give me understanding,
That I may know Thy TESTIMONIES.
ע 126 YHVH's time for action is come:
They have made void Thy LAW.
ע 127 Therefore I love Thy COMMANDMENTS
More than gold[b]—more than fine gold[b].   [b] Ps. xix. 10
ע 128 Therefore all (Thy) PRECEPTS in all things I approve;
Every false way I hate.

God's Word, i.e. all that proceedeth out of the Mouth of God, is that by which man lives.

פ 129 Marvellous are Thy TESTIMONIES,
Therefore my (very) soul keeps them.
פ 130 The revelation of Thy WORD giveth light,
Making the simple wise[c].   [c] Ps. xix. 8
פ 131 I opened my mouth and drew in my breath,
I have such longing for Thy COMMANDMENTS.
פ 132 Turn Thou to me and shew me favour;
As JUDGEMENT[d] should be to those that love Thy Name.   [d] i.e. *as Thy manner is to...*

---

v. 122. This verse is without one of the eight words. The verb in the first line has two meanings (*a*) *to be sweet*, (*b*) *to be surety*. The Prayer Book Version follows the former "Make Thou Thy servant to delight in &c." a rendering which could scarcely be justified grammatically as a paraphrase. The other meaning, *of surety*, is undoubtedly correct. Compare Is. xxxviii. 14, "I am oppressed; be surety for me."

PSALM CXIX.

ס 133 Uphold my steps in Thy ORACLES;
So shall no wickedness obtain the rule over me[a].   [a] Ps. xix. 14
ס 134 Redeem me from the oppression of man;
So shall I observe Thy PRECEPTS.
ס 135 Make Thy face to shine upon Thy servant,
And teach me Thy STATUTES.
ס 136 Mine eyes flow streams of water;
For that they[b] have not observed Thy LAW.   [b] or, *men*

<small>God's Word is "tried" and *righteous* and is also the trier of hearts to make them *righteous*.</small>

צ 137 Righteous art Thou, O YHVH,
And right are Thy JUDGEMENTS.
צ 138 Thou hast enjoined the righteousness of Thy TESTI-
MONIES;
And in exceeding faithfulness.
צ 139 My zeal hath consumed me,
Because mine adversaries have forgotten Thy WORDS.
צ 140 Thy ORACLE is tried[c] exceedingly,   [c] i.e. as by fire Ps. xix. 9 (note)
And Thy servant loveth it.
צ 141 I am small and despised,
(But) I do not forget Thy PRECEPTS.
צ 142 Thy righteousness is an everlasting righteousness,
And Thy LAW is truth.
צ 143 Trouble and anguish have found me out,
(Then) Thy COMMANDMENTS were my delights.
צ 144 The righteousness of Thy TESTIMONIES is everlasting;
Grant me understanding and I shall live.

<small>God's Word is music in the night (cf. letter *Zain*).</small>

ק 145 I cry with my whole heart;
Answer me, O YHVH, I would keep Thy STATUTES.
ק 146 I cry unto thee, Oh save me,
For I would keep Thy TESTIMONIES.
ק 147 I anticipate the dawn and cry aloud,
For Thy WORD do I hope.
ק 148 Mine eyes anticipate the night-watches[d]   [d] cf. v. 55
To meditate in Thy ORACLES.
ק 149 Hear my voice according to Thy lovingkindness;
Quicken me, O YHVH, according to Thy JUDGEMENT.
ק 150 They draw near who follow iniquity,
From Thy LAW they are estranged.

THIRD COLLECTION, ALPHABETICAL PSALMS.

ק 151 (But) near art Thou, O YHVH,
And all Thy COMMANDMENTS are truth.
ק 152 I know that Thy TESTIMONIES are of old,
That Thou hast established them for ever.

God's Word sums up the 'many things' in the one thing needful, which is Truth.

ר 153 See mine affliction and rescue me,
For I do not forget Thy LAW.
ר 154 Plead Thou my cause and redeem me;
Quicken me after Thy ORACLES.
ר 155 Safety is far from the wicked,
For they seek not Thy STATUTES.
ר 156 Many are Thy compassions, O YHVH,
Quicken me according to Thy JUDGEMENTS.
ר 157 Many are my persecutors and adversaries,
(Yet) I swerve not from Thy TESTIMONIES.
ר 158 I saw the treacherous-dealers and was grieved;
Because they have not observed Thy ORACLES.
ר 159 See how I love Thy PRECEPTS,
Quicken me, YHVH, according to Thy lovingkindness.
ר 160 The sum of Thy WORD is truth:
Each righteous JUDGEMENT of Thine is eternal.

God's Word brings perfect Peace to the heart that loves it and accepts it as a whole.

שׁ 161 Princes have persecuted me without a cause;
Yet my heart is in awe of Thy WORDS.
שׁ 162 I rejoice over Thy ORACLES
As one that findeth great spoil.
שׁ 163 Lies I hate and abhor;
Thy LAW do I love.
שׁ 164 Seven times a day do I praise Thee,
Because of Thy righteous JUDGEMENTS.
שׁ 165 Great peace there is to those that love Thy LAW,
And to them there is no stumbling-block.
שׁ 166 I hope for Thy salvation O YHVH,
And perform Thy COMMANDMENTS.
שׁ 167 My soul observeth Thy TESTIMONIES,
And loveth them exceedingly.
שׁ 168 I observe Thy PRECEPTS [and Thy TESTIMONIES],
For all my ways are before Thee.

v. 168. The structure of the Psalm leads us to expect only one of the eight synonyms for Law in each verse, whereas the Hebrew text in this verse has two viz. PRECEPTS and TESTIMONIES. Of these, TESTIMONIES may easily have been copied from verse 167.

PSALM CXIX.

<small>The letter *Tav* signifies *desire* (Job xxxi. 35) and also a *mark* or *cross* (Ezek. ix. 4, 6).</small>

ת 169 Let my plaint draw nigh before Thee O YHVH,
  Give me understanding according to Thy WORD.
ת 170 Let my supplication come before Thee;
  Give me deliverance according to Thy ORACLES.
ת 171 Let my lips overflow with praise-song;
  Because Thou teachest me Thy STATUTES.
ת 172 Let my tongue respond to Thy ORACLES;
  Because all Thy COMMANDMENTS are righteous.
ת 173 Let Thy hand be to help me,
  Because I have chosen Thy PRECEPTS.
ת 174 I long for Thy salvation O YHVH,
  And Thy LAW is my great delight.
ת 175 Let my soul live and it shall praise Thee,
  And let Thy JUDGEMENTS help me.
ת 176 I have wandered like a sheep that is lost;
  Seek Thy servant: for I do not forget Thy COMMANDMENTS.

<small>v. 172. Here again, according to the structure of the Psalm, we should not expect to find ORACLES and COMMANDMENTS in one verse. The parallelism too with v. 171 would lead us rather to expect that as 'my lips overflow with praise-song' so 'my tongue responds *with words.*' Such a reading would only require the omission of one letter in the Hebrew, that being the letter with which the next word begins.</small>

PSALM CXLV.

In this, the last of the Alphabetical Psalms, the division into stanzas is by no means clearly defined, there is however a sequence of thought which is indicated in the marginal notes. After an Introduction of two verses we have four verses in praise of God's *Greatness* followed by four verses in praise of His *Mercy* as revealed in the Covenant Name (Exod. xxxiv. 6; cf. Ps. cxi. 4). This completes what we may call the first half of the Psalm in ten verses. The second half repeats and expands the same two thoughts. It begins with three verses (or four, if we grant the genuineness of the נ verse) on the *Greatness* of God in His Kingdom on Earth; followed by six verses on His *Mercy*: these six verses are again subdivided, the first three (vv. 14—16) denoting God's mercy towards His creatures generally, the second three (vv. 17—19) denoting His mercy towards His own people who call upon Him. Thus, granting the genuineness of the נ verse, the second half of the Psalm would consist of ten verses, divided like those of the first half, between the Greatness and the Mercy of God with more special reference to His Kingdom upon Earth. The Psalm concludes, as it opens, with a summary of two verses (vv. 20 and 21) which should be compared with vv. 1 and 2. Possibly v. 20 should be read with vv. 17—19. If so I should be inclined to think that the author of the Psalm had intentionally omitted the נ verse in order that the verses in praise of God's greatness and mercy might form a ten-stringed lute in the second half just as they do in the first half.

PSALM CXLV.

Introduction.	א	1	I will extol Thee, my God, as King,
			I will bless Thy Name for ever and ever.
	ב	2	Every day will I bless Thee,
			And praise Thy Name for ever and ever.
His greatness.	ג	3	GREAT is YHVH and highly to be praised[a], • Ps. xlviii. 1
			His greatness is unsearchable.
	ד	4	Generation to generation shall laud Thy acts,
			And proclaim Thy mighty deeds.
	ה	5	The splendour of the glory of Thy majesty shall they tell,
			And of thy wondrous works will I meditate.
	ו	6	Of the might of Thy works of awe they shall speak,
			And I will recount Thy greatness.
His mercy.	ז	7	The Memorial-Name of Thy abundant goodness[b] shall [b] Vulg. suavitatis
			they utter,
			And ring out with songs to Thy righteousness.
	ח	8	"GRACIOUS and COMPASSIONATE is YHVH,
			LONG-SUFFERING and of GREAT KINDNESS."
	ט	9	YHVH is GOOD to all,
			His tender mercies are over all His works.
	י	10	All Thy works praise Thee, O YHVH,
			And Thy saints bless Thee.

v. 7. "*The Memorial...shall they utter.*"—God's Memorial is His Covenant-Name (see p. 64). That Name was revealed as Mercy "unto thousands of generations" (Exod. xxxiv. 7). The words "*they shall utter*" imply an exuberant speech which breaks out like the waters of a fountain (Prov. xviii. 4; Ps. cxix. 171; Ps. xix. 2 (3)).

v. 9. "*His tender mercies are over all His works.*"—The canopy of heaven always remains centred over us whichever way we go;—so it is with God's Love, we never reach its bounds (Eph. iii. 19) but it remains as completely ours as if we alone formed the Centre of the Universe. The interesting passage on God's mercy in *Wisdom* xi. 23—26 is quoted by Neale.

v. 10. "*All Thy works praise Thee...And Thy saints bless Thee.*"—This verse sounds the key-note of the Psalm. Throughout the Universe God's works have only one meaning of "Glory" (cf. Ps. xxix. 10) but this is not so dear to Him as His "little human praise," the heartfelt *blessing* of His saints (cf. on Ps. xix.). Man is Nature's priest; he must present the offering of "all flesh." But this soulless character of Nature is only for a time; for, through man the Creation itself shall pass into the liberty of conscious Sonship (Rom. viii. 19 ff.). I find a hint of this in *v.* 21 which reverses the thought of *v.* 10 thus:—"My mouth shall speak the praise of YHVH, And let all flesh bless His holy Name for ever and ever."

THIRD COLLECTION, ALPHABETICAL PSALMS.

His greatness.	כ 11	They speak of the glory of Thy Kingdom, And proclaim Thy might.
	ל 12	Manifesting His mighty deeds to the sons of men, And the glory of the splendour of His Kingdom.
	מ 13	Thy Kingdom is a Kingdom of all ages, And thy dominion to all generations.
	נ	[Missing verse supplied in Septuagint.]
His mercy (towards His creatures).	ס 14	YHVH is the STAY[a] of all that are falling, The UPLIFTER of them that are bowed down. [a] Ps. xxxvii. 24
	ע 15	The eyes of all wait upon Thee, And Thou givest them their food in its season.
	פ 16	Thou openest Thy hand, And satisfiest the desire of every living thing.
His mercy (towards His own people).	צ 17	RIGHTEOUS is YHVH in all His ways, And LOVING in all His works.
	ק 18	NEAR[b] is YHVH to all that call upon Him, To all that call upon Him in truth. [b] Deut. iv. 7
	ר 19	He will perform the desire of them that fear Him, Will hear their cry and will help them.
Conclusion.	ש 20	YHVH is the GUARDIAN of them that love Him, But all the wicked will He destroy.
	ת 21	My mouth shall speak the praise of YHVH, And let all flesh bless His holy Name for ever and ever.

v. 14. "*YHVH is the stay...the uplifter...*"—Thus Shakespeare says:—

"What's in Prayer, but this two-fold force—
To be forestalled ere we come to fall
Or pardoned, being down?"

In verses 7—9 we have the attributes of Divine mercy as they exist in God, but in verses 14—16, 17—19 we have the application of these attributes to the needs of the world as it is.
The relation between these verses may perhaps be indicated as follows:—

God's nature in Itself is	{ "Gracious" "Compassionate" "Long-suffering" "Of great kindness" "Good to all" }	Therefore towards the World and especially towards His own people He is	{ "The Stay" of the falling. "The Uplifter" of the fallen. "Righteous" "Loving" "Near" to His own. }

v. 21. "*And let all flesh bless...*" This verse which closes the Psalm must be compared, not only with the opening v. 1, but also with v. 10 which closes the first half of the Psalm. In v. 10 it was *man* alone who *blessed* God, but here "*all flesh*" is called upon to *bless* Him. "All flesh" includes the whole animate Creation (see Gen. vi. 12, 13, 17, 19; vii. 15, 16, 21 &c.; Ps. cxxxvi. 25). The words therefore involve a prophecy and should be compared with Ps. lxv. 2 (3) "unto Thee shall all flesh come."

'DAVIDIC' PSALMS RESUMED.

N.B. The Alphabetical Psalms being now completed the order of the 'Davidic' Psalms of the First Collection is resumed at Ps. xi. All that comes between pages 18 and 67 must be regarded as a parenthesis.

It would, no doubt, have been more logical to have placed the Alphabetical Psalms of the First Collection as an Appendix to the First Collection and the Alphabetical Psalms of the Third Collection as an Appendix to the Third Collection (the Second Collection having no Alphabetical Psalms), but it seemed to me that the advantage of studying all the Alphabetical together in one group outweighed the objections that might be urged on the other side.

PSALM XI.

The circumstances of the Psalm would seem to be similar to those of Ps. cxx. The 'Servant' of God is in danger, not so much of open foes as, of treacherous calumny. The "pillars," whether they be great men of the time or the foundations of society, are being cast down and righteousness seems in vain (*v*. 3; cf. Mal. ii. 17; iii. 14 f.). At such a time the 'Servant' was tempted to a policy of earthly expediency (Stanza I.) but meets it by the fact that he has once for all taken shelter (*v*. 1; cf. Ruth ii. 12) under the wings of the Eternal (cf. Ps. xxxvi. 7 (8); lvii. 1 (2); lxi. 4 (5); xci. 4). In Stanza II. he comes to the central thought—The Eternal is, even now, passing calm judgement in Heaven. Stanza III. then answers the temptations of Stanza I. but in the reverse order (see marginal notes). The feeling of useless failure (*v*. 3) 'What can the righteous effect in such disorder?' is answered by (*v*. 5), God is *testing* him by that very failure. The wounding words of the wicked (*v*. 2) recoil on their own heads (*v*. 6). The simple fleeing to God for refuge (*v*. 1) is accounted to God's Servant for righteousness and the reward is to see His Face.

The Psalm might be classed as a Psalm of the "two ways" and compared with Pss. i., v. and vii.

Thus:—

{ i. 6 "For YHVH taketh note of the way of the righteous,
    And the way of the wicked perishes."
  xi. 7 "For YHVH, the Righteous, loveth righteousness:
    The upright shall behold His Face."

Again, as in Ps. v. 11, 12 it is God's "trusting ones" (i.e. those who have "taken refuge" in Him) who are gladdened by the joy of His Presence and called "the righteous" in *v*. 12. So Ps. xi. begins "In YHVH *I have taken refuge*" and ends (*v*. 7) "The upright shall behold His Face." Once more; if we compare Ps. vii. we find still more striking resemblance:—

{ vii. 1 "YHVH...in Thee I have taken refuge."
  xi. 1 "In YHVH I have taken refuge."

  vii. 6 ff. YHVH sitting in Judgement; cf. xi. 4 ff.

{ vii. 9 "Elohim the Righteous is the Trier of hearts, &c."
  xi. 5 "YHVH trieth the righteous."

  vii. 13 God's burning arrows; cf. xi. 6.

PS. XI.

(a) God only shall be my Refuge.

1 In YHVH I have taken refuge—
How say ye then to my soul,
"Flee as a bird[a] to your mountain[b]:   [a] Lam. iii. 52

(b) True, the wicked wound us with words like arrows.

2 For lo, the wicked bend the bow,   [b] Gen. xix. 17
They fit their arrow on the string,
To shoot[c], in the dark, at the upright of heart: [c] Ps. lxiv. 3 f.

(c) True, all is confusion and the righteous is helpless.

3 When the pillars[d] are torn down,   [d] Is. xix. 10. only
What can a righteous man do?"

God's in His heaven—All's right with the world.

4 YHVH is in His holy Temple[e],   [e] Palace
YHVH's throne is in Heaven.
His eyes behold,
His eyelids try the sons of men.

(c₁) The righteous is being tested for his good.

5 YHVH trieth the righteous,
But the wicked and lover of violence
His soul hateth.

(b₁) The arrows of the wicked will recoil (cf. Ps. cxx.) in a rain of fire upon themselves.

6 May He rain coals[f] on the wicked,   [f] So Sym.
Fire and brimstone[g] with scorching blast,   [g] Gen. xix. 24
(Such be) the portion of their cup.

(a₁) I shall (when tried) see Him as He is.

7 For YHVH, the Righteous, loveth righteousness:
The upright shall behold His Face[h].   [h] 1 John iii. 2; Rev. xxii. 4

---

v. 1. "*In YHVH I have taken refuge.*"—The E.V. "In the Lord put I my trust" is too vague. The verb is constantly used of that *trust which takes shelter* e.g. under the shadow of *protecting wings* (Ruth ii. 12; Pss. xxxvi. 7 (8); lvii. 1 (2); xci. 4; cf. Jud. ix. 15; Is. xxx. 2) or under a *shield* (II Sam. xxii. 31; Pss. xviii. 30 (31); Prov. xxx. 5; cxliv. 2) or under a protecting *rock* (Deut. xxxii. 37; II Sam. xxii. 3). The word is never used of that *trust* which may exist between equals but always of the refuge which the weak must find in the strong.

v. 1. "*Flee as a bird &c.*"—Nothing is more easy, nothing more dangerous, than to suggest historical allusions; but without assigning the Psalm to Nehemiah we may illustrate it from the noble answer he gave to his faithless advisers: "Should such a man as I flee? and who is there, that, being as I am, would go into the Temple to save his life?" (Neh. vi. 11). History repeats itself. It is rash to assume that because a Psalm suits a certain occasion it was necessarily written for that occasion.

PS. XII.

Worldly men are making an end of us!	1 Save, O YHVH, for the godly is no more: For faithfulness^a is ended because^b of the sons of men. 2 Falsehood they speak, Each one to his fellow, With lip of flattery, With a double heart do they speak.
May God judge the levity of their words.	3 May YHVH destroy all flattering lips! The tongue that speaketh great things. 4 Who say, "We are masters of our tongues, Our lips are our own, Who is lord over us?"
God *will* judge: His words are anything but levity.	5 "Because of the oppression of the poor, Because of the sighing of the needy, Now can I arise," saith YHVH, "I can place (him) in the safety he longs for." 6 The oracles^c of YHVH are pure oracles, Silver smelted^d from dross in the crucible, Seven times refined.

Marginal notes:
a. or, *the faithful*
b. or, *from among*
c. Ps. xviii. 31
d. Prov. xxx. 5

v. 1. "*For faithfulness is ended because of the sons of men.*"—The words "sons of men" must be interpreted by the last line of the Psalm. In themselves they denote mankind from a low point of view (Ps. lxii. 9 (10) &c.) but occasionally they denote the low worldly party which is opposed to God; e.g. Ps. lvii. 4 (5) "I lie among them that are set on fire, even the sons of men, whose teeth are spears and arrows," also Ps. lviii. 1 (2) "Do ye judge uprightly, O ye sons of men?" This, I think, is their significance in the present Psalm.

v. 6. "*The oracles......are pure oracles.*"—There is nothing in English which answers to the Hebrew *imra*. We cannot use *word*, for that is required for *davar*; *saying* is feeble. Perhaps we might naturalize the Greek *logia*, meanwhile *oracles* seems least objectionable. For a note on this word and its special connexion with a *fiery test* see p. 52. We have seen that this word, which occurs so often in Ps. cxix., is used also in connexion with the *promises* of God which are all "yea" (II Cor. i. 19; Rom. xi. 29). These promises can be trusted to the uttermost, they are therefore here called "pure oracles" and are contrasted with the vain words of the wicked in the preceding stanza (*v.* 4). The connexion between verses 5 and 6 is, I think, as follows: God longs to fulfil His promises and to come to the help of His saints; but this Divine longing is conditioned by human action; hence there arises a fiery trial in which the promises of God "are tried" even as silver is tried.

It should be noted that, whereas in the preceding Psalm (xi. 4 f.) God "tries" ($\sqrt{bhn}$) men by delaying His help, in the present Psalm the Divine Word or promise is itself "tried" ($\sqrt{srf}$) by a still severer test (cf. note on Ps. cv. 19, p. 52).

The cry of the oppressed (*v.* 5) sets God free to act (cf. Exod. iii. 7 f.).

He will keep us, and His promise; the wicked rise only as scum.	7 Thou YHVH wilt preserve us^a, Wilt keep us from this generation, for ever. 8 The wicked go their round, As the rising of the scum of the sons of men.	^a So Sept., Heb. *them*

v. 8. "*As the rising of the scum of the sons of men.*"—What is vile and worthless rises to the top by its very levity. In verse 4 we hear the levity of the words of the wicked which, in verse 6, is put in sharp contrast to the weighty words of God which have run out, as it were, pure metal from the crucible. Thus the contrast between pure metal and dross is still in the poet's mind when, in verse 8, he would picture the end of the wicked. They rose only as dross; as dross they will be rejected.

The Septuagint read a different text, not easy to account for. See Schleusner's lexicon s.v. πολυωρέω.

PSALM XIII.

This Psalm falls naturally into three Stanzas after the manner of Psalm vi., with which it should be closely compared.

The first Stanza is all *Despondency*; the second is all *Prayer*; the third is all *Joy*.

Despondency, though it may have many causes, is always the result of earth-born clouds. The soul must fight its way through these clouds with the weapon of All-Prayer (cf. Jas. v. 13 ff.). By Prayer we do not mean the lip-service of "Lord, Lord" but the patient performance of unpraised duty. Matthew Arnold has truly said

> "We cannot kindle when we will
> Thy fire, which in the heart resides ;
> The spirit bloweth and is still,
> In mystery our soul abides :
>   But tasks in hours of insight willed
>   Can be through hours of gloom fulfilled."

The Psalmist teaches a still deeper lesson. Every vision of God's Face involves a task; God then stands aside; the servant is being tested; his first feeling is of Despondency (Exod. iii. 11; Is. vi. 5, 8; Jer. i. 6, &c.); then follows Prayer, the task is done, and the servant comes out into the Joy of still nearer vision of God. This threefold movement of an upward widening spiral gives the law of all growth.

PSALM XIII.

The relation which we have pointed out between the three Stanzas of the Psalm will bear minute subdivision. Thus :—

Despondency. { *v.* 1 Desertion of God.
{ *v.* 2 Hostility of man.

Prayer. { *v.* 3 for God's Presence in answer to *v.* 1.
{ *v.* 4 for protection against enemies in answer to *v.* 2.

Joy. { *v.* 5 God's Presence experienced. Cf. *vv.* 1, 3.
{ *v.* 6 Thanksgiving for a victory over foes. Cf. *vv.* 2, 4.

PS. XIII.

Despondency.
{ 1 How long, YHVH! wilt Thou utterly forget me?
{ How long wilt Thou hide Thy face from me?
{ 2 How long must I plan in my soul in daily heart-grief?
{ How long^a must mine enemy exalt himself against me?   ^a Ps. vi. 3

Prayer.
{ 3 Consider, and answer me, O YHVH my God ;
{ Lighten mine eyes lest I sleep the (sleep of) death^b;   ^b Ps. vi. 5
{ 4 Let not mine enemy say "I have mastered him,"
{ Let not my foes^c exult when I stumble.   ^c Ps. vi. 7

Joy.
{ 5 As for me—in Thy kindness I trust,
{ My heart shall exult in Thy salvation.
{ 6 Let me sing unto YHVH because He has dealt lovingly^d   ^d Pss. cxvi. 7; cxlii. 7
{   with me.
{ [*Yea, I will praise the name of YHVH, Most High.*]^e   ^e Sept., not in Heb.

v. 6. "*Yea, I will praise* &c." Though this occurs only in the Septuagint the symmetry of the Psalm would seem to require a line here. Thus :—

v. 1^a. "How long wilt Thou forget...!" } answered { *v.* 5^a. Absolute trust in God's kindness.
v. 1^b. The sense of God's Face hidden! }   by   { *v.* 5^b. A heart that exults in salvation.
v. 2^a. How long this lonely grief!   } answered { *v.* 6^a. A heart-song of gratitude.
v. 2^b. How long must the enemy triumph!} by   { *v.* 6^b. I have triumphed in God.

The four '*How longs*' seem to require four corresponding lines in the last Stanza, so that the Prayer Book rendering, which inserts a line from the Septuagint, may possibly be correct.

The reader will not fail to note how the four prayers of the middle Stanza take the four sorrows of Stanza I. and change them into the four joys of Stanza III.

Perhaps Trench's sonnet on Prayer is the best comment on this Psalm.

PSALM XIV.

This Psalm, which occurs again in an Elohistic form as Ps. liii., would seem to belong to a period of practical atheism. The "fool" (v. 1) is one who ignores God and thus becomes no better than the brutes that perish. Verse 2 brings to mind Gen. vi. 12 "And God looked upon the earth, and, behold, it was corrupt; for all flesh had corrupted his way upon the earth." St Paul was therefore justified in giving to our Psalm (Rom. iii. 10 ff.) a wider meaning than its author probably intended and in making it prove that both Jews and Gentiles "are all under sin."

The text of the Psalm, especially in vv. 5, 6, is corrupt. A careful comparison with the duplicate Psalm liii. obliges us to conclude that the variations sprang from one original text.

I would refer the Hebrew scholar to a short article on the texts of Psalms xiv. and liii. which I published in *Hebraica*, July 1886, p. 237 ff.

The translation I now offer is based upon the text there suggested, and as I am writing for English readers I have not thought it necessary to reproduce the arguments there used.

As the *seventh* Psalm is a Psalm of Judgement so the *fourteenth*, which closes the second group of seven, is also a Psalm of Judgement. The allusions to Genesis vi. are certainly not accidental.

PS. XIV.

Godless oppressors as in Gen. vi. 1—4.

1 The fool hath said in his heart
"There is no God."
They are vile and corrupt in their ways^a,
There is none doeth good.

God "looks upon the earth" (Gen. vi. 12).

2 YHVH from heaven looketh forth
On the children of men,
To see if there were that took heed,
That sought after God.

PSALM XIV.

"And behold it was corrupt..." (Gen. vi. 12).	3 But all was perverse, One and all were corrupt, There was none doing good, No not one!^a
These are "like natural brute beasts..." (2 Pet. ii. 12 f.; Jude v. 10).	4 They do not know^b God, They are all evil-doers, Eating^c My people As they eat bread. They do not call^d upon YHVH.
Sudden judgement (as on the Babel builders).	5 There they feared a fear, For God has scattered the oppressor. 6 The counsel of the hypocrite He hath put to shame, For YHVH hath spurned them.

[a] P. B. V. inserts three verses here
[b] Jer. x. 25; Ps. lxxix. 6
[c] Jer. x. 25; Ps. lxxix. 7
[d] Jer. x. 25; Ps. lxxix. 6

Possibly a later addition.	7 O might but Israel's help come forth from Zion, When YHVH brings back His captive people Jacob shall rejoice, Israel shall be glad.

vv. 3, 4. The three verses inserted in the P. B. V. "Their throat is an open sepulchre......before their eyes" are taken from the Septuagint, where they were doubtless inserted from Rom. iii. 13—18. St. Paul, in quoting our Psalm (Rom. lii. 10 ff.), coupled with it similar passages from Ps. v. 10; Ps. cxl. 4; Ps. x. 7 and Is. lix. 7 f. These passages thus found their way into the Septuagint, Vulgate and P. B. V.

v. 4. For the interrogative ה I suggest either the usual contraction for the Divine Name or the word *El* "God" (cf. Ps. lxxxv. (6) 7, where the Septuagint read *God* for the interrogative ה). This reading brings out the parallelism "They have not known God......they have not called upon YHVH," and is well illustrated by the kindred passage in Jer. x. 25 "Pour out Thy wrath upon the heathen *who know Thee not* and on the families that *call not upon* Thy Name, for *they have eaten* Jacob, and *eaten him up...*"

v. 5 f. "*There they feared a fear.*" The parallel text of Ps. liii. adds "*where no fear was.*" This is probably a gloss but is true in thought and is best explained by the interpretation of the plague of darkness given in *Wisdom* xvii.

The last line of *v.* 5 and *v.* 6 in the present Hebrew texts runs thus:

"For Elohim is in the generation of the righteous
The counsel of the poor ye put to shame
But YHVH is his refuge,"

or in text of Ps. liii.

"For Elohim hath scattered the bones of thy besieger (LXX. of the hypocrites)
Thou (?) hast put them to shame
For Elohim hath spurned them."

These two passages, which differ so widely, are represented in the Hebrew by similar sounding words, so that a common text can be reproduced with some degree of certainty.

PSALM XV.

The question of verse 1, 'Who can dwell as a guest with God?' is answered in four stanzas which postulate perfection, in *heart, tongue, eye and hand*, while the three lines of each stanza follow the threefold division of a "*godly, righteous*, and *sober*" life, i.e. duty to God, to man, and to self. This has been indicated in the marginal notes. We may also observe that these four stanzas represent, alternately, positive and negative virtues. Thus, every way, an absolute perfection is predicated for the Man who shall ascend to God. The Psalm should be studied in connexion with Ps. xxiv., both being proper Psalms for Ascension Day. There is an interesting paraphrase of this Psalm in the Poems of Henry Vaughan.

PS. XV.

God's guest must be perfect	1 YHVH, who can sojourn^a in Thy Tent? Who can dwell in Thy Holy Mountain?	^a i.e. *as a*
in *heart* (*a*) toward God. (*b*) toward man. (*c*) toward self.	2 One that walketh blameless; That doeth justice; And that communes truly with himself;	

v. 1. The first verse must be taken as the question which is answered in the other verses of the Psalm "Quod ergo interrogavit propheta, nunc respondet Spiritus Sanctus. Et quid ei dicit? Vis scire, O propheta, quis habitabit in tabernaculo meo, aut quis requiescet in monte sancto meo? Audi quae sequuntur: si haec feceris quae sequuntur, habitabis in monte sancto meo." (S. Hieron. Presb. *Tract. in Psalmos* p. 28, Morin's Edition.)

v. 1. Cheyne has well shewn that the idea of dwelling as a *guest* with God was common to the early Semitic religions. The Psalmist takes this idea, which to the heathen was an empty form, and shews what dwelling with a holy God must involve. His words go further than he himself probably intended and fit the Psalm for its use on Ascension Day. (See also on Ps. xxiv.)

v. 2. The *blameless* walk is the walk with God (Gen. xvii. 1: 2 Sam. xxii. 24, 26).

"*That doeth justice.*" Few words have gone through such significant phases of meaning as the Hebrew word for *righteousness* or *justice*. The context here decides for the latter meaning of justice between man and man. I am glad to see that Jerome takes this view of *justice* in the passage before us. "Other virtues give pleasure to him who possesses them; *justice* gives pleasure, not to him who possesses it, but to outsiders. If I am wise, my wisdom delights myself; if I am brave, my courage delights myself; if I become chaste, my chastity is my own joy; but *justice* bestows its benefits, not on the man who possesses it, but on other wretched creatures who possess (it) not.... Justice knows neither brother, nor father, nor mother; what it knows is the truth, it accepts not persons, it imitates God" (*Tract. in Psalmos* Vol. III. Part ii. p. 29, Morin's Edition).

"*and that communes truly with himself,*" lit. "that speaketh the truth in his heart." The participle Kal of *dabar* has, not unfrequently, an inward sense, as of a voice speaking within the

PSALM XV.

in *tongue*
(a_1) toward God.   3 That never let his tongue go slandering,
(b_1) toward man.   Nor wrought his fellow wrong,
(c_1) toward self.   Nor dealt in tales against his neighbour.

in *eye*
(a_2) toward God.   4 One in whose eyes the vile is despicable,
(b_2) toward man.   And that honours the fearers of YHVH,
(c_2) toward self.   That sweareth to his hurt, yet changeth not.

in *hand*
(a_3) toward God.   5 That doth not put his money out to usury,
(b_3) toward man.   Nor take reward against the innocent.
(c_3) toward self.   And doing such-like things he never swerves.

man, e.g. "the angel *that communed* with me," lit. "*that spake in me*" (Zech. i. 9, 13, 14, 19 (ii. 2); ii. 3 (7); iv. 1, 4, 5; v. 5, 10; vi. 4; cf. Gen. xvi. 13: Jonah iii. 2). In the present passage it denotes not merely truthfulness of speech but that inner communing which places self in true relation (altruistic) to the whole. Thus it is parallel to St Paul's ἀληθεύοντες...ἐν ἀγάπῃ (Eph. iv. 15).

v. 3. "*That never let his tongue go slandering.*" Only in one other passage is this word used of *slandering* (viz. 2 Sam. xix. 27 (28)). Elsewhere it signifies to *go about as a spy*. The connexion of thought between *v.* 2 (*a*) and *v.* 3 (a_1) is the same as in Jas. iii. 2, the "perfect man" is the man who does not offend with his tongue.

v. 4. "*One in whose eyes the vile is despicable.*" The words are difficult. We may certainly dismiss the P. B. V. "He that setteth not by himself, but is lowly in his own eyes," for humility does not require that a man should hold himself as "vile" and "despicable." The key to the passage may possibly be found in Jer. vi. 30, "despicable silver shall men call them, for YHVH hath despised them" (cf. Ps. liii. 5 (6)). Thus we might paraphrase 'One who holds vile that which God holds vile.'

v. 5. "*That doth not put...to usury.*" At first sight it might appear that this is rather the fulfilment of a duty towards *man* than towards *God*. But it is not so. See Levit. xxv. 36—38.

"*And doing...he never swerves.*" This line must be interpreted by the parallel line of the preceding Stanza; we then read that 'if he swear to his own hurt he changes not,' so here, there is a fixedness of purpose in all he does. Compare Horace, Ode III. iii.

It is suggestive that a Psalm (xiv.) which declares that the earth is corrupt, that 'there is none that doeth good, no not one,' should be followed by a Psalm (xv.) which makes nothing less than perfection the condition of dwelling with God! Such Divine paradox is often found in the Old Testament and is full of promise.

PSALM XVI.

The writer of this Psalm lived at a time when the world, the flesh and the devil were expressed in a voluptuous idolatry. But, says he, I choose God above all things (*v*. 2)... I know the end of idolatry (*v*. 4)... Having God I have all things (*v*. 5)... Just as Levi had no portion in the division of the Land but the Lord was his portion (Deut. xviii. 1 f.). So God is my Portion... This Portion is, in my eyes, most lovely (*v*. 6)... This for two reasons:—

(*a*) His Presence means my *progress under His guidance* (*v*. 7 ; cf. Ps. lxxiii. 24)... Even pain contributes to this...(note on *v*. 7).

(*b*) His Presence means also my *security from falling* (*v*. 8)... It was not always easy to realise His Presence...but "I have set the Lord always..." thus it has become to me a second nature. I now live in the strength of His Presence... Thus I know to whom I have entrusted each day's work... My labour is not in vain in the Lord (*v*. 8).

Hence I find peace. Spirit, soul and body trust Him absolutely for death and all that is beyond it (*vv*. 9, 10)...

Beyond the grave God will still be mine ; and therefore the work will go on... "Thou wilt acquaint me with the path of Life."

(a_1) Then, as now, Thy Presence will mean my progress—but not, as now, through pain. "The fulness of joy (is) in Thy Presence"...

The Presence constitutes the joy...

(b_1) Then too Thy Presence will be my *security from falling*...my *security for retaining those joys*. "Pleasures that, in thy right hand, are evermore" (see note) No need there to "set the Lord alway before me"...

The Son of Man has already gone through this experience.

He chose God above all earthly good.

His "Father" became to Him a "lovely heritage" (St John xvi. 15).

He thanked His Father for "giving Him counsel" even when that counsel crossed His human will (St John iv. 34: vi. 38). "Even so, Father."

He set His Father always before Him so that He remained unmoved by world or flesh or devil.

Thus He looked calmly at death and saw beyond it (*vv*. 9, 10).

Through death He entered immediately on "the path of Life": body, soul and spirit entered with new powers into "the fulness of joy."

And into the reward which the Love of the Father and the gratitude of the redeemed makes ever new.

PS. XVI.

I choose God above all things.	1 Preserve me O God^a for in Thee I take refuge. 2 As to YHVH I say: "Thou art my Lord^b, My good, beyond which there is none."	^a *El* ^b *Adonai*
I reject idolatry and all its works.	3 As to "the holy ones," that are in the earth, And mighty ones whose joy is all in them (I say): 4 "Many shall be their pangs that wed with a stranger-god, I would not pour their blood-libations, Nor take their (very) names^c upon my lips."	 ^c Exod. xxiii. 13
Having God I have all things.	5 YHVH, mine allotted portion and my cup! Thou Thyself dost uphold^d my lot! 6 The lines are fallen unto me in pleasant places, Yea a beauteous inheritance is mine.	 ^d or *make wide*
His Presence means (*a*) my *progress*, though through pain, and (*b*) my *security* from falling.	7 I bless YHVH for giving me counsel^e, Yea nightly my reins instruct me. 8 I have set YHVH always before me^f, While He is at my right hand I shall not be moved.	^e Ps. lxxiii. 24 ^f Acts ii. 25

v. 3. The meaning of (*Q^edoshim*) "*holy ones*" may be determined from the following passages taken from the Revised Version:

Job iv. 18, v. 1. "Behold, He putteth no trust in His servants;
And His angels He chargeth with folly:
. . . .
. . . to which of the *holy ones* wilt thou turn."

Job xv. 15. "Behold He putteth no trust in His *holy ones*;
Yea the heavens are not clean in His sight."

Ps. lxxxix. 5—7. "The heavens shall praise Thy wonders, O Lord;
Thy faithfulness also in the assembly of the *holy ones*."
. . . .
"Who among the sons of the gods (*margin*) is like unto the Lord?
A God very terrible in the Council of the *holy ones*."

Compare also Dan. viii. 13, where the "holy ones" are angels (cf. Dan. iv. 13 (20); also Zech. xiv. 5; Hos. xi. 12 (xii. 1)). It is therefore evident that, in our Psalm, the word is not to be translated "*saints*" (for which *ḥasidim* would have been used as in *v.* 10) but "*holy ones*" in a semi-mythological sense (cf. *v.* 4). This interpretation was, I find, suggested long ago by Kennicott. So also with *addirim*, "*mighty ones*": the word is never used to denote the moral quality of "excellent" (E.V.) but rather of *power* and *splendour*. The reading I have adopted, "whose joy is all in them" for "all that delight in them," involves only a slight change in the vowel points. The "mighty ones" are the "nobles" who delight in idolatry.

v. 7. God's "counsel," in this life, is the *guidance* of His eye (see on Ps. xxxii. 8, where the same word is used). This involves the trial of faith, therefore the Psalmist goes on to say "*Yea*

80   FIRST COLLECTION, 'DAVIDIC' PSALMS.

<blockquote>

Therefore spirit, soul, and body trust Him for the future.

9 So my heart^a is glad,
And my glory^a rejoices,
Yea my flesh^a too can rest secure.
10 For Thou wilt not abandon my soul to Sheòl,
Nor wilt Thou let Thy loved-one see the Pit^b.

Then, as now, His Presence will mean (a_1) my *progress*, in joy, and (b_1) my *security* in retaining joy.

11 Thou wilt acquaint me with the path of Life;—
The fulness of joy, which is Thy Presence:
Pleasures that, in Thy right hand, are evermore.
</blockquote>

nightly my reins instruct me" or "*my reins also chasten me etc.*" The same word signifies both to *instruct* and to *chasten*. The *reins* are the seat of feeling and emotion. God tries the hearts and reins (Ps. vii. 9 (10); xxvi. 2; Jer. xi. 20; xvii. 10; xx. 12). When then it is said "my reins instruct me" it implies a discipline which the man himself consents to and for which he even blesses God, knowing it to be for his good.

 v. 11. According to the punctuation the "fulness of joy...pleasures," &c. are an expansion of the thought contained in "the path of Life." The "fulness of joy" results directly from the "Presence," and the fact that the "Pleasures are evermore." i.e. *lasting pleasures*, is because they are "in (not *at*) God's right hand to give, and therefore are eternal like Himself.

PSALM XVII.

This Psalm contrasts the ideal of the children of this world with that of the children of light. The Psalmist speaks in the name of Israel, indeed he drops accidentally into the *plural* in *v.* 11.

In *vv.* 1—5 the child of light claims, not indeed perfection, but the steadfast will and purpose of following God (Righteousness).

Because God is Righteous, therefore He must at last mark the difference between His children and the children of the world (*vv.* 6—8), who are then described in all their proud hostility (*vv.* 9—12). Their ideal, their whole desire, for their present, is eating, drinking and pleasure (*v.* 14, see note); and, for their future, there is no thought beyond having children and leaving their all (!) to others (*v.* 15, see note).

In contradistinction with this ideal the child of light gives his own in *v.* 16. This verse consists of two lines, of which the first answers to *v.* 14, the second to *v.* 15. The first gives Israel's ideal for the present, "As for me, in righteousness I behold Thy Face," i.e. in striving to follow God (*vv.* 1—5) I gain even now a growing vision of His Face; all things in nature, all events in history, all sorrows and all joys become outward and visible signs of His Presence, so that I find "God, always, everywhere, and all in all." Then, as to the future, "I would be satisfied, in the upwaking, with Thy Image"—i.e. I look forward to a time when I shall see Thee, not as now, "in Righteousness," but, in bodily *Form* (see note) on Earth.

PS. XVII.

Thou knowest I am set to do right (cf. Ps. xviii. 20—23).	1 O YHVH hearken unto righteousness[a], Attend my cry—Give ear unto my prayer— from lips unfeigned.	[a] Cf. v. 16
	2 Let judgement for me come forth from Thy presence[b], Let Thine eyes regard uprightness[c].	[b] Cf. v. 16 [c] i.e. my just cause
	3 Thou hast tried my heart—hast visited me by night— Hast tested[d] me—yet findest nothing: No evil thought shall pass my mouth;	[d] i.e. as by fire
	4 As for the works of men—by the word of Thy lips I have kept me from the paths of the robber[e].	[e] Dan. xi. 14
	5 My steps have held fast to Thy tracks, My footsteps did not slip.	
Therefore Thou wilt distinguish between me and	6 As for me I call on Thee, for Thou, God, wilt hear me; Incline Thine ear to me; hear Thou my speech; 7 Distinguish (such) with Thy favour, O Saviour of them that trust, From such as resist Thy right hand. 8 Keep me as the very apple of an eye; Hide me under the covert of Thy wings.	
my proud persecutors.	9 Because of these wicked ones that would destroy me, My foes that greedily encompass me. 10 They are enfolded in lusty strength; With their mouth they speak out proudly. 11 Even now they dog our steps, Their eyes are set to cast us to the ground. 12 Like as a lion that is famished for prey, And like a young lion lurking in the coverts. 13 Arise, O YHVH! Meet him to the face and bow him low; Deliver my soul from the wicked—who is Thy sword. From men—Thy instruments[f] O YHVH—	[f] Thy hand
Their ideal for the present,	14 From men who wholly are of earth, Whose portion is in living; Whose bellies Thou fillest with Thy treasure[g].	[g] Cf. Job xxi. 7—14

v. 4. "*I have kept...paths of the robber.*" The word translated *robber* (cf. Jer. vii. 11: Ezek. vii. 22 &c.) signifies literally *one who breaks through*. It seems to be used here, and in Dan. xi. 14, to denote those lawless Israelites who sympathised with heathen ways as opposed to "the old paths" (Jer. vi. 16). Possibly the Hebrew word was in our Lord's mind when He said "He that entereth not by the door...the same is...a robber" (John x. 1). The Psalmist is not one of these—"My steps have held fast to Thy tracks."

FIRST COLLECTION, 'DAVIDIC' PSALMS.

for the future.
My ideal for the present, for the future.

15 They are satisfied with children,
And leave their plenty to their offspring[a]!

16 As for me, in righteousness I behold Thy Face[b],
I would be satisfied, in the upwaking, (with)[c] Thy Image.

[a] Job xxi. 11
[b] Presence
[c] or *of Thy Image.* See Greek versions

v. 15. "*They are satisfied with children.*" The word "satisfied" is far too weak both here and in *v.* 16. It signifies a *satiating*, a *filling to the full*. God is good to the just and the unjust (Matt. v. 45). He opens His hand and all things are "*satiated* with good" (Ps. civ. 28). But each thing can receive only according to its *desire* (Ps. cxlv. 16). The earth is "satiated" with rain (Ps. civ. 13); the beast with food (Ezek. xxxii. 4); the good man with God. The desire of the children of this world as to their future does not rise beyond having children, founding a family, and leaving their abundance to others! God gives them their desire. Compare Browning's Poem, *Christmas-Eve and Easter-Day*, xxii. to end.

"*And to leave their plenty...*" There is a solemn irony in the word we translate "plenty." It signifies literally *all that is left* of them! but has occasionally a secondary meaning of "excellency" (Gen. xlix. 3). The irony lies in the combination of the two meanings exactly as in Job iv. 21, "Doth not their *excellency* (which is) in them go away? they die even without wisdom." We are reminded of the Parable of the Rich Fool.

v. 16. "*As for me, in righteousness...*" These words are in sharp contrast with *v.* 14 as though he said, 'They are carnal, I am spiritual. They are of this world, I am not of this world.' *Righteousness* has many meanings in the Old Testament: in the present passage we must interpret it from *v.* 1. As there he confidently appealed to God to "hearken unto righteousness," so here he is assured that by following whatsoever things are right he gains an ever clearer vision of God's Face.

"*I would be satisfied...Thy Image.*" Here again we note the contrast with *v.* 15. The children of this world are "satisfied" to have children in their own likeness, etc. but the children of light can only be "satisfied" with God and with the Divine Image. The word *Temunah* here translated Image is never used of likeness of *character* but always of likeness of *form*. Thus the Israelites are forbidden to represent God by an *image* of any thing (Exod. xx. 4 : Deut. iv. 16, 23, 25; v. 8) because they "saw no image" (E.V. *similitude* Deut. iv. 12, 15). On the other hand, of Moses it is said, "With him will I speak mouth to mouth,...and the *image* of YHVH shall he behold" (Numb. xii. 8). Job also saw the "image" of a spirit that stood before him (Job iv. 16). These are the only other passages in which the word occurs, it is therefore evident that, in our Psalm, it must have an objective sense so that we must not translate "*after Thy likeness*" but "I shall be satisfied...*with Thy Image.*" The Psalmist expects, in the future, a far nearer vision of God—almost in human *form*. Compare the Vulgate "Satiabor cum apparuerit gloria tua." The key-note of the Psalm is the twice-repeated "as for me" (*v.* 6 and *v.* 16). In *v.* 6 this introduces the ground of Israel's hope, viz. the righteousness which he can claim as contrasted with the Nations of the world. This 'righteousness' he sets forth very boldly in the Introduction (*vv.* 1—5). In *v.* 16 the words "as for me" again mark sharply the contrast between the aim and the end of Israel and that of the World-Nations. The children of this world have but one object for the present, a mere animal existence (*v.* 14). And but one hope for the future, to transmit their goods to others (*v.* 15). Israel, on the other hand, has a *present possession*, not of goods but of God, discerned through that single eye which is here called 'Righteousness,' and a *hope for the future* in the upwaking of the Divine Form on Earth.

Another interpretation of the *upwaking* is however quite possible, viz. that it is used in contrast with the state of *vision* in the first member of the verse. In that case we should translate

"As for me, in righteousness, I have a vision of Thy face.
I would (fain) be satisfied in the upwaking, with Thy Image."

The sense would then be similar to that of St Paul,

'We now in a glass darkly:—
But then face to face.'

In either case the Psalmist's hope for the future is fixed on such a Presence of God as has been granted to us in the Incarnation.

PSALM XVIII.

This Psalm occurs also, with some slight verbal changes, in 2 Sam. xxii. The author, whoever he may have been, makes frequent allusions to the Exodus. He was clearly familiar with the Book of Deuteronomy (see marginal references). This alone makes the Davidic authorship absolutely impossible; unless we are prepared to set aside all the results of modern scholarship. The title runs as follows: "*To the Precentor: (A Psalm) of [David], the servant of the Lord, who spake to the Lord the words of this song (Shirah) in the day the Lord delivered him from the hand of [all his enemies], and from the hand of [Saul]; and he said:—*" I would suggest that an ancient title which originally alluded to Israel, the "servant of the Lord," has been modified by a later writer who intended to imply that the deliverance of Israel out of Egypt was repeated in the deliverance of David from his enemies. The original title would probably have run somewhat as follows:— *For the servant of the Lord, who spake to the Lord the words of this Shirah in the day when "the Lord delivered him from the hand of the Egyptians and from the hand of Pharaoh"* (Exod. xviii. 10). Kay who maintains the Davidic authorship notes that *Shirah*, "song," is "a rare form;—used of the two songs of Moses (Exod. xv. 1; Deut. xxxi. 19 ff.), of the song of Israel on the borders of the wilderness." He accounts for "the prolonged reference to the Exodus in the early part of this Psalm" by asserting that "David's deliverance out of Saul's hand was not less God's own deed than the deliverance of Israel out of Pharaoh's was." The fact is that the Psalm refers to Israel.

Verses 4 to 24 depict in vivid colours the Baptism (1 Cor. x. 2) of Israel in the Red Sea (and at Sinai). When Israel went down into the Sea he was like Jonah (compare *vv.* 4—6 with Jonah ii.). Like Jonah he cried to God (*v.* 6; cf. Exod. xiv. 10). Then, in a passage of marvellous poetic beauty, God is depicted as coming to his help (*vv.* 7—19). No doubt the shaking earth, the fire and the darkness remind us rather of Sinai (Exod. xix. and xx.) but we must not forget (Exod. xiv. 19, 20) that the Pillar of Cloud was changed and became "cloud and darkness" to the Egyptians and that St Paul tells us that the fathers "were all baptized...in the Cloud and in the Sea" (1 Cor. x. 2).

The 10th verse, "He...came swooping on wings of the wind," reminds us of Ex. xix. 4, "...how I bare you on eagles' wings, and brought you unto Myself."

In the 14th verse—" He sent forth His arrows and scattered them, He shot out His lightnings and *routed* them"—we clearly have the same picture as in Exod. xiv. 24, "And...the Lord looked unto the host of the Egyptians through the pillar of fire and of cloud, and *routed* the host of the Egyptians." And again in the Asaph Psalm (lxxvii. 16 ff.), "The waters saw Thee, O God, &c..." Compare also the grand Theophany in Habac. iii.

So too, v. 15, "The bed of the waters was seen...at the blast of the breath of Thy nostrils," is best explained by the song of Moses, Exod. xv. 8, "And with the blast of Thy nostrils the waters were gathered together, the floods stood upright as an heap, the depths were congealed in the heart of the sea."

The following passages should also be compared:—

Deut. xxxii.	Ps. xviii.
v. 4 *He is the Rock, His way is perfect.*	God as *the Rock*, vv. 2, 31, 46; v. 30 *His way is perfect.*
vv. 11, 12 God coming as an *eagle* to Israel's help.	v. 10 Same image in the word "swooping."
v. 13 *He made him to ride upon the high places...*	v. 33 *He maketh me tread the high places.*

St Paul would seem to have recognised our Psalm as relating to Israel when, in Rom. xv. 9, 10, he quotes it *in connexion with Deut. xxxii.* to prove that the Gentiles share with Israel in the deliverance of God:—"And that the Gentiles might glorify God for His mercy; as it is written,

Therefore will I give praise unto Thee among the Gentiles
And would sing unto Thy name (Ps. xviii. 49).

And again he saith,

Rejoice, ye Gentiles, with His people" (Deut. xxxii. 43).

We conclude, therefore, that this Psalm depicts the Baptism of Israel, God's "Beloved," in the 'Cloud and in the Sea,' including in that Baptism the Sinai covenant wherein God willing to save the world chose Israel as a nation (cf. v. 19: see Exod. xix. 5 f.), and Israel chose God's service (Exod. xxiv. 3). This pure intention constitutes Israel's 'righteousness' (see vv. 20—24 of our Psalm: v. 22 especially should be compared with Deut. vi. 2; vii. 11; viii. 11). The connexion of thought in v. 25 f. is, I think, as follows:—The 'Cloud and the Sea' are the (seeming) terrors into which Israel in his obedience goes down, but in as far as he is 'loving,' 'perfect,' 'pure' the Cloud is a guiding light, the Sea a protecting wall. To the Egyptians, on the other hand, who 'contend' with God, the Cloud becomes a stormy terror and the Sea an overwhelming destruction. This verse is the central verse of the Psalm and contains the central thought.

If the interpretation I have here sketched be correct the Christian application becomes a very interesting one: Christ is in truth what Israel was only in part, the Beloved; He too had a 'baptism to be baptised with' when He obediently went down into "the overflowings of ungodliness," but inasmuch as He was absolutely "loving," "perfect" and "pure" He saw the Fatherhood through all and the Father came to His aid and highly exalted Him, giving Him a glorious deliverance not for Himself alone but that He might be God's salvation unto the ends of the world.

PS. XVIII.

1 Thee will I love, O YHVH, my Strength!
2 YHVH my Cliff, my Fortress, my Deliverer,
My Strong-One, the Rock^a I can trust in!
My Shield^b, my Horn of Salvation, my Tower!
3 I call upon YHVH the Praised-one,
And from my foes I am saved!

_{Israel at the Red Sea.}

4 The toils^e of Death came round me,
The floods of Chaos terrified me,
5 The toils of Sheol were round me,
The fetters of Death confronted me.

6 In my distress (I thought)
"I will call^d upon YHVH,
And will make my cry to my God:
He will hear my voice from His Palace-temple,
My crying will come before Him, even into His ears^e."

_{Israel delivered at the Red Sea by a Theophany.}

7 Then Earth itself quivered and quaked^f,
The mountains' foundations were troubled,
Yea, they quivered because He was wroth.
8 There went up a smoke from His^g nostrils,
And a fire consumed from His mouth,
Yea, flames were kindled from Him.
9 So He bowed down the Heavens and came,
With the Darkness under His feet.
10 He rode on the Cherub and flew,
Came swooping^h on Wings of the wind.
11 He made darkness His covert,
His pavilion all round Him—
The dark of abysses—dense clouds of the skies.
12 Through His splendour opposing His dense clouds removed,
There was hail with flames of fire.
13 For YHVH thundered in heaven,
The Most High uttered His voice—
[There was hail with flames of fire.]ⁱ

^a Deut. xxxii. 4, 37
^b Deut. xxxiii. 29

^e "breakers of Death," II. Sam. xxii. 5
Cf. Jonah ii.

^d Exod. xiv. 10

^e Exod. ii. 23

^f Ps. lxviii. 8
Ps. lxxvii. 16 ff.
Cf. also the Psalm in Hab. iii.
Exod. xix. and xx.
^g Deut. xxxii. 22

^h Deut. xxviii. 49, Jer. xlviii. 40, xlix. 22

ⁱ Omitted in Sept. and in II. Sam. xxii.

14 He sent forth His arrows and scattered them,
   He shot out His lightnings and routed^a them.
15 Then the bed of the waters was seen,
   The foundations of Earth were laid bare,
   At the blast of the breath^b of Thy nostrils.

^a Exod. xiv. 24
^b Exod. xv. 8

16 He reaches from high, He takes me,
   Draws me forth from many waters,
17 Frees me from my mighty foe,
   From enemies too strong for me.
18 They confronted me in the day of my weakness,
   So YHVH became my stay.
19 He brought me forth at large,
   He frees me because He loves^c me.

Cf. v. 4
Ps. lxviii. 22;
Is. lxiii. 12
Cf. v. 5
Cf. v. 6

^c lit. "takes pleasure in me"

Israel is now keeping the Law and conscious of no defection from God.

20 YHVH requites me according to my righteousness,
   Renders me according to the cleanness of my hands.
21 Because I have observed the ways of YHVH,
   And not gone wickedly against my God.
22 Because all His ordinances are before me,
   And His statutes I put not from me.
23 And I am become perfect^d with Him,
   And have kept me from mine iniquity.
24 So YHVH rendered me according to my righteousness,
   According to the cleanness of my hands in His eyesight.

Deut. vi. 2; vii. 11; viii. 11

^d i.e. wholehearted

v. 16. "*He reaches from high, He takes me*, &c." This description of the sudden deliverance of Israel in answer to the cry of misery may be compared with Browning's *Instans Tyrannus*:

> "When sudden...how think ye, the end?
> Did I say 'without friend'?
> Say rather, from marge to blue marge,
> The whole sky grew his large,
> With the sun's self for visible boss,
> While an Arm ran across,
> Which the earth heaved beneath like a breast,
> Where the wretch was safe prest!
> Do you see? Just my vengeance complete,
> The man sprang to his feet,
> Stood erect, caught at God's skirts, and prayed!
> —So, *I* was afraid!"

v. 19. Israel sums up God's dealings in this one line.—Such a Providence manifests a purpose of love for the future. Possibly the Psalm at one time ended here. A different word is used (*v.* 1) of Israel's love of God. Israel's love springs out of God's choice: "We love Him because He first loved us."

PSALM XVIII.

<table>
<tr><td>Therefore Israel's future is assured.</td><td>25 With the loving Thou shewest Thyself loving,
    With the perfect man Thou shewest Thyself perfect.
26 With the pure Thou shewest Thyself pure,
    And with the contentious Thou shewest^a Thyself a contender.
27 Surely it is Thou that wilt save the lowly People,
    And abase (all) lofty looks.
28 Surely it is Thou that ^bwilt light^b my lamp,
    YHVH, my God, will make my darkness shine.
29 Surely through Thee I can break^c a host,
    Yea, through my God I can leap the wall.</td><td>Wisdom xvi., xix.
^a Prov. iii. 34

So II. Sam. xxii. 28
^b not in II. Samuel xxii.
^c so Lagarde</td></tr>
<tr><td>God's way is thorough: through pain to glory.</td><td>30 As for God^d, His way is perfect^e,
    The promise^f of YHVH is tried to the proof.
    A Shield He is to all that trust in Him.</td><td>^d El
^e Deut. xxxii. 4
^f lit. oracle. See note, Ps. xii. 6</td></tr>
</table>

v. 25. "*With the loving*, &c." Delitzsch expresses the meaning thus:

(α) "Towards the *loving* Thou shewest Thyself *loving*,
(β) Towards the man of *entire surrender* Thou shewest Thyself *giving*,
(γ) Towards him that *purifieth himself* Thou shewest Thyself *pure*" (i.e. bright and clear).

We may regard (α), (β), (γ) as the three upward steps to the Clear Vision of God.

(α) "*Loving*" (ḥasid) very rarely applied to God, but often to men as *attached to God*, i.e. "*godly*," cf. the word "saint" in the New Testament. Towards such God *shews Himself loving*.

(β) The second step is *entire surrender*.—The word denotes *whole-hearted men*—such men as forsook all and followed Christ. To such God *shews Himself giving* (Matt. xix. 29). God never lets His servants out-do Him in generosity.

(γ) But there is something better than giving gifts and that is giving ourselves: and there is something better than receiving God's gifts and that is receiving God. So the last step is *to purify oneself*—a word much wider than moral purity, denoting that single-hearted self-surrender which keeps nothing back from God. Such men would see God bright and clear. "O righteous Father, the world hath not known Thee; but I have known Thee, and these have known that Thou hast sent Me" (St John xvii. 25).

v. 26^b. "*With the contentious Thou shewest Thyself a contender.*" As the upward course ends in the Clear Vision of God through growing inner light so the downward course ends in putting out the eyes of the soul.—"How great is that darkness!" The eye only sees what it brings the power of seeing—for good or evil—hence "to the scorner God Himself seems a scorner" (Prov. iii. 34). If he "seek wisdom it (simply) does not exist" (Prov. xiv. 6). Reproof and kindness are useless upon him (Prov. ix. 7; xiii. 1; xv. 12). The Pharisees were very near this stage when they said "This fellow doth not cast out devils but by Beelzebub the prince of the devils" (Matt. xii. 24, cf. *v.* 31).

> "For I say, this is death and the sole death,
> When a man's loss comes to him from his gain,
> Darkness from light, from knowledge ignorance,
> And lack of love from love made manifest."

Thus the soul may create for itself a world without God! I know nothing in literature more terrible than Richter's Vision of a soul awaking in such a world.

The thought in these two verses of our Psalm seems to me to be alluded to and expanded in Rev. xxii. 11 (R.V. margin).

v. 30. "*As for God, His way is perfect...*" The thought is similar to that of the 'Asaph' Psalm lxxvii. 13 (see ad loc.). There is a *thoroughness* about God's way which does not stop at

FIRST COLLECTION, 'DAVIDIC' PSALMS.

31 For who is God other than YHVH,
Or who is a Rock save our God?
32 As for God^a He girdeth me with strength,
And hath made my way perfect.
33 He giveth me feet like the hind's,
And letteth me tread^b the heights.
34 He traineth my hands for war,
So the steel bow is snapped^c by my arms.
35 Thou hast given me the shield of Thy help,
Thy right-hand sustains me,
Thy lowliness^d exalts me.
36 Thou makest me room to tread,
And that my feet should not falter.

A vision of Israel's future.

37 I shall follow my foes and o'ertake them,
Nor shall I turn back till I have destroyed them.
38 I shall smite them that they be not able to rise,
They shall fall under my feet.
39 Thou hast girded me with strength for war,
Thou humblest mine adversaries under me.
40 Thou hast given me the grip of my enemies,
And I cut off those that hate me.
41 They cry—but there is none to help—
To YHVH—but there is none that answers them.

pain. By this very fact that "*His* way is perfect," He "hath made *my* way perfect" (*v.* 32).
"Perfect I call Thy plan:
Thanks that I was a man!
Maker, remake, complete,—I trust what Thou shalt do!"

"*The promise (or word) of YHVH is tried to the proof.*" Just as God's *way* does not stop at pain so His *promise* does not stop at fire, but comes out as gold from the fiery trial (see note p. 52). All the promises of God are without repentance (Rom. xi. 29). From these two facts it follows that God is "A shield to all that trust in Him" (cf. *v.* 35).

v. 35. "*...the shield of Thy help.*" As in *v.* 30 the Psalmist explains the shield of God's help by two sharply contrasted thoughts:—
(a) "Thy right-hand (i.e. Thy power) sustains me,"
(b) "Thy lowliness (i.e. Thy condescension) exalts me."
For similar contrast see Ps. cxiii. 5 f.; cxxxviii. 6: Is. lvii. 15. God's *power* sustains Israel in life and makes room for him to go along the way; while God's *lowliness*, which is always closely akin to His *Word* moved in Israel as "the hope of glory" before the days of the Incarnation.

v. 41. "*To YHVH.*" The thought of the enemy crying unto YHVH is certainly strange. Possibly the name *Elohim* originally stood here: the Psalm has many points of contact with the Elohistic 'Asaph' Psalms. If the Editor who arranged the Psalms had placed it in the Jehovistic 'Davidic' group he may very possibly have changed Elohim into YHVH.

PSALM XVIII.

₄₂ I beat them as small as the dust before the wind:
I pour them out as the mud of the streets.
₄₃ Thou deliverest me from the strivings of the people;
Thou makest me the chief of the nations:
A people I knew not obeys me.
₄₄ They but hear[a] of me with rumour's ear: [a] Exod. xv. 14 f.
And aliens pay me homage.
₄₅ Aliens fail—
They come trembling out of their strongholds.

₄₆ YHVH liveth, and blessed is my Rock,
And exalted[b] be the God of my salvation.   [b] Exod. xv. 2
₄₇ As for God[c] He granteth me vengeance,   [c] *El*
And hath subdued the peoples under me.
₄₈ He delivers me from mine enemies:
Yea from mine adversaries Thou settest me up on high;
From the violent Thou rescuest me.
₄₉ Therefore I thank Thee among the nations O YHVH,
And would strike the harp to Thy Name.
₅₀ As One who giveth great salvation to His King,
And sheweth loving-kindness to His Anointed,
To David and his seed for evermore.

---

v. 50. "*His King...His Anointed...David.*" It is clear that these words refer to one and the same person; but are we therefore compelled to interpret them of David the son of Jesse? Those who say Yes must account for the following passages written long after David's death:

Hos. iii. 5. "They shall seek unto YHVH their God and unto David their King...in the latter days."

Jer. xxx. 9. "And they shall serve YHVH their God and David their King, whom I will raise up for them."

Ezek. xxxvii. 22 and 24. "One King shall be King to them all"..."David My Servant (shall be) King."

FIRST COLLECTION, 'DAVIDIC' PSALMS.

PS. XIX.* PART I.

The Light of Nature.

Day I.	1 The heavens are telling the glory of God[a],	[a] *El*
Day II.	And the firmament sheweth his handiwork.	
Day III.	2 Day unto day abounds[b] with speech,	[b] Ps. cxix. 171
Day IV.	And night unto night discourseth knowledge.	
	†[3 Not speech, not words—without their voice being heard].	
Day V.	4 Through all the earth is gone forth their strain,	
Day VI.	Their words through the confines of the world.	

The blessings that it brings.

Day I.	He appointed the sun to tent in them.
Day II.	5 And he, like a bridegroom goes forth from his canopy,
Day III.	Rejoicing as a giant in running his course.
Day IV.	6 His ingress is upon one bound of heaven,
Day V.	His regress on the other bound thereof,
Day VI.	So that nothing is hid from his heat.

* For the Introduction to this Psalm see page 94.
† Regarded as a gloss by Olshausen and Wellhausen.

v. 1[a]. The *Glory* of God is His manifestation to the world. Its natural emblem is *Light*. The first Day tells of the creation of Light, from which all else follows. Thus, by way of parable, the first Day tells the whole story of creation as the Manifestation of God. We notice that the parallel line of Part II (i.e. *v*. 7[a]) contains the parallel thought:—just as "All Creation is one act at once—the birth of light," so all Revelation is one act at once—the birth of Thora. If any word of God ever came to man that word must ultimately reach to the highest expression.—"In the beginning was the Word—And the Word became flesh." Our Psalm is appointed fitly for Christmas Day. There is also, I believe, a correspondence between the two stanzas of Part I, so that the line 1[a] answers to the line 4[c], "The heavens are telling the Glory of God," because "He appoints the sun to tabernacle in them."

v. 1[b]. "*And the firmament sheweth...*" The *firmament* was the work of the second Day. There is a thought of firmness and stability in the word which is quite foreign to our modern conception. The firmament was a partition between the upper and lower worlds (cf. Gen. i. with Ezek. i. 22—26). It gave stability to the Universe, upon it was the Throne of God (Ezek. i). What the firmament "sheweth" of God's handiwork is that it is *sure* and stable. If we compare the parallel line in Part II we find the parallel thought that "The TESTIMONY of VHVH is *stable*." The TESTIMONY of VHVH (see p. 51) is that which He has attested, limited and defined, as a rule of human conduct. The word was in later times specially applied to the Decalogue (Exod. xvi. 34, xxv. 16, 21 f. &c., &c.) though it would be rash to assume that the "Ark of the Testimony," and "the tabernacle of Testimony," were originally so called because they contained the "tables of Testimony"! Indeed, when the word "Testimony" stands alone, as in Exod. xxvii. 21, Numb. xvii. 4 (19), it seems to require a wider meaning.

In a difficult passage, Ps. lxxxix. 37, we read

"...his throne is as the sun before Me.
It is established for ever as the moon,
And as the witness in the sky it is sure."

PS. XIX. PART II.

<table>
<tr><td>The Light of Revelation.</td><td></td></tr>
<tr><td>Sphere I.</td><td>7 The LAW of YHVH is perfect—life-reviving,</td></tr>
<tr><td>Sphere II.</td><td>The TESTIMONY of YHVH is stable—making wise the simple.</td></tr>
<tr><td>Sphere III.</td><td>8 The PRECEPTS of YHVH are upright—gladdening the heart,</td></tr>
<tr><td>Sphere IV.</td><td>The COMMANDMENT of YHVH is bright—enlightening the eyes.</td></tr>
<tr><td>Sphere V.</td><td>9 The WORD[a] of YHVH is pure—enduring for ever.</td></tr>
<tr><td>Sphere VI.</td><td>The JUDGEMENTS of YHVH are truth—righteous altogether.</td></tr>
</table>

[a] or "ORACLES ...are pure"
Ps. cxix. 140
Ps. lxix. 62, 106

The blessings that it brings.

<table>
<tr><td>Sphere VI.</td><td>10 O more desirable (are they) than gold!—than much fine gold!</td><td></td></tr>
<tr><td>Sphere V.</td><td>Sweeter are they than honey[b],—and the dripping honey-comb.</td><td>[b] Ps. cxix. 103</td></tr>
<tr><td>Sphere IV.</td><td>11 Thy servant too gets warning-light[c] from them,</td><td>[c] Ps. cxix. 105</td></tr>
<tr><td>Sphere III.</td><td>In keeping them the after-gain[d] is great.</td><td>[d] Ps. cxix. 112</td></tr>
<tr><td>Sphere II.</td><td>12 Who can comprehend his errors?</td><td></td></tr>
<tr><td>Sphere I.</td><td>From hidden (faults) Oh cleanse me!</td><td></td></tr>
</table>

Probably a later addition.

[13 Also from proud ones keep Thou back Thy servant,
Let them not master[e] me. So shall I be perfect,   [e] Ps. cxix. 133
And clean from much transgression.
14 Let the words of my mouth and the meditation of my heart
be acceptable in Thy sight O YHVH, my Rock
and my Redeemer.]

Is this "witness in the sky" the firmament? If so it would be an interesting comment on the words of our present Psalm.

The second line of stanza i. should also be compared with the second line of stanza ii. (i.e. *v.* 1[b] with *v.* 5[a]). The 'canopy' from which the sun goes forth is the 'firmament.'

v. 2[a]. "*Day unto day abounds with speech.*"—Literally '*bubbles over with....*' There is a wellspring of joy and meaning too full for utterance. This is the work of the Third Day. There is an old Jewish tradition that 'Praise-songs to God arose on the Third Day.' (See Hebrew Poem by R. Judah Ha-Levi in 'Treasures of Oxford,' p. 59). The line should first be compared with the third line of stanza ii. This wellspring of joy in Creation is due to the sun, 'Rejoicing as a giant in running his course.' Next we should compare it with the third line in Part II (*v.* 8[a]) "The PRECEPTS of YHVH are right, gladdening the heart,' i.e. Revelation regarded as the sacred deposit (see on PRECEPTS, page 52) finds its answering echo in the heart (cf. Ps. cxix. 128) which it fills with joy.

v. 2[b]. "*Night unto night....*" This fourth line corresponds with the work of the fourth Day. On that Day the luminaries were placed in the firmament to give light upon the earth. By this means 'night unto night discourseth knowledge.' The fourth line of stanza ii. tells us of the sun that 'his ingress is upon one bound of heaven....,' but the words *ingress* and *regress* of *v.* 6 must not be confined to the daily rising and setting of the sun: they refer rather to his yearly movement among the Signs

12—2

FIRST COLLECTION, 'DAVIDIC' PSALMS.

of the Zodiac or the Spheres. The word we have translated *regress* always denotes in Biblical Hebrew "*the turn*" of the year (Ez. xxxiv. 22; 1 Sam. i. 20; 2 Chr. xxiv. 23; Ps. xix. 6 (7) are the only passages). In later Hebrew it was used to denote the solstices. The Babylonian Year was a repetition of the day on a larger scale. As the day consisted of equal periods of light and darkness so their year consisted of six months (decline), during which the sun was moving from his birth to his death, and six months (ascent), during which he was moving from his death to his birth. Thus the thoughts of day and night were transferred to the year: each night he went "beneath the waters" and traversed the underworld, so in what we may call the night of the year he was "beneath the waters." This gives a much deeper meaning to the words of verse 6 "and nothing is hid from his heat." Compare the hymn, *Veni Redemptor Gentium*, of St Ambrose, quoted by Neale:

> "From God the Father He proceeds;
> To God the Father back He speeds:
> Proceeds—as far as very hell,
> Speeds back—to light ineffable."

If we compare the fourth line of Part I with the fourth line of Part II we are reminded at once of the work of the fourth Day; as on that Day the luminaries became "for signs and for seasons" causing "night unto night to discourse knowledge" so (in the world of Revelation) the "commandment," which is likened to a *lamp* (Prov. vi. 23), shone out in man's darkness—"bright, enlightening the eyes" so that man can say (v. 11ᵃ) "Thy servant too gets warning-light from them."

v. 4ᵃ. "*Through all the earth is gone forth their strain.*"—This, omitting the gloss, is properly the fifth line. In Creation the fifth Day introduces for the first time the marvel of animated life:—for the first time too we read "And God blessed them." The birds are God's preachers. To them, as giving voice to Creation's Hymn, we might apply the words, "Through all the earth is gone forth their strain." We must compare this line with the fifth line of Part II (v. 9ᵇ), "The oracles of YHVH are pure &c...." The oracles of YHVH (see note, p. 51) are those Divine utterances 'whose very sweetness yieldeth proof that they were born for immortality'; while they satisfy the heart they enlarge it for a wider fulfilment to come. In this sense they are "enduring for ever."

If the reader now passes to *v.* 10ᵇ which we have coupled with *v.* 9ᵃ he will note how the thought is expanded. "Sweeter are they than honey—and the dripping honey-comb." The words are almost identical with Ps. cxix. 103, "How sweet are Thy oracles unto my taste—more so than honey to my mouth."

v. 4ᵇ with 9ᵇ. "*Their words, &c.*" "*The judgements of YHVH...*" This *sixth line* answers to the work of the *sixth Day*. In the world of Nature the "Heavens" arrive, on the sixth Day, at articulate speech in the creation of Man, so that, through him "their words (go) through the confines of the world." So too in the world of Revelation the sixth Day is associated with God's *judgements* (see notes on 'Asaph' Psalms), thus it is said, "The judgements of YHVH are truth"—not merely *true* but *truth* itself, the final expression of His thought seen and justified before men and angels. So it is added—"righteous altogether." The same idea is expressed Ps. cxix. 160, "The sum of Thy word is truth. Each righteous judgement of Thine is eternal."

v. 4. "*their strain.*"—The Hebrew text gives "their line," i.e. their measuring-line. The going forth of a measuring-line implies the establishment of a claim (cf. Jer. xxxi. 39), which would give a very possible sense here. But the parallelism seems to suggest that we should read (with LXX), and Wellhausen קֹלָם instead of קַוָּם, and translate "their voice" or "their strain."

v. 9. The text reads "*The fear of YHVH.*" I am, however, convinced that the text here is wrong, and that instead of יראת יהוה, "the fear of YHVH," we ought to read אמרת יהוה, "the *word*, or rather the *oracles*, of YHVH. And this for the following reasons :

1st. The other five terms *Law, testimony, precepts, commandments, judgements*, are all synonyms for the Law (see notes on Ps. cxix. page 50 f.), consequently we should expect some such expression as "the *oracles* of YHVH are pure and endure for ever," instead of the present text, which scarcely makes sense.

2nd. The very expression is found in Ps. xii. 6 (7) "The oracles (אמרות) of YHVH are pure oracles, silver purified (צרופה)..." And again, Ps. cxix. 140, "*Thy word* (i.e. *oracles*, אמרתך) is *purified* (צרופה). And again, Ps. xviii. 31 (30) and 2 Sam. xxii. 31, "*The word of YHVH is pure.*" Thus we find that this particular name for the *word* (or *oracles*) of God is constantly

PSALM XIX.

coupled with the idea of *purity from a fiery trial*. A similar thought is found in Ps. cv. 19, "The word (אמרת) *of YHVH purified him* (צרפתהו)," i.e. tried him as by fire [cf. Heb. iv. 12 f.].

Thus I conclude that the proper reading in our Psalm is "The *word* (אמרת) of YHVH is pure and endureth for ever," i.e. the *oracles* of YHVH have stood the fiery test and abide. If the reader object that the words "יראת and "אמרת were not likely to be confounded, I reply that the Septuagint have actually made this confusion in Prov. i. 29, where the Hebrew has "the *fear* of the Lord," and the Greek "the *word* of the Lord."

vv. 13, 14. Wellhausen regards *v.* 14 as a gloss, but the 13th verse is also very different in style and reads like a pious prayer written on the margin of a hymn. Probably it was suggested by the mention of "errors..." "hidden faults" in *v.* 12. The scribe feels that there is one other class of sins from which he must pray for deliverance—viz. *sins of presumption*. "*Errors*"..."*hidden* (things) mean to the Psalmist much more than the "*ignorances*"..."*hidden sins*" of the scribe. The cry, "Who can comprehend his errors" is not the wail of "an infant crying in the night...and with no language but a cry." It is rather man's thanksgiving for the Revelation as the Light of Life—'Apart from that Revelation who would have known right from wrong? but now that Light makes the simple wise.'

Since however the gloss has become part of the text we must interpret it according to the later and more dogmatic theology of the scribe. In his eyes *ignorances...hidden sins...proud ones* denote the three steps on the downward road which ends in *the great transgression*. 'Ignorances' are sins which the sinner did not know to be sinful (Levit. iv. and v.). 'Hidden sins'—literally 'Hidden things.' Not secret faults which the sinner tries to hide from God and man, but sins which are hidden from himself, pitfalls into which he might sink unawares. Thus when Saul of Tarsus with a clear conscience persecuted the Church it was a sin of 'ignorance,' but when Abimelech took Sarah (Gen. xx.) it was 'hidden sin.' In the former case light was needed to the conscience, in the latter light to the intelligence. For all such sins of 'ignorance' the Jewish Law provided atonement through sacrifice (Numb. xv. 27 f.). Not so with 'proud sins,' i.e. sins of presumption; for these no sacrifice was provided (Numb. xv. 30 f.). Though there might be forgiveness for such, as in the case of David, yet it was beyond the Covenant; therefore the scribe prays 'also from proud ones hold Thou back Thy servant.' Man without the Divine Word (Law) would be like a universe without its sun; he would have no light to his conscience whereby he might avoid sins of ignorance, no light to his intelligence whereby he might escape hidden sins, no restraint upon life to keep him within the orbit of his being, and by force of attraction hold him back from ruin.

It is however only fair to say that the word we have translated "proud ones" might refer to "proud men" as in the closely parallel passage Ps. cxix. 122—125.

PSALM XIX.

I have shewn in my Akkadian Genesis that the six "Days" of Creation correspond with the six *spheres*, each having, according to Babylonian thought, its presiding planet or deity. The sun's course through these six spheres completed the ancient year of six months. This being so, the 'music of the spheres' is not an idle dream of the poets. Each season has its meaning and is a parable to the wise:—

> "These, as they change, Almighty Father, these
> Are but the varied God. The rolling year
> Is full of thee!"

This nineteenth Psalm interprets the music of the spheres. The Psalm consists of two parts, which are so different in style that many suppose them to have been originally distinct. Whether this be so or no the two parts have now a close relation to one another. Part I is a magnificent poem, setting forth the office of the sun as giving voice and meaning to the whole universe, which, but for him, would be a silent instrument, dumb to the glory of God, but which now brims over with such joy and praise as can scarcely find expression. All this new meaning which awakes in the heavens is due to the sun which 'tabernacles' among them and is, as the poet seems to suggest (*v*. 5), the Bridegroom of Nature.

Part II (*v*. 7 to end) is wholly different in style, and reminds us of Psalm cxix. It is all in praise of the Law. We should however be greatly mistaken if we supposed that the *Law* which the Psalmist found to be light and life was the letter of the Mosaic code; on the contrary, it was the Living Voice of God speaking through Priest and Prophet, sufficing for every need as it arose. To the Psalmist *Law* (*Thora*) was almost identical with *Revelation*. It is only when we have realized this that we can appreciate the relation between the two parts of the Psalm.

What the sun is in the world of nature that the *Law* (*Thora, Divine Word*) is in the world of men. Without this inspiration, or Divine Word, which indwells the ages, the world of man would be a voiceless chaos, but, with it, all things "mean intensely and mean well" (cf. Is. xlv. 18).

In Part I the Divine Name is *El*, as the God of Nature: in Part II it is YHVH, as the God of the Covenant.

The style of Part I is very different from that of Part II, but, on the other hand, they are similar in structure. Both (if we omit the portions marked as gloss) consist of two stanzas of six lines each, which seem to have reference to the six 'Days' or Spheres of Creation (see notes). Part II is much more artificial in its structure, and its two stanzas correspond in reverse order: it probably belongs to the same period as Ps. cxix., whereas Part I *may* be much earlier.

PSALM XX.

This Psalm is best interpreted from the story of Jacob at Peniel (Gen. xxxii. 24 ff.) There God "answered him in the day of his trouble" (Gen. xxxv. 3), shewing him that the Divine Name (Nature) could not be won without the struggle. The life of Jacob (Israel) was felt to be in this respect a type of the Nation (Israel): cf. Hos. xii. 3 f.

The mission of Israel is to win God's Name by struggle and to express that Name to the World. This involved separation from the World, and therefore the hatred of the World. Israel becomes the "Suffering Nation." Israel must conquer the World not by might or by strength but by winning and by imparting the Divine Name. Let the Psalm now be read with this meaning in view.

The lives of the Prophets (e.g. Jeremiah) led to the expectation that God's Ideal for Israel must find expression in the life of a Perfect Man. The world being what it is, such a Man *must* be a Sufferer (cf. Plato *Rep.* II. p. 44; *Davies and Vaughan's translation; Wisdom of Sol.* ii. *vv.* 13—20).

But the world will not always be what it is. The Redeemer will at last receive the gratitude of the redeemed. "This Psalm is the prayer which the Church might be supposed offering up, had all the redeemed stood by the Cross, or in Gethsemane, in full consciousness of what was doing there" (A. A. Bonar, quoted in *Treasury of David*).

Let *vv.* 1—5 be now read in this light—

We Christians know how the Father did "answer Him in the day of His trouble," and how the "Name above every name" became His Name and "set Him on high." Knowing this we can take to ourselves the lesson and comfort of *vv.* 6—8.

The chief division of the Psalm comes between verses 5 and 6. Many commentators from Ewald downwards suppose that a sacrifice had been offered at this point and that the second half of the Psalm (*vv.* 6—10) denotes the acceptance of this sacrifice. This is by no means improbable. The student should carefully compare the thought and structure of this Psalm with that of Psalm xxviii. which may be called its octave.

PS. XX.

The Vision of Victory

1 YHVH answer thee in the day of *trouble;
   The Name of Jacob's God set thee on high^b!
2 Send thee thy help from the Sanctuary^c;
   And sustain thee from out of Zion!
3 May He remember all thy offerings;
   And graciously accept thy sacrifice!
4 Grant thee thy very heart's desire^d;
   And accomplish^e all thy purpose!

realized as an historic present.

5 We sing for joy in Thy salvation,
   We exult in the name of our God;
   YHVH accomplishes all thy requests.

Comfort from the Vision.

6 Now know I that YHVH helpeth His Anointed,
   That He answers him from His holy heaven,
   With the saving help of His right hand.
7 Some—in chariots, and some, in horses^f!
   But we—we make mention of the Name of YHVH our God,
8 As for them, they sink and they fall;
   But we, we arise and stand firm.

9 O YHVH save!
   In the day when we call the King answers us.

---

v. 1. The Yalkut sees in these words a reference to Gen. xxxv. 3, where Jacob says, "Let us go up to Beth-el; and I will make there an altar unto God, *who answered me in the day of my trouble*." The verb we have translated "*set thee on high*" has also the kindred meaning of *safety*. From the same root we have the Hebrew word for a "*high tower*." The two meanings are again combined in Prov. xviii. 10. "The name of YHVH is a strong tower, the righteous runneth into it *and is safe* (marg. *set aloft*)." Compare Prov. xxix. 25, "Whoso putteth his trust in YHVH *shall be safe* (marg. *set on high*)." The word is again coupled with the Name of God in Ps. xci. 14, "*I will set him on high* because he hath known my Name" (cf. Pss. lix. 1 (2); lxix. 29 (30); cvii. 41). When then it is said, "The Name of Jacob's God set thee on high" it must imply that as Jacob became Israel through partaking of the Name (Nature) of God, so too it must be in the history of Jacob's seed.

v. 9. Many commentators here, following the Septuagint, disregard the accents, and translate

"*O Lord save the King,
He hears us* (or *and hear us*) *in the day when we call*."

This interpretation probably led to the use of the Psalm in the Accession Service.

The *Yalkut* draws attention to the fact that the Psalm ends as it began. It began, "YHVH answer thee in the day of trouble." It ends, "In the day when we call the King answers us."

The *Midrash* explains the readiness of the answer from the words,

"He shall call me and I will answer him,
I (myself) am with him in trouble..." (Ps. xci. 15).

Though God may allow His People to be afflicted yet "in all their trouble He is troubled," (Is. lxiii. 9).

PSALM XXI.

The "King" in this Psalm is a reflex of God. In him God is well-pleased (vv. 1—3). God gives him an endless life (v. 4). God puts of His own Majesty upon him (v. 5). Through him God fulfils the old promise that all the world shall be blessed and makes him radiant of the very brightness of the Shechina (v. 6). This King places his whole trust in God and never can be moved (v. 7; cf. Is. xlii. 4).

Can such a description have been intended to apply to any monarch who ever sat upon a throne? I refuse to believe it. The fulsome flattery of Eastern hyperbole is alien to the spirit of the Old Testament. Early kings, like Saul and David, lived on familiar terms with their people, and, in later times, Isaiah ridicules with stinging words the god-like pretentions of the heathen kings (Is. xiv. 12 ff.).

The fact is that, from the very earliest time, God Himself was felt to be "the King" of Israel (1 Sam. xii. 12). When a king was afterwards appointed he "sat upon the throne of God" (1 Chron. xxix. 23). The Prophets looked forward to a time when the Kingship of God over Israel, and even over "the whole earth" (Zech. xiv. 9), would become a realized fact (Is. xxiv. 23; lii. 7 &c.). This thought finds expression in the Psalms of the Theophany (see on Pss. xciii. &c.). Side by side with this expectation of a visible reign of God upon earth we find another channel of expectation, not clearly defined, in which the Divine reign on earth is to be realized through an ideal "David" who should, as it were, so completely fill "God's throne" that what is said of God may fitly be said of him. Thus:— Hos. iii. 5, "They shall seek unto YHVH their God and unto David their King..."

Jer. xxx. 9, "And they shall serve YHVH their God and David their King..."

Ezek. xxxvii. 22 and 24, "Our King shall be King to them all..." "David My servant (shall be) King."

It is in this sense that I understand the word 'King' in many passages of the Psalms, e.g.

Ps. xviii. 50 (51) "Who giveth great salvation to His King
And sheweth loving-kindness to His Anointed,
To David and his seed for evermore."

The Jewish tradition is therefore to be accepted which asserts that the King in Psalm xxi. is none other than King Messiah (see *Yalkut*).

The division of the Psalm is as follows:—

Verses 1—6 are addressed to God.

Verses 8—12 are addressed to the King. (This is evident from v. 9b). Verse 7 is addressed neither to God nor to the King but forms a connecting link between the two main portions of the Psalm. Verse 13 drops, as it were, the parable of the King and claims for the People that triumph which strictly belongs only to their ideal Representative.

The first main division of the Psalm may be described as *the arming of the King*. The weapons of his warfare are all spiritual. God puts such Majesty upon him that he becomes the effulgence of His Glory, the expression of His essence (Heb. i. 3). But this same Glory that makes him a fount of endless blessing to his own People makes him a terror to his foes (contrast v. 6 with v. 9).

Thus in the second main division of the Psalm the King is seen armed with terrors which remind us of Milton's description in *Paradise Lost*, Bk. vi. 824—866.

In vv. 9, 10 the imagery is, I think, coloured by associations connected with Molok, "the King." To those who refuse the joy of God's Presence (v. 6) that Presence becomes a consuming fire. It is a fearful thing to reject God and "fall into the hands" of the Laws of Nature (Heb. x. 31).

PS. XXI.

The arming of the King.
Our King becomes the reflex of God and dispenser to us of His blessings.

1 O YHVH, in Thy might the King rejoices;
O how exceeding glad he is through Thy Salvation!
2 Thou gavest him his heart's desire^a;   ^a Ps. xx. 4
Thou didst not withhold the request of his lips.
3 But didst meet^b him with blessings of goodness;   ^b anticipate
Setting on his head a crown of gold.
4 Did he ask life of Thee?—Thou gavest it—
A length of days to all eternity!
5 Great is his glory through Thy Salvation;
Splendour and majesty^c Thou layest upon him.   ^c Ps. viii. 5
6 For Thou makest him an endless blessing^d;   ^d Gen. xii. 2
Gladdening him with the joy that is Thy Presence.

Central thought.

7 For the King trusteth in YHVH,
Through the lovingkindness of the Most High he shall never be moved.

The victory of the King.
Our King (*Melek*) becomes to his enemies a very *Molok*.

8 Thy hand shall reach all thine enemies;
Thy right-hand shall reach them that hate thee.
9 Thou shalt make them as a fiery furnace in the time of thy Presence;
YHVH will devour them in His anger, the fire will consume them.
10 Thou destroyest their fruit from off the earth,
Their seed from among the children of men.
11 Though they plotted evil against thee,
They devised a device—but were powerless!
12 For thou turnest them to flight,
Aiming thy bow-strings at their faces.

Our victory, too, is only in God.

13 O YHVH be Thou exalted in Thy might^e: ^e v. 1
We sing, we strike the harp, through Thy power.

PSALM XXII.

The Suffering Servant feels himself forsaken in spite of prayer (*vv.* 1 and 2). He looks back to a time when men had only to cry and be helped (*vv.* 4 and 5) but not so now! The Sufferer must bear the reproach of being forsaken by God in whom he trusts (*vv.* 6—8). Yet he knows that God Himself caused him to be born and that the blind instinct of an infant's mother-trust had behind it the mother-care of God (*vv.* 9 and 10: compare Aug. *Confess. Book* 1. [VI.] 7); therefore, like an infant "crying in the night" his one prayer is "*be not far*" (*v.* 11). His thought turns naturally to the *strength* of the enemy (cf. *bulls* and *lions*, *vv.* 12, 13), and to his own *weakness* (*vv.* 14 and 15): next, the *cruelty* of the enemy (cf. *dogs*, *vv.* 16—18), and his own *meek submission* in their hands. Again the Sufferer commits himself to God with the same prayer "*be not far*" (*v.* 19): he prays to be delivered from the *cruelty* of the *dog* (*v.* 20), from the *strength* of the *lions* and *bulls* (*vv.* 20 and 21)—While this prayer is yet on his lips there breaks the full assurance that *God has answered him* (*v.* 21); instead of the *bulls* he sees now *brethren*, instead of the *assembly of evil doers* like *dogs* (*v.* 16) he sees now a *Great Congregation* of worshippers (*v.* 22). The Sufferer has gone through the experience of Joseph and, like Joseph, now proclaims God's name to reconciled brethren.

Here the Psalm may be said to end. All that follows is the utterance, not of the Sufferer, but of the Congregation of Israel which, as a Chorus, draws the lesson from the Sufferer's experience. Thus (*vv.* 23 and 24);—All believers are called upon to thank God because the Sufferer's pain was *not* in vain and the Sufferer's prayer was *not* unheard. Since *his* pain was not in vain, all earth's suffering-ones can "feast and be filled" (*v.* 26). Since *his* prayer was not unheard, all "seekers of God" can praise Him so that his experience is the *Sursum Corda* of humanity (*v.* 26). But further—the Suffering Servant will bring the whole world to the feet of God (*vv.* 27 and 28); through him life's happiness becomes a sacrificial feast, life's misery a devoted homage (*v.* 29); all this is seen to spring from the fact that the Sufferer *did not save himself* (*v.* 29). Therefore an undying seed shall serve him, ever springing to tell new truths of his righteousness and of the finished work that he hath done.

Christians believe that this has found its fulfilment in Christ.

> "Glory on glory compasseth Him round,
> From henceforth unto all the deathless years;
> The smile of God wherewith He sitteth crowned,
> More sweet because the memory of tears
> Is in His heart, and dieth not away;
> And in exchange for every weary day
> He spent on earth, some blessèd soul forgiven,
> Some face once darkened with our sin and night,
> Is lifted up to Him in cloudless light,
> And addeth glory to those days of heaven."
>
> [Quoted by Bourne in *The King of Sorrow*, p. 58.]

PSALM XXII.

But though I would maintain most strongly that the full meaning of the Psalm is to be found alone in Christ I have no wish to close my eyes to the fact that, in the mind of the writer, the Sufferer was Israel. This will appear in the notes. Meanwhile there is no fact in the Life of our Lord more certain than that He regarded Himself as sent to fulfil God's ideal of Israel. This appears at His baptism—in His Temptation in the Wilderness—in His choice of the name "Son of Man" (compare Dan vii. 13, 27)—in His forecast of His sufferings and the glory that should follow. When then, upon the cross, He takes upon His lips the first words (Matt. xxvii. 46) and probably the last words (John xix. 23) of the Psalm, we may conclude that the Psalm as a whole was in His mind and was His strong comfort in death.

Thus Jerome, commenting on *v.* 1, says, "Hoc versiculo Dominus in cruce pendens usus est: ex quo animadvertimus totum Psalmum a Domino in cruce posito decantari" (*Comment. in Psalmos*, p. 32).

PS. XXII.

A cry of wonder but not of doubt.

1 My God^a, my God^a, why hast Thou forsaken me? ^a Matt. xxvii. 46, *Eli, Eli*
Far from my help, from the words of my complaint!
2 O my God^b I cry in the daytime, but Thou answerest not, ^b *Elohim*
In the night-time also, but there is no rest for me:
3 Yet Thou art Holy,
Throned on the Praise-songs of Israel.
4 In Thee our fathers could trust,
They trusted and Thou didst deliver them;
5 Unto thee they cried and escaped,
They trusted and were not shamed:

6 But I am a worm and no man,
The reproach of men, the despised of the people.
7 All that see me mock^c at me,   ^c Luke xxiii. 35
They shoot out the lip, they wag^d the head.   ^d Mark xv. 29
8 "He casts (his burden) on YHVH—let Him release him,
Let Him deliver him, since He delighteth^e in him."   ^e Matt. xxvii. 39, 43

vv. 1—5. Israel cries to his Father; not doubting His goodness but asking to see the meaning of his sufferings, cf. Lam. v. 19 f. "Thou O Lord, remainest for ever; Thy throne from generation to generation. Wherefore then dost Thou forget us for ever, and forsake us so long time?" But though "Zion said, the Lord hath forsaken me" (Is. xlix. 14) still Zion knew, "For a small moment have I forsaken thee, but with great mercies will I gather thee" (Is. liv. 7, cf. lxii. 4). The promise to Jacob, "I will not forsake thee until I have done all that I have spoken to thee of," was the promise to Israel (Deut. xxxi. 6). Still, while the suffering lasts it is strange:—strange that the Holy should let His Holy One suffer:—all the more strange in that the past history of Israel was a record of temporal blessings and deliverances (*vv.* 4, 5).

vv. 6—8. The language of these verses is elsewhere applied to Israel, e.g. *worm*. "Fear not, thou *worm* Jacob" (Is. xli. 14). *Reviled of men...despised of the people.* "Thus saith ..the Redeemer

FIRST COLLECTION. 'DAVIDIC' PSALMS.

9 Yet it was THY doing I came from the womb,
Thou wert my cause of trust upon my mother's breasts.
10 On Thee have I been cast from my birth,
Thou art my God^a from my mother's womb.   ^a *Eli*
11 BE NOT FAR from me, for trouble is nigh,
And helper is none!

The strength of the foe.
12 Many bulls are come about me,
Mighty ones of Bashan ring me round.
13 They open their mouths at me,
As a lion that rends and roars.

The weakness of the sufferer.
14 I am poured out like water,
All my bones are out of joint,
My heart is become like wax,
It is melted within my body.
15 My strength^b is dried up like a potsherd,   ^b or, *my pa..* Reading for *khi*
My tongue cleaveth to my jaws,
And in the dust of death Thou art laying me low.

The cruelty of the foe.
16 For dogs are come about me,
The assembly of evil-doers have closed me round,
They pierce^c my hands and my feet.   ^c ? text

The meekness of the sufferer.
17 I may count all my bones,
They^d look on!—they gloat over me.   ^d emphatic

of Israel...to him whom *man despiseth*, to him whom a nation abhorreth..." (Compare also Jer. xlix. 15, where Edom is said to be "*despised among men*.") *All...mock at me*, compare Neh. ii. 19; 2 Chr. xxx. 10. *They wag the head*, "They hiss and *wag their head*" (Lam. ii. 15). *v.* 8 should be compared with the remarkable passage *Wisdom* ii. 16, 17, which marks the transition between the thought of the righteous *Nation* and the righteous *Man*.

vv. 9—11. The thought goes back to the difficulty which remained unsolved in *vv.* 1—5 but there is less of wonder, more of child-like trust. The God who has led me all my life through from helpless infancy will not leave me now in my distress.

If to any reader the language of these verses should seem to bespeak a love too individual to be applied to Israel he is invited to consider such passages as the following:—"Hearken unto me, O house of Jacob, and all the remnant of the house of Israel, which are borne (by Me) from the belly, which are carried from the womb. And (even) to (your) old age I (am) He; and (even) to hoar hairs will I carry you..." (Is. xlvi. 3 f. cf.; Hos. xi. 1, 3).

vv. 12—21. The Sufferer is laid at Death's door *by God Himself* (*v.* 15). His foes take this opportunity of shewing their hatred. Their blindness, ferocity and cowardice is described under the imagery of bulls, lions, dogs. The words "They pierce (lit. *they have dug through*) my hands and my feet" since they are used of *dogs*, probably imply the cowardly attack that a band of Syrian dogs would make upon a man who was lying helpless. I speak now only of the primary meaning. Those who believe in Inspiration will admit that the word may have been so chosen as to fit even the details of the Crucifixion. For my own part, were it proved that, in the Crucifixion, the feet of Christ were not pierced, the words would lose none of their force as a picture of His sufferings on the Cross.

While the Sufferer is crying to God, not merely for deliverance, but for a solution of the mystery of suffering (see on *vv.* 1—5), the sudden answer comes (*v.* 21). *Thou hast answered me!*

PSALM XXII.

_{His strong crying unto Him that is able to save.}

18 They part^a my garments among them,
 And for my vesture they cast lots^a.
19 But Thou, O YHVH, BE NOT FAR!
 O my Strength, haste to my help!
20 Deliver my soul from the sword,
 My dear-life from the power of the dog.
21 Save me from the mouth of the lion,
 From the buffalo horns—

^a Mark xv. 24; Luke xxiii. 34; Matt. xxvii. 35; John xix. 24

_{The answer comes.}
 Thou hast answered me.

_{The sufferer sees the joy set before him.}

22 I can declare Thy name unto my^b brethren,
 In the midst of the Congregation I shall praise Thee.

^b Heb. ii. 11, 12, cf. Matt. xxviii. 10; John xx. 17

(The Congregation of Israel now speaks and draws the lesson from the above.)

_{The Chorus of Creation.}

23 O ye fearers of YHVH, give Him praise;
 O all ye seed of Jacob, give Him honour;
 All ye seed of Israel, shew him reverence ;
24 For He did *not* despise—He did *not* spurn the Sufferer's pain,
 He did *not* hide His face from him,
 But while he was crying unto Him He hearkened.
25 Thou art my theme of praise in the great Congregation,
 I pay my vows amidst His worshippers.
26 The lowly shall feast and be filled,
 Seekers of YHVH shall praise Him,
 "May your heart live for ever."
27 All the ends of the earth shall remember and turn unto YHVH,
 All the families of the Nations shall worship before Him.
28 For (now) the Kingdom is YHVH's,
 And He rules among the Nations.
29 All earth's richest worship as they feast,
 All that go down to the dust kneel before Him,
 For His own life He did not save!
30 A seed shall serve Him,
 It shall be counted as the "Lord's people."
31 They shall come and tell of His righteousness,
 To a people yet to be born—how He hath finished^c it.

^c John xix. 2.

vv. 22—31. This answer, so far as Israel is concerned, gives the solution of the Second Isaiah. The suffering of Israel is not in vain. He becomes the reconciliation of the World. He gathers in the Gentiles. God's Kingdom, at last, is set up on earth.

PSALM XXIII.

Nothing can exceed the exquisite beauty of this Psalm unless it be its spiritual depth.

The Psalm falls naturally into two Stanzas of three verses each. In the *first* we see the Divine Shepherd caring for the *natural* needs of His sheep; in the *second* for the *spiritual* needs of man; or, to put the same thought in other words, the *first* stanza relates to what we call *joys*, the second to the deeper experience through what we call *trials*, including therein death itself.

In Stanza I we note 3 thoughts in the 3 verses.

(*a*) The all-embracing security of the Divine Shepherd's presence (*v.* 1).

(*b*) The green pastures and restful waters that He prepares (food and drink) for His sheep (*v.* 2).

(*c*) The kindly restoring guidance whereby He brings back the weary and the wanderers, and sets them in the track of His flocks (*v.* 3).

In Stanza II we find the same three thoughts, though, from the nature of the case, it was not possible to keep so closely to the image of the sheep when dealing with human trials.

Thus (a_1) the security of the Divine Shepherd's presence in the "Dark Valley" (*v.* 4) of pain, sorrow or death, is as all-embracing as the thought in *v.* 1 to which it corresponds.

(b_1) The feast that the Shepherd spreads in *v.* 5 answers to the green pastures and restful waters of *v.* 2; but there is now an added thought: it is "*in the presence of foes.*" These spiritual enemies so far from hindering the feast are but evidence of the guardian care of the Shepherd.

(c_1) The same kindly guidance which brought back the weary wandering sheep in verse 3 is seen in verse 6 to work through all the changes and chances of life so as to make them all "work together" for good in bringing man to God his home. The word 'pursue' gives just a hint of hostile forces, but the same enchantment which had changed the Dark Valley has also changed the 'foes' to a 'feast' (*v.* 5) and the pursuers to 'goodness and mercy' (*v.* 6).

The words (*v.* 6) which we have translated "I am homed in the House..." lit. "I return into &c...." cannot, according to the Hebrew pointing, signify "I dwell in...." The analogy of verse 3 also requires the sense of *return*; as, in *v.* 3, the Shepherd brings the sheep back and sets it in the right tracks, so, in *v.* 6, He brings the man back, by many devices of love, to the only true home which is Himself.

PSALM XXIII.

All spiritual utterances are capable of meanings wider than the speaker's thought. Our Psalm may therefore justly be applied to the relation between God and the individual soul; still, even this relation will best be understood by interpreting it first of the relation between God and Israel, then between God and Christ (which gives the basis for individualism), and lastly between God and the Church (the true Israel). God is "the Shepherd of Israel" (Ps. lxxx. 1 (2); Is. xl. 11; Ezek. xxxiv. 12). The Wilderness was, for Israel, the "Dark Valley" (Jer. ii. 6), but the Shepherd of Israel 'turned this Shadow of Death into morning' (Amos v. 8) by the felt nearness of His Presence (cf. Is. xliii. 2; lxiii. 9; Ps. xci. 15). Thus, through the Wilderness life (Deut. viii. 2 f.) Israel was intended to learn these three lessons of trust.

(a_1) *The absolute security of the Divine care.*

It was in the Wilderness that Israel (God's "Son," Exod. iv. 22) learnt to lean on his Father's Presence. His Father was "with him in trouble" (Ps. xci. 15). "In all his afflictions He was afflicted, while the Angel of His Presence was saving them" (Is. lxiii. 9). Thus the Wilderness was eminently a season of Revelation, "I did know thee in the Wilderness, in the land of great drought" (Hos. xiii. 5).

(b_1) Again, in the Wilderness Israel learnt *the 'Providence' of the Divine Shepherd.* The gift of the Manna explained the hunger as well—"He suffered thee to hunger and He fed thee with manna...that He might make thee know that man doth not live by bread alone, but by everything that proceedeth out of the mouth of the Lord doth man live" (Deut. viii. 3).

(c_1) Lastly, in the Wilderness Israel learnt that the Divine Shepherd had *guided them* in ways that to them were strange. "Thou leddest Thy people like a flock," (Ps. lxxvii. 20; cf. Is. lxiii. 12, 13; Ps. lxxviii. 14, 53). When the Land of Promise was reached, Israel might say, 'Naught but goodness and kindness pursue me all the days of my life, and I am homed in the House of YHVH for ever and ever.'

But though Israel may have been said to have learnt these lessons there was only One who truly learnt them, and he was God's 'Only' Son—the Lamb of God.

(a_2) In the 'Dark Valley' of this world he "learned obedience by the things that he suffered" (Heb. v. 8). Every desertion of earth brought the Father's Presence nearer. "Thou art with me"—"I am not alone because the Father is with me." Thus the Dark Valley became a Revelation to man and God; to *man*, of a Divine Fatherhood; and to *God*, of a perfect human Sonship.

(b_2) In the Dark Valley of a hostile world God 'spread a feast' for him— He who could say 'My meat is to do the will of Him that sent me' must have found all life a feast. God 'anointed him with the oil of gladness above his fellows' and even his "cup" of sorrows was "fulness itself" of joy.

(c_2) His life was preeminently a *guided* life. He did not come of himself, the Father sent him. All through his ministry he 'did nothing of himself' (S. John v. 19, 30; viii. 28; ix. 4; xii. 49; xiv. 10). The Father guided him through the grave and gate of death up to the highest place at His right hand; so that, looking back on sorrows such as no other life has known, he can confess, "Naught but goodness and kindness pursue me all the days of my life and I am brought home to the House of YHVH for ever and ever" (cf. Heb. xiii. 20).

If we believe that Jesus is the Son of God we shall understand that "green pastures" and "restful waters" cannot mean for us the idle life of the well-fed beast but the 'food convenient' for the man.

> "In pastures green? not always; sometimes He
> Who knoweth best, in kindness leadeth me
> In weary ways, where heavy shadows be—
>
> Out of the sunshine warm and soft and bright,
> Out of the sunshine into darkest night;
> I oft would faint with sorrow and affright—
>
> Only for this—I know He holds my hand;
> So, whether in the green or desert land,
> I trust, although I may not understand.
>
> And by still waters? no, not always so;
> Ofttimes the heavy tempests round me blow,
> And o'er my soul the waves and billows go:
>
> But when the storm beats loudest, and I cry
> Aloud for help, the Master standeth by,
> And whispers to my soul, "Lo it is I."
>
> ....
>
> And more than this: where'er the pathway lead
> He gives to me no helpless broken reed,
> But His own hand sufficient for my need.
>
> So where He leads me I can safely go:
> And in the blest hereafter I shall know
> Why in His wisdom He hath led me so."
>
> —*Anon.*

PS. XXIII.

(*a*) The Shepherd's Presence is all-sufficing.	1 YHVH is my Shepherd^a, I can lack^b nothing!	^a Gen. xlviii. 15 (Heb.) ^b Deut. ii. 7
(*b*) Makes life a feast.	2 In green pastures He maketh me lie down; He gently leads^c me by the restful waters.	^c Is. xlix. 10
(*c*) Gives restoring guidance.	3 He restoreth my soul; He guideth me in the right tracks; for His own Name's sake.	
(*a*₁) The Shepherd's Presence is all-sufficing.	4 Yea when I go through the Dark-Valley^d I fear no ill, for Thou art with me; Thy staff and stay—they comfort me.	^d Jer. ii. 6
(*b*₂) Makes life a feast.	5 Thou spreadest a table for me in the sight of my foes; Thou enrichest my head with oil, And my cup is fulness itself!	
(*c*₁) Gives restoring guidance.	6 Naught but goodness and kindness pursue me All the days of my life! And I am homed^e in the House^f of YHVH, for ever and ever!	^e am returned, cf. 1 Pet. ii. 25 ^f Exod. xv. 17

v. 1. "*Shepherd*"—In the Old Testament when this title is applied to God it is always as the Shepherd of the People, not of the individual soul. See Is. xl. 11; Ezek. xxxiv. 11 ff.; Pss. lxxviii. 72; lxxix. 13; lxxx. 1, etc. There is, I believe, only one exception, viz. Gen. xlviii. 15 f. where Jacob says, "The God that was my Shepherd (EV *fed me*) all my life long unto this day, the Angel which redeemed me from all evil...." But this is really no exception because Jacob's life is a type and prophecy of that of Israel as a Nation. The promise, "Lo I am with thee" (Gen. xxviii. 15) was the secret of Jacob's life just as the Presence of the Shechina was that of Israel's (Exod. xiii. 21 f.; xiv. 19; Numb. x. 33; Deut. i. 33). By reason of this Presence every hostile event became to *Jacob* a blessing in disguise (Gen. xxxi. 25—55; xxxii., and xxxiii. etc.) and also to *Israel*, *e.g.* the Red Sea...Amalek...etc.

But if God be the Shepherd of Israel, and of Christ, how is Christ the Good Shepherd? The answer is in Ezek. xxxiv. where God after speaking of Himself as the Shepherd (*vv.* 11—22) says, *v.* 23, "And I will set up one shepherd over them, and he shall feed them, (even) my servant David; he shall feed them, and he shall be their shepherd." A Shepherd was needed upon earth who should be to men all that the Father is to him (cf. St John x. 14, 15 with Bp. Westcott's note).

v. 4. "*The Dark-Valley*"—Literally *the valley of gloom*. A mistaken derivation, which is at least as old as the vowel points, has given rise to "*the Valley of the Shadow-of-death*," but this sense has become so embedded in the language and literature of the Bible that it is mere pedantry to ignore it. I have intended by "*The Dark-Valley*" to hint at this, but, at the same time, not to exclude all those wider meanings which "the Wilderness" had for Israel (Jer. ii. 6) and which we include under 'the Wilderness of Temptation.'

v. 6. "*All the days*"—In the Septuagint the same words are used as in the promise of Christ's Presence with His Church (Matt. xxviii. 20).

PSALM XXIV.

An old tradition, preserved by the Septuagint, assigns this Psalm to the *first day of the week*. Now the *first day* is the beginning of the Creation of God—the birth of Light. But Light in Nature is only a parable of the "Glory of the Lord" (cf. John i. 9 and Ps. xix.). We might indeed modify the Poet's words and say that 'All Creation is one act at once, the incoming of God's *Glory*.'

The Psalm is a Dedication-Psalm and will be best understood from the Vision that Ezekiel saw of the Dedication of his Temple. When the Temple at Jerusalem was lying in ruins God shewed Ezekiel a Vision of another Temple unlike the former (Chaps. xl.—end). Ezekiel describes its Gates and all its measurements most minutely; for everything was symbolical. But what avails a Temple unless God dwell in it? And Ezekiel had seen the "Glory of the Lord" desert the Temple at Jerusalem, being driven away by the sins of the People (Chap. xi. 22 f.). Will God then return to the Temple of the future?

This question is answered in Chap. xliii. 1 ff., "Afterward He brought me to the Gate, the Gate that looketh toward the East: And behold the Glory of the God of Israel came from the way of the East and His voice was like the noise of many waters: and the earth shined with His Glory... And the visions were like the visions that I saw by the river Chebar; and I fell upon my face. And the Glory of the Lord came into the House by the way of the Gate whose prospect is towards the East. So the Spirit took me up and brought me into the inner Court; and behold the Glory of the Lord filled the House" (xliii. 1—5)... That 'Glory' was not a Pillar of Cloud and Fire but "Upon the likeness of the Throne was the likeness as the appearance of a Man" (Chap. i. 26). Such was to Ezekiel the Dedication of the Temple of the future. God would not leave His Temple of the Universe, though men were sinners; He would enter that Temple through its eastern Gate, He would pass through the inner Gate into the inmost Shrine and His Glory would be "the likeness as the appearance of a Man upon the Throne" —a "King of Glory."

Let us now turn to the Psalm (v. 1 f.) "*The earth is YHVH'S...upon the Ocean-floods.*" The Temple of Creation is finished... But what avails a Temple if God Himself dwell not in it?... The sin of man has driven God away... The Glory has deserted this Temple! There is no communion between God and man! Therefore the Psalmist says "Who can ascend..." [See vv. 3—6 with marginal notes.]

To man this seemed impossible. But God had promised "As truly as I live, all the earth shall be filled with the Glory of the Lord" (Numb. xiv. 21). As in vision Ezekiel saw the Glory enter in through the Gates into the Temple, so now the Psalmist sees that same Glory enter, as a "King of Glory," through the Gates of Earth and Heaven; and, filling all things with His Glory, restore the broken Communion between God and Man —"Lift up your heads..." [See vv. 7—10 with marginal notes.]

If we ask 'How has this been fulfilled?' the answer is (*vv.* 3—6) One Man *did* "ascend the Mountain of the Lord..." He was "clean of hands...pure of heart..." He did "bear away a blessing from VIIVII..."

Just in so far as the Christian lives in the presence of this great Fact all "Heaven is opened" (John i. 51) for him... All life is transfigured. Earth becomes to him

"The broad foundation of a holy place,
Man's step to scale the sky."

All things are his, the world, or life, or death, or things present, or things to come; all are his, for he is Christ's; and Christ is God's (1 Cor. iii. 23).

Thus he can say, with a new meaning, "The earth is the Lord's and the fulness thereof" (*v.* 1, see footnote).

The Psalm then is, in the fullest sense, a Psalm of Creation. In His Eternity all is "one act at once"; the incoming of the King of Glory. This being so the Psalm lends itself to all the stages of His incoming.

Milton was justified in applying it to the first creation of the worlds by the Son of God:

"heaven open'd wide
Her ever-during gates, harmonious sound,
On golden hinges moving, to let forth
The King of Glory, in his powerful Word
And Spirit, coming to create new worlds." (Book VII. 205—209.)

And again, on His completion of this work:

"Up he rode,
Follow'd with acclamation...
The heavens and all the constellations rung,
The planets in their station listening stood,
While the bright pomp ascended jubilant.
Open, ye everlasting gates! they sung;
Open, ye heavens! your living doors; let in
The great Creator, from his work return'd
Magnificent, his six days' work, a world." (Book VII. 557 ff.)

The Gospel of Nicodemus was justified in applying the Psalm to the entrance of Christ into Hades since this was one stage of His creative work:

"Then came again the voice, saying, 'Lift up your gates, ye princes! and be ye lift up, ye everlasting doors, and the King of Glory shall come in!'"

"And Hades, hearing the voice, the second time, answered, as one forsooth unwilling, 'Who is this King of Glory?' And the Angels of the Lord answered, 'The Lord strong and mighty, the Lord mighty in battle.' And straightway, with that word, the brazen gates were broken, and the bolts of iron torn asunder, and the bound in death were loosed from their chains, and we with them. And the King of Glory entered, in form even as a man, and all the dark places of Hades were lighted up" (see the whole passage in Bp. Forbes on *Article III.* and compare the use of the Psalm for Easter Eve, in the Latin Church).

But by far the most obvious use of the Psalm is for Ascension Day, as is appointed in our own Church.

PS. XXIV.

As the Heaven so the Earth is God's de jure.

1 The earth is YHVH'S and the fulness thereof[a] :
The world, and the dwellers therein.
2 For He it was that built it on the Waters,
That founded it upon the Ocean-floods.

[a] Quoted in I Cor. x. 28

But no road from Earth to Heaven except a man could be

3 Who can ascend the Mountain of YHVH?
Who can stand within His Holy Place?

v. 1[a]. St Paul quotes this passage (1. Cor. x. 26) to shew that all God's creatures of food may be dedicated to God's use (cf. Ps. l. 12). "It is used in a very glorious sense by the Eastern Church in her Funeral Service, when at the moment in which the coffin is let down into the grave the Priest exclaims, '*The Earth is the Lord's, and the fulness thereof*;' that is, the multitude of the bodies of the faithful who there are awaiting His Second Coming" (Neale). Both these interpretations are but special instances of the great truth implied by the Psalmist. If we seek his original meaning it may be found from such passages as the following: "Behold the *Ark* of the covenant of *the Lord of all the earth* passeth over before you..." (Josh. iii. 11, 13), and "As truly as I live, *all the earth* shall be filled with the *Glory of the Lord*" (Numb. xiv. 21). When the Priests and Levites moved upwards in procession round the walls of Jerusalem (see later, on the *Songs of Ascents*) they were not merely 'dedicating' the *City* but were claiming the *whole earth* for God. Hence the "gates" and "the everlasting doors" are not so much the Gates of Zion as of the Heavenly Jerusalem of which Zion was the pledge. Many commentators, missing the connexion between *v.* 1 and *v.* 7, have followed Ewald in assigning *vv.* 7—10 to another writer.

The connexion of the verses may be traced as follows:

v. 1. *The Earth is YHVH'S and the fulness thereof*"—This is the claim of the Seraphim. "The fulness of the whole earth is His Glory" (Is. vi. 3) but it is only prophetically true "The whole earth *shall* be filled with His Glory" (Ps. lxxii. 19), but at present "The Heavens are the Lord's Heavens but the Earth He has given to the children of men" (Ps. cxv. 16)—given to men to make it His. But herein comes a break in the Glory (i.e. the Manifestation) of God, for all men have "sinned and come short of the Glory" (Rom. iii. 23); therefore our Psalm says—

v. 3. "Who can ascend the Mountain of YHVH?" The "Mountain of YHVH" is the Heaven of Heavens which ought to have been conterminous with Earth so that every Earthly beauty and delight should have led up naturally to its Eternal counterpart in the Heavens. The life of man would then have been an Enoch-walk with God; the days of earth and the days of Heaven would have been 'linked each to each in natural piety.'—But now "Who can ascend...?" If *one* could be found of perfect purity and perfect truth (*v.* 4) he might walk that way that leads to God—nay more, (*v.* 5) hints that such an one might open the road for others, "He might bear away a blessing from YHVH..." (cf. the Psalm of the ideal King, Ps. xxi. 6). But alas 'no man in heaven, nor in earth, neither under the earth was able to open this (road) neither to look thereon' (Rev. v. 3). But now there comes to the Psalmist the same vision of victory that St John saw (Rev. v. 5—14). He sees the ideal King coming along that Road and he cries as a challenge to the Gates of Heaven "Lift up your heads, O ye gates...that the King of Glory may come in!"

The title "King of Glory" is unique. The *Glory* is the Manifestation of God: the King of Glory must therefore be the King who lies open to and reflects God, i.e. He is the ideal King of whom we read in Ps. xxi. All others had 'come short of the Glory' but He is the King of

PSALM XXIV.

Pure { outwardly, inwardly;	4 One clean of hands, And pure of heart,	
True { inwardly, outwardly.	That never set his mind to what is false, Nor swore in order to deceive,	
Such an one might open the way for God to man and for man to God.	5 He might bear away a blessing[a] from YHVH, A boon of righteousness from the God of his salvation. 6 Such must be the race of those that seek Him; Of those that seek Thy face—A very Jacob[b]!	[a] Gen. xxxii. 29 [b] John i. 47—51
The Conqueror is seen coming	7 "Lift up your heads, O ye gates, Be ye lift up ye everlasting doors, That the King of Glory[c] may come in!" 8 "Who then is the King of Glory?"	[c] 1 Cor. ii. 8; James ii. 1
as the "Hero-God."	"YHVH, a mighty one and a hero, YHVH, a hero in battle.	
The Conqueror is not alone, He comes with His "Hosts."	9 Lift up your heads O ye gates, Lift yourselves ye everlasting doors, That the King of Glory may come in!" 10 "Who is He then—the King of Glory?"	
As the Heaven so the Earth is God's *de facto*.	"YHVH of Hosts—He is the King of Glory."	

Glory—ἀπαύγασμα τῆς δόξης (Heb. i. 3). The Psalmist feels the mystery of this Holy Being so he cries—or hears a Voice that cries—(v. 8) "Who then is the King of Glory?"—The answer reminds us of the "Mighty God" of Is. ix. 6 and of the Conqueror from Edom (Is. lxiii. 1—6). As, in the latter passage, the Conqueror was "alone, and of the people there was none with him." So here, at the first entry, he enters alone,

"YHVH, a mighty one and a hero,
YHVH, a hero in battle."

But now the Vision changes; the Conqueror is seen not alone but with ten thousands of His saints. Once more the challenge sounds, "Lift up your heads O ye gates...." Once more the question, "Who then is He—the King of Glory?"—but the answer is significantly different, "YHVH of Hosts...."

The Lord of *Hosts* is not here a mere title of the God of battles as though this verse were an idle repetition of v. 8, but the *Hosts* are the 'hosts' of His redeemed (cf. Exod. xii. 41, 51; vii. 4 &c.) with whom He is seen now to enter into the Heavenly City. Thus we see that verses 7 and 8 speak of a single entry won through conflict and therefore correspond with verses 3 and 4; while verses 9 and 10 speak of the entry of all the redeemed and thus correspond with the hinted promise of verses 5 and 6.

"For lo! there breaks a yet more glorious day;
The Saints triumphant rise in bright array:
The King of glory passes on His way.
Halleluia!"

This Psalm is one of our Ascension Day Psalms. The reader would do well to study it in connexion with the Proper Preface for Ascension Day and the Sanctus, Sanctus, Sanctus that follows.

(Ps. xxv. is among the Alphabetical Psalms. See p. 26.)

PSALM XXVI.

This is essentially a pilgrim-Psalm. Doubtless it was composed for the use of those Processions which at the Feast of Dedication and at other times encompassed the Temple of God (see note on *v.* 6 f.). Such sacred Processions, rising upward from Court to Court, were felt to be a type of life's pilgrimage to God. (This will be seen more clearly when we come to the 'Songs of Degrees'.) It is evident that, to our Psalmist, the Procession was no mere empty form but a representation before God of his own life-struggle upwards to its goal. At the start he claims, not "*innocency*" P.B.V. but "*singleheartedness.*" As his feet are aiming at the Upper Temple Court so his life is aiming at Truth (*vv.* 3 and 11). This implies that he leaves behind him (renounces) the lower World (*vv.* 4, 5). The brasen laver (Exod. xxx. 18 ff.) suggests to him that sanctification without which no man can see the Lord. While he washes in it he is washing, not in water, but *in innocency* (*v.* 6) for his whole being is set toward God. We might have expected the Psalm to end here. It does indeed come to a climax in verse 6, which is the middle verse of the Psalm. The six verses which follow take up the same thoughts *but in inverted order* (see marginal notes, the law of the Psalm being $\alpha \beta \gamma \gamma_1 \beta_1 a_1 + \gamma_2$).

Thus the conditions would be exactly satisfied if we suppose it to be sung by two Processions, the one ascending, the other descending (the turning point being the Altar-Court, i.e. at $\gamma \gamma_1$); one singing the Stanzas $\alpha \beta \gamma$ as it ascends the three Courts to the Altar; the other singing Stanzas $\gamma_1 \beta_1 a_1$ as it descends through the same three Courts and comes at last to γ_2 the Court of the Gentiles.

The order will be best understood from the following sketch.

The life of the ideal Israel is an ascending to God (Altar Court) as a Priest and a descending to bring God down to men (Court of the Gentiles). Thus the words (*v.* 12) "My foot has its stand on the level" have a double meaning (see note and γ_2 in sketch). When Israel reaches the Court of the Gentiles so that "In full Congregation he blesses YHVH" (*v.* 12 see note) then his work is done, "his foot standeth right." When γ_2 answers to γ_1 then all the World will be an Altar-Court. The above sketch would also explain the allusions to the "Congregation" in β and β_1 since this is the Court of Israel. Every true life has in it these two movements, ascending to God, descending to the World; and these two movements answer so closely the one to the other that they are always one movement in God's sight and form together the Dedicated walk with God.

PS. XXVI.

PART I. (*The ascent, from the World to God.*)

(a) I. God's Pilgrim, am whole-heartedly with Him.

1 Judge me, O YHVH, for I walk in singleheartedness[a],   [a] v. 11
In YHVH I trust, I waver not.
2 Test me YHVH and try me,
Prove[b] my reins and my heart.   [b] i.e. as by fire. See Sept. and Vulg.
3 For Thy mercy is before mine eyes,
And I walk in Thy truth.

(β) I renounce the Congregation of Satan.

4 I have not sat with worthless men,   cf. Ps. i.
And with the hypocrites I have no intercourse.
5 I hate the congregation[c] of evil doers,   [c] Vulg. *ecclesiam*
And with the wicked I will not sit.

(γ) God's Altar represents my goal.

6 I would wash[d] mine hands in innocency,   [d] Exod. xxx. 19f.
And would encompass Thine Altar, O YHVH :

vv. 1—3. Man's life here below is a pilgrimage to God. 'Israel,' God's Pilgrim, walks with a *single heart* (*v.* 1ª) towards God's *truth* (*v.* 3ᵇ) and with a step that is *unwavering* (*v.* 1ᵇ) because it never loses sight of God's *mercy* (*v.* 3ª). But this ideal needs the support of the prayer in *v.* 2 which is practically repeated in *v.* 11, "But I in singleheartedness would walk, Redeem me and shew me mercy." The *past* tense in *v.* 1ª and the *future* in *v.* 11ª should be noted. The Pilgrim begins by claiming for himself the *single heart*; he ends by praying for it! In the outset he says "Thy mercy is before my eyes"; but when he has seen more of it, he cries "Redeem me and shew me mercy!"

v. 4. "*Hypocrites*"—literally "hidden ones," i.e. "dissemblers." The Talmud has another word with a similar meaning, viz. "dyed ones," on which Buxtorf quotes T.B. Sota 22ᵇ, "He not afraid of Pharisees, nor of those who are not Pharisees, but of the *dyed ones* who seem like Pharisees, whose deeds are the deeds of Zimri and who seek for the reward of Phineas."

v. 5. "*The congregation of evil doers.*" The Jewish commentators illustrate this by "the congregation of Korah." The Vulgate has "ecclesiam pessimorum."

It is evident from verses 4, 5 and the corresponding verses 9, 10 that the sinners were not heathen but apostate Jews.

v. 6ᵇ. "*And would encompass Thine Altar.*" The verb here must signify movement either round or partially round the Altar; for, as Delitzsch has well noted, it may be used "even of compassing in a semicircular fashion (Gen. ii. 11 ; Numb. xxi. 4)." As a matter of fact we know from Jewish sources that Processions round the Altar formed part of the ritual of the Feast of Tabernacles. The Altar was indeed a Temple in miniature; it rose in three terraces (Edersheim, *Temple*, p. 131); the inclined plane running round it lent itself to the same symbolism as the three Courts of the Temple. What that symbolism was will be explained in our Introduction to the Songs of Degrees and the Levitical Psalms. (See also on Ps. xxix.)

FIRST COLLECTION, 'DAVIDIC' PSALMS.

PART II. (*The descent, from God to the World.*)

(γ_1) This goal of mine shall be the goal of others.

{ 7 In order to make heard the voice of the Thanksgiving,
  In order to recount all Thy wonders.
  8 YHVH, I have loved Thy Temple's Home,
  The place of the Shrine of Thy Glory.

(β_1) Let me not be numbered with the Congregation of Satan.

{ 9 O gather not my soul with the sinners,
  Nor my life with men of blood:
  10 In whose hand is crime,
  And their right-hand is full of bribes.

(a_1) Let me become whole-hearted.

{ 11 But I in singleheartedness^a would walk,
  Redeem me and shew me mercy.

^a *v.* 1

(γ_2) I have reached my second goal (the Court of the Gentiles).

{ 12 My foot has its stand on the level,
  In full-congregation^b I bless YHVH.

^b Vulg. *in clesiis*

v. 7. "*In order to make heard the voice of the thanksgiving.*" The "thanksgiving" was so closely associated with the religious processions that Nehemiah uses the same word for both. Thus:— xii. 31, "I appointed two great *companies of them that gave thanks* (lit. 'thanksgivings')." Cf. also 38 and 40. This passage will be fully considered later: suffice it now to remark that Nehemiah's two processions moved in opposite directions just as I have supposed the two choirs to do in my introduction to this Psalm.

The reader will observe that *v.* 7 may either be read with *v.* 6 or with *v.* 8. In either case the meaning is the same. Israel aspires to God that he may make God known. 'For their sakes I dedicate myself that they also may be dedicated.'

v. 9. "*O gather not...*" The word *asaph* signifies "*to gather in.*" The *Asiph* was the Feast of *Ingathering* at the end of the year, Nature's great yearly Parable of the final *ingathering* of souls. In the present passage this thought is latent. There are two homes, the home of sin and the home of God. The Psalmist, like Dante, has looked upon the home of sin. His words are rather a shudder than a prayer, "*O gather not my soul with the sinners,* &c." In the parallel passage of the following Psalm he uses the same word to express his own confidence in God's mercy, "Though father and mother should forsake me, yet let YHVH (or *YHVH will*) *gather me in.*" See further on the word *asaph* under the '*Asaph*' Psalms.

v. 12^a. The word here translated "*the level*" is often used of *plain*, i.e. level country, but it is also used of *equity* (Is. xi. 4; Ps. xlv. 6 (7) &c.). Sometimes, as in our Psalm, the two meanings are combined, e.g. Ps. xxvii. 11, "lead me in a *plain* path (marg. 'way of plainness' E.V.)." When then our Psalmist says, 'My foot stands in the level,' I believe that he uses the word in its double meaning and thus interprets the ritual of the Procession: 'My foot stands on the level, for I have literally reached the lower Court, the Court of the Gentiles, and in full-congregation I bless God,' also 'My foot standeth in equity (cf. Mal. ii. 6) for the end of Israel's pilgrimage is to turn the Gentiles to God.'

v. 12^b. "*In full-congregation...*" A different word, though from the same root, is used in verse 5; there the thought was on the Congregation itself but here the form of the word fixes the thought rather on the place where the Congregation meets, i.e. the Court. The end of the Pilgrimage is reached at last.

PSALM XXVII.

Here again we have a Psalm of man's pilgrimage to God. It is closely related to Ps. xxvi. both in language and structure (see marginal notes). Both Psalms consist of two Parts, and in each case Part II differs so widely in its sad tone from the exultation of Part I that commentators who have not understood the connexion have resorted to the theory of independent Psalms.

Psalms xxvi. and xxvii. are both explained by the theory which I have suggested. Part I is an ascent, in three stages, from the World to God. Part II is a descent, in three stages, from God to the World. We might express this somewhat differently by saying that Part I gives the *ideal*, Part II the *actual*; Part I, the life of devotion, Part II, the life of service; the work of Israel (and of man) being to make the two coincide. The Processions ascending and descending the three Temple Courts gave, I believe, the outward form and clothing to these thoughts; but it would shew a marvellous lack of poetical imagination and of spiritual insight if we were to suppose that the "One thing" (*v.* 4), the goal of the Psalmist's life, could have been nothing more than to reside in the Temple! The commentator on Dante gives him credit for meaning within meaning; the thoughts of the Psalmist go quite as deep as those of Dante.

Psalms xxvi. and xxvii. should be carefully studied together. Both give God's ideal of Israel, who walks the dedicated Way, and by self-dedication brings all the Nations to God. This being so both Psalms find their full meaning only in Christ who 'dedicated Himself' that we men 'might be dedicated also in truth.' There is no doubt a difference in tone between these two Psalms. In Ps. xxvi. there is more of struggle, in Ps. xxvii. there is more of repose. The former is a Psalm for Gethsemane, the latter for the victory of the Cross. The Latin Church, guided by a true instinct, appointed the latter Psalm for Good Friday and Easter Eve.

PS. XXVII.

PART I. (*The ascent, from the World to God.*)

(a) I, God's Pilgrim, walk safely, through His Presence. He is the Way.

1 YHVH is my Light and my Salvation,
  Whom should I fear?
  YHVH is my life's defence,
  Whom should I dread?
2 When the wicked made onslaught upon me,
  To eat up my flesh[a]—
  Those oppressors and foes of mine—
  It was they that stumbled and fell.
3 Though a camp should encamp against me,
  My heart should not fear.
  Though there rose up war against me,
  I still should be confident.

(β) "One thing" I desire; to be God's guest. He is the Truth.

4 One thing have I asked of YHVH,
  And it I will seek ;
  That I may dwell in YHVH'S House
  All the days of my life,
  To behold the fair-beauty of YHVH,
  And meditate in His Palace.
5 For He would hide me in His pavilion,
  In the day of evil,
  Would cover me in the covert of His tent,
  Would set me high upon the rock.

v. 2. "*To eat up my flesh.*" In the late form of the language (Chaldee) a false accuser is called by a word which Aben Ezra explains as 'an eater of the flesh.' This derivation is not certain since the Hebrew word *to eat*, like the Latin *edere* came to have two meanings, *to eat* and *to edit* or *promulgate* (see Buxtorf s. v. *akl*), but, as Delitzsch well remarks, "even in Job xix. 22, to eat up one's flesh is equivalent to persecute one even to destruction by evil speaking (in Aram. by evil reports)." Thus we see that the enemies in verse 2 and the "false witnesses" of *v.* 12 are identical.

v. 3. "*Though a camp should encamp....*" When Jacob saw the Angels he said, "This is God's host (or *camp*): and he called the name of the place *Mahanaim* (the *two hosts* or *two camps*)," Gen. xxxii. 2 (3). When men fear God they have no cause for other fear; "the angel of the Lord *encampeth* round them and delivereth them" (Ps. xxxiv. 7 (8)). God promised this protecting Presence to Israel (Zech. ii. 5 ; ix. 8).

PSALM XXVII.

(γ) I have gained my goal. The Altar is the pledge of it. He is the Life.

    6 And now my head is high
       Above mine enemies.
       I have encompassed and sacrificed in His Tent
       Sacrifices of Jubilee^a.
       I sing, I hymn unto YHVH.

^a See Sept. and Vulg. Cf. Ps. xxvi. 6

PART II. (*The descent, from God to the World.*)

(γ₁) Leaving the Altar I need that pledge in the world.

    7 Hear, O YHVH, I cry with my voice,
       Shew me mercy^b, and answer me.
    8 Thine—says my heart—is "Seek ye My Face,"
       Thy Face, O YHVH, I seek.

^b Ps. xxvi. 11

(β₁) Turn not Thy guest from Thy door.

    9 Hide not Thy Face from me,
       Turn not away Thy servant in anger,
       Thou that hast been my help!
       Cast me not off, forsake me not,
       O God of my salvation!
    10 Though father and mother should forsake me,
       Yet let YHVH take^c me in.

^c Josh. xx. 4

v. 6. The Vulgate, following the Septuagint, has here an interesting reading. "Circuivi, et immolavi in tabernaculo ejus hostiam vociferationis." The word *circuivi*, "I have encompassed," is obtained by taking the Hebrew word, which the E.V. translates "round about," as a verb. It cannot be denied but that the usual rendering "above mine enemies *round about me*" gives good sense, but the harder reading suggested by the Septuagint and Vulgate ought surely to be preferred when we bear in mind the fact that the same verb occurs in the same sense in the parallel verse of the parallel Psalm, i.e. Ps. xxvi. 6, "I would *encompass* Thine Altar...." If the view that I have suggested be correct the 6th verse in each of these Psalms represents the turning point of the Processions The origin and significance of these Processions will be explained more fully when we come to the Songs of Degrees.

"*Sacrifices of Jubilee.*" Vulg. "*hostiam vociferationis*," Jer. "*hostias jubili.*" The Hebrew word is translated in many ways in the E.V. Thus Lev. xxiii. 24, "blowing of trumpets"; xxv. 29, "the jubilee" (marg. "*loud of sound*"); 11 Sam. vi. 15, "shouting"; Ps. lxxxix. 15 (16) "the joyful sound" (but see note). The leading thought in the word both at the Feast of Trumpets and at the Jubilee is the *loud cry* (whether of shouting or of trumpets) in answer to which God has promised to come down to the deliverance of His people. The following passages in which the word occurs should be carefully considered: Numb. x. 8—10; Ps. xlvii. 5 (6), see note; 11 Chron. xiii. 12. As far as we can gather from Scripture the trumpets were never blown over the sacrifices of an individual but always over the sacrifices of the Community; hence our view is confirmed that the speaker in our present Psalm is Israel.

v. 7. "*I cry with my voice.*" These words denote a loud cry. We picture the Procession leaving the Altar-Court, going down, as it were, into the temptations and sorrows of the World with a loud cry to God. If we apply the Psalm to Christ we have a parallel in Heb. iv. 7, "in the

FIRST COLLECTION, 'DAVIDIC' PSALMS.

(a₁) Be Thyself the Way. So shall Thy Pilgrim be safe.

    11 Teach me, O YHVH, Thy way,
       And lead^a me in a level^b path,
       Because^c of mine enemies^c.
    12 Give me not over to the will of mine oppressors,
       For false witnesses have risen against me
       That breathe out cruelty.

^{a} Ps. v. 8
^{b} Ps. xxvi. 1
^{c} cf. v. 6

cf. v. 2 (note

(γ₂) The Altar is a pledge: therefore Israel can afford to wait (cf. γ and γ₁).

    13 Oh^d if I did not believe to enjoy the goodness of YHVH
       in the land of the living!—
    14 Wait for YHVH, be strong and let thy heart be firm,
       And wait for YHVH.

^{d} Sept. differ

days of His flesh having offered up prayers and supplications *with strong crying....*" It may be worth noting that the 7th verse of Ps. xxvi. begins the descent with the *voice* of thanksgiving just as this verse does with the *voice* of supplication.

v. 13. "*Oh if I did not believe....*" If I had not, as it were, gone up into the third Heaven and there contemplated God's goodness as it is (Part I), I should not have been able to understand the mystery of the World's sorrows (Part II); but now that I have gone into the Sanctuary (see note on Ps. lxxiii. 17), I understand His growing purpose; therefore I can say "*Wait for YHVH.*"

PSALM XXVIII.

This Psalm, in point of structure, has much in common with its octave, Ps. xx. The chief division, as in that Psalm, is between verses 5 and 6. The latter half, as in Ps. xx, implies some outward, visible sign of God's favour, possibly an accepted sacrifice, which is the pledge of Israel's victory in the future. But our Psalm has also points of contact with Pss. xxvi. xxvii. (See marginal references.) There is the same thought of the two Congregations (viz. the Congregation of God's People, and the Congregation of the wicked) that we saw in Ps. xxvi (cf. xxvi. 9 with xxviii. 3). Israel, conscious of choosing God, yet conscious of much failure, feels the horror of being "gathered in" at last with the sinful nations of the World. If God were to leave him such a fate must be his (v. 1); but the whole Ritual of Sacrifice is a pledge that God will *not* leave him to himself; this is his "*supplication*...as he lifts up his hands to the Shrine of the Holy Place" (v. 2).

In verse 6 there comes the full assurance that God "hath heard the voice of this *supplication.*" (Compare the 6th verse of Pss. xxvi. and xxvii.) The Sacrifice has been accepted (cf. Ps. xx. 6). The whole character of the Psalm is now one trumpet-peal of victory. a *Gloria in Excelsis.*

PS. XXVIII.

God is my portion. How terrible if He were not to hear me!	1 Unto Thee, O YHVH, I cry: Thou art my Rock, be not deaf towards me; For shouldst Thou be silent unto me I am become like those that go down to the pit. 2 Hear the voice of my supplications[a] as I cry unto Thee, As I lift up my hands to the Shrine of Thy Sanctuary[b].
If He were to number me with the wicked!	3 Draw me not in with the wicked[c], Nor with the workers of wrong, Men that speak peace to their neighbours While evil is in their hearts.
whose work I hate, and whose end I know too well!	4 Give them as their work is, As the evil of their deeds, As the work of their hands give to them! Requite them as they do deserve. 5 Because they have no understanding of the doings of YHVH[d], Nor of the work of his hands; He shall pull them down, And not build them up.
Nay but God has heard me.	6 Blessed be YHVH! For He hath heard the voice of my supplications[e]. 7 YHVH is my Strength and my Shield, In Him my heart trusted and I am helped. So that my heart exulteth, And I praise Him beyond[f] my song. 8 YHVH is a Strength for His People[g], A Defence[h] of safety to His Anointed. 9 Oh save Thy People! Bless Thine Inheritance[i]! Tend them and bear[j] them up for ever!

Side notes: [a] cf. v. 6; [b] Ps. xx. 2; [c] cf. Ps. xxvi. 9; [d] Rom. i. 21; [e] cf. v. 2 and Ps. xx. 6; [f] i.e. *more than song can tell*; [g] so Sept.; [h] Ps. xxvii. 1; [i] Deut. ix. 29; [j] Is. lxiii. 9; Mic. vii. 14.

v. 4. These words need not be regarded as an imprecation. They denote that sensitive shrinking from Evil which springs from the desire of God's Presence (cf. notes on Pss. v. 4—10; vi. 8). We must, in justice to the Psalmist, exclude all thought both of personal enmity and of eternal condemnation; when then the Psalmist says "*Requite them as they do deserve*" he does not go beyond St. Paul's denunciation of Alexander, "The Lord reward him according to his works" (2 Tim. iv. 14). There are eyes so blinded that nothing but the flash of judgement can make them see. What would perfect Charity pray for in such a case? Meanwhile until our charity be perfect it is safer for us to apply all such passages only to God's enemies who are fighting in our own hearts and striving to hinder us from communion with Him.

v. 5. *"Because they have no understanding..."* Their minds may have been enlightened but "their foolish heart was darkened" (Rom. i. 21). The "fool" in Scripture is the man who puts out the eyes of his own soul.

v. 7. *"And I praise Him beyond my song"*—Compare *"Sacrifices of Jubilee"* Ps. xxvii. 6. When words have done their utmost there must still be that homage of Creation's Chorus of which the Trumpet of Jubilee is a type:

"The shout of the King is among them. One King and one song,
One thunder of manifold voices harmonious and strong,
One King and one love, and one shout of one worshipping throng." (c. Rossetti.)

v. 9. *"Oh save..."* This verse is not so much a prayer as a *Hosannah*. The certainty of God's help was attained in verse 6, which is exactly parallel to the 6th verse of Psalm xx. In Ps. xx. 9 we also read "O YHVH save!" just as here we have, "O save Thy People!"

The last words of this verse are a Pastoral Symphony with allusions to Deut. ix. 29 and Is. lxiii. 9, "They are Thy People and Thine *Inheritance* which Thou broughtest out by Thy great power..." "In all their affliction He was afflicted, and the Angel of His Presence *saved them*: in His love and in His pity he redeemed them; and He *took them up and bare them up* all the days of old." It is a singular coincidence that this passage from Isaiah should also be quoted in the *Midrash* on Ps. xx. 9 (see note).

As the good shepherd carries the feeble lambs so will God carry His People.

PSALM XXIX.

It is impossible to understand this Psalm until we can dismiss from our minds the prevalent idea that it is "a magnificent description of a thunderstorm." It is true that the "Voice" of the Lord sometimes signifies the thunder. It is true also, that the Seven Voices of our Psalm and the Seven Voices and Seven thunders of Rev. viii. and x. have one and the same origin as we shall presently see, in the Symbolism of the Feast of Tabernacles: but no Commentator has been found to assert that Rev. viii. or x. is "a magnificent description of a thunderstorm which passed from north to south over the Isle of Patmos."

The very structure of the Psalm points to a mystical meaning. It consists of five Stanzas. Of these the first and last correspond as Introduction and Conclusion and each contains the Divine Name in every line. The body of the Psalm consists of the three middle Stanzas which alone contain the Seven Voices (see margin).

We learn from the Title of the Psalm in the Septuagint that it was assigned by tradition to the last day of the Feast of Tabernacles. This "last day, the great day of the feast" (St John vii. 37 ff.) was I believe not the eighth day but the seventh day, i.e. *Hoshannah Rabba*, the day of the water-drawing Festival on which the Jews used to surround the Altar seven times (Mishna, *Sukkah* iv. 5. See Appendix C in my translation of the *Yalkut on Zechariah*). This interesting tradition, preserved by the LXX., is also confirmed by the *Zohar* (*Parasche* יצ) where, as Delitzsch states, "Ps. xxix. is connected with the pouring out of water on the seventh day of the Feast of Tabernacles (*Hoshannah Rabba*), since it is said, that by means of the seven 'Voices' (answering to the seven compassings of the Altar) seven of the Sephiroth open the flood gates of heaven."

Now the Feast of Tabernacles was in the *seventh* month. It closed the cycle of the Jewish Feasts. The *seventh* day of this Feast was closely associated with the gift of rain (and fruitful seasons) for the coming year. The *seven* compassings of the Altar represented, I believe, the cycle of the completed year which ended in the seventh month, each compassing representing one month. If this be so the seven 'Voices' of our Psalm would represent the course of God through the year that was closing; each 'Voice' answering to a month.

It need scarcely be said that the cycle of the year pointed onwards to God's increasing purpose and the coming of His Kingdom. Thus to sum up :— The Jewish year began with the Vernal Equinox: it ended with the Autumnal Equinox in the *seventh* month; the first day of that month being called "New Year's Day." The Feast of Tabernacles, in this *seventh* month was the Sabbath of the year and was a thanksgiving for the Seasons and also a spiritual interpretation of God's great purpose for the world as seen in the seven cycles of months. We can now see why "'The Voice of YHVH" is repeated *seven* times in the Psalm and why it should have given rise to the "seven thunders" of Rev. x. 3.

The *first* Voice is "*upon the waters*" (April); for the Spring of each year is a repetition of the Day when God's Spirit first "brooded upon the waters"; in Spring as Shelley says

"Through wood and stream, and field and hill and ocean,
A quickening life from the earth's heart has burst,
As it has ever done, with change and motion,
From the great morning of the world! when first
God dawn'd on chaos."

The *second* and *third* Voices are *with power* and *with Majesty* as the purpose of the year expands in May and June.

The *fourth* Voice *breaketh the Cedars*, for July is the month of the tempest's power.

The *fifth* and *sixth* Voices *cleave out the flaming fire* and desolate the *wilderness-pastures*, for this season is the season of greatest heat, the fifth month being called by the Babylonians "*the descent of fire.*"

The *seventh* Voice is at the Autumnal Equinox; it *strips the forests bare*.

"When yellow leaves, or none, or few do hang
Upon those boughs which shake against the cold,
Bare ruin'd choirs; where late the sweet birds sang."

The best comment on the whole Psalm is to be found in the beautiful words in which Thomson gathers up the lessons of the Seasons. The coincidence here is certainly undesigned.

cf. Voices I and II verses 3 and 4.	"These as they change, Almighty Father, these Are but the varied God. The rolling year Is full of Thee! Forth in the pleasing Spring Thy beauty walks, Thy tenderness and love. Wide flush the fields; the softening air is balm; And every sense, and every heart, is joy.
cf. Voices III, IV and V verses 4_b– 7.	Then comes Thy glory in the Summer months, With light and heat refulgent. Then Thy sun Shoots full perfection through the swelling year; And oft Thy voice in dreadful thunder speaks; . . . .
cf. Voices VI and VII verses 8—9.	Thy bounty shines in Autumn unconfined, And spreads a common feast for all that lives. . . . . with clouds and storms Around Thee thrown, tempest o'er tempest roll'd Majestic darkness! On the whirlwind's wing Riding sublime Thou bidd'st the world adore. . . . .
cf. verse 1. cf. verse 9.	Nature, attend! Join every living soul Beneath the spacious temple of the sky, In adoration join; and ardent raise One general song! . . . .
cf. verse 10. cf. verse 11.	for the great Shepherd reigns And this unsuffering Kingdom yet will come."

The connexion of Psalm xxix with the octave of Psalms (xx.—xxviii.) which it closes is suggestive. If from this octave we omit the Alphabetical Psalm (xxv.) we obtain a series of Altar-Psalms with frequent allusions to an accepted sacrifice (e.g. Pss. xx. and xxviii.; xxvi. and xxvii.), also to a 'King' who goes forth to war (Ps. xx.), who fights only with spiritual weapons (Ps. xxi.) and who appears again as the "King of Glory" opening the Way to Heaven (Ps. xxiv.). We also find in this group of Psalms at least two allusions to the "encompassing" of the Altar (Pss. xxvi., xxvii.), while Ps. xxix., the Psalm of the seven 'Voices,' is directly connected by Jewish tradition with the seven "encompassings" of the Altar on the seventh day of Tabernacles. May we not venture to suggest that the whole group formed, as it were, a Passion Play for the Season of Tabernacles?

PS. XXIX.

1 Give unto YHVH, ye sons of God[a],
Give unto YHVH glory and strength[b],
2 Give unto YHVH His Name's due glory,
Worship YHVH with hallowed[c] pomp.

[a] or *of the mighty*
[b] v. 11
[c] Sept. differs

Voice I.   3 The VOICE of YHVH is upon the waters,
           YHVH is on the great waters.
Voice II.   4 The VOICE of YHVH is with power,
Voice III.   The VOICE of YHVH is with majesty.

v. 1. The reading of the P.B.V., which is derived from the Vulgate and *Sept.*, is an interesting example of a reading creeping into the text from the margin of a manuscript. Originally the Sept. would have read

"Bring unto the Lord, O ye sons of God,
Bring unto the Lord glory and honour."

But since the Hebrew words here translated "*sons of God*" are somewhat unusual and might be translated "*sons of rams*," a scribe must have written this in the margin as an alternative rendering. A later scribe inserted it in the text. Hence the P.B.V.

"Bring unto the Lord, O ye mighty,
[Bring young rams unto the Lord],
Ascribe unto the Lord worship and strength."

v. 3. "*The Voice...upon the waters...the great waters.*" The waters are the origin of all things. In Creation the Spirit of God moved upon the face of the waters. Each year the Parable of Creation begins afresh in Spring. Voice I. is therefore either the first month of the Year or the first voice of creation of which that month is a type. The "great waters" in *v.* 3 and the "Water-flood" in *v.* 10 are practically the same. It is true that the word *mabbul* occurs only in *v.* 10 and in Gen. vi.—xi. and that in Genesis it always signifies the Deluge, but to give it the sense of Deluge in the Psalm would be to introduce a thought quite alien to the context. As I understand it verse 10 sums up the lesson of the Seven Voices, God's Kingdom began with Creation (from the Waters) and His Kingdom continues for ever,

"YHVH sat enthroned at the Water-flood,
And YHVH sitteth as King for ever."

If, as I have suggested, this Psalm was the Psalm for *Hoshannah Rabba*, the great Water Festival, then there would be an additional reason for tracing the origin of all things to the Waters.

After *v.* 3ᵃ the text inserts "The God of Glory thunders." This line clearly destroys the structure and parallelism of the verse, while on the other hand a line is needed after *v.* 7ᵃ. I have therefore restored it to what I believe to have been its original position.

124   FIRST COLLECTION, 'DAVIDIC' PSALMS.

Voice IV.   5 The VOICE of YHVH breaketh the cedars,
                   YHVH shattereth the cedars of Lebanon.
                6 He maketh them^a skip like a calf,   ^a i.e. the ce[dars]
                   Lebanon and Sirion like a young antelope.
Voice V.   7 The VOICE of YHVH cleaveth the^b flames of fire,   ^b or *with*
                   [The God of Glory thunders]^c.   ^c Transpos[e]
                                                                        from v. 3

Voice VI.   8 The VOICE of YHVH casteth the wilderness in birth-pangs,
                   YHVH casteth in birth-pangs the wilderness of Kadesh.
Voice VII.   9 The VOICE of YHVH maketh the oaks to cast their birth
                   and strippeth the forests,
                   And throughout His Palace-temple it all proclaimeth
                   "GLORY."

v. 6. "*He maketh them skip...*" i.e. the *cedars*, not *the mountains*. The up-and-down motion of a wind-swept wood is here compared to the skipping of a calf. Though Lebanon and Sirion are mentioned in v. 6^b the thought is centred, not upon the mountains, but, upon the woods that clothe them. To make the mountains skip (as in Ps. cxiv. 4, 6) destroys the unity of thought which belongs to each 'Voice.'

The Septuagint mistook two words in this verse and thus obtained a translation which is of no interest except to those who would study the origin of mistakes.

v. 7. "*The Voice of YHVH cleaveth the flames of fire.*" The word here translated *cleaveth* is often used for *hewing* rock or stone or even for *digging* a well. Once in the E.V. it is translated *cut*, viz. Is. li. 9 "Art Thou not it that hath *cut* Rahab and wounded the Dragon?" Cf. Chap. xxvii. 1 with Cheyne's note. The expression in the Psalm is no doubt remarkable. Wellhausen would read "YHVH's voice splitteth [rocks, YHVH's voice sendeth forth] flames of fire." There is however no need for this. The word was probably chosen because of some association of semi-mythological thought similar to that in Is. li, 9. It should be observed that the oldest name of the *fifth* month signified "*fire making fire*," and that the Assyrians called it the month of *the descent of fire*: so in our Psalm it is the *fifth* 'Voice' that "heweth out the flames of fire." I agree however with Wellhausen when he says "As the verse reads at present, it is incomplete." There is no other verse in the Psalm consisting of one line. The line which I have inserted from v. 3 exactly meets the difficulty. In v. 3 it was redundant; but here it is required by the parallelism.

v. 9. "*The Voice of YHVH maketh the oaks to cast their birth.*" The usual translation, "maketh the hinds to bring forth young!" destroys the parallelism, drags in a thought which is alien to the whole passage and ends in an almost inconceivable bathos—"Parturiunt montes; nascetur ridiculus mus!"

The fact is that the Hebrew word not only for *ram* but also for *stag*, *hind*, is derived from a root signifying *strong*, from which also the words for *oak* and other *strong trees* is derived. This similarity has not unfrequently given rise to confusion. [See the Greek versions on Gen. xlix. 21; Ps. xlii. 2; Is. lxi. 3 &c.] Dr Schiller-Szinessy, in his Hebrew note on this passage, in his edition of Qimchi on the Psalms, says "I have no doubt" but that the sacred writer intends to imply, not hinds but "some kind of strong trees such as the oak, &c." Though this view was, long ago, propounded by Lowth it has, strange to say, met with little or no acceptance. My reasons for advocating it are as follows:—1st. The verb which I have translated "*cast their birth*" is another voice of the same verb which in verse 8 I have translated "*casteth in birth-pangs.*" This being so the thought is clearly continuous in vv. 8, 9. The *Wilderness* (not the *desert*) is in *birth-pangs* at the touch of Autumn while the next 'Voice' makes the *strong trees* to *cast their birth* as it *strips the forests bare*.

PSALM XXIX.

10 YHVH sat enthroned at the Water-flood,
And YHVH sitteth as King for ever.
11 YHVH will give strength* to His people,   * v. 1
YHVH will bless His People with peace.

The thought of *birth-pangs* led the writer to make the words for *oaks* and *forests* feminine though in both cases the feminine was unusual. Rosenmuller states that the verb, which in Hebrew has the sense of "*strips bare*," has in Arabic the sense of *causing abortion*. If this be so we see how the poet so chose his language as to convey the double thought. In any case there is an allusion to the birth-pangs of a new Creation caused by the near approach of God and earth (cf. Pss. xcvii. 4; cxiv. 7; Hab. iii. 10; Rom. viii. 22).

"*And throughout His Palace-temple.*" God's Palace-temple is the Universe. All the seven 'Voices' of the Year are, in their ultimate meaning summed up in one word and that is "Glory." The Glory of God is the Manifestation of God. All God's Voices in Nature point to this. The Feast of Tabernacles, in the seventh month, with its seven circuits round the Altar was felt to be an acted Parable of the final goal of Creation. Compare Rev. x. 4 ff. (R.V.) "And when the seven thunders uttered (their voices) I was about to write: and I heard a Voice from heaven saying, Seal up the things which the seven thunders uttered, and write them not. And the angel which I saw standing upon the sea and upon the earth lifted up his right hand to heaven, and sware......that there shall be time no longer; but in the days of the voice of the seventh angel, when he is about to sound, then is finished the mystery of God...."

v. 11. "*YHVH will give strength to His People...peace.*" In verse 10 we see God's Kingdom come on earth; while verse 11 shews us the effect of this upon His People. To His People He gives that attribute of "*Strength*" which became most peculiarly His own (cf. *v.* 1b with 11a) and crowns it with that "*Peace*" which is the perfection of His own Unity—"That they may be One even as we are One." According to Old Testament thought *Peace* is the bond of perfectness which reconciles all things in heaven and in earth (see notes on Ps. cxxii.). Thus the *Yalkut* on this passage "R. Simeon ben Ḥ'lafta says, Great is Peace. When the Holy One, blessed be He, created His Universe He made Peace between the upper and the lower worlds. On the *First Day* He created from both *upper and lower worlds*, as it is said, 'In the beginning God created the *Heavens* and the *Earth*.' On the *Second Day* (He created) 'the Firmament,' i.e. from the *upper world*. On the *Third Day* 'Let the waters be gathered together,' i.e. from the *lower world*. On the *Fourth Day* 'Let there be lights &c.,' i.e. from the *upper world*. On the *Fifth Day* 'Let the waters bring forth &c.,' i.e. from the *lower world*. On the *Sixth* (*Day*) He created 'Man,' whose body is from the *lower world* and whose soul is from the *upper world*." The object of the writer is to shew that the promise of the First Day is fulfilled in the Sixth. Man is the Microcosm. Through Man God must at last reconcile all things whether in Heaven above or in the Earth beneath.

Delitzsch may well say "How expressive in such a Psalm as this is the concluding word '*with Peace!*' It overarches it like a rainbow. The beginning of the Psalm shews us the heavens open, and the throne of God in the midst of the angelic songs of praise, and the conclusion of it shews upon the earth..., His people victorious and blessed with peace. *Gloria in excelsis* is the beginning, and *pax in terris* the close."

PSALM XXX.

Here again the Title to the Psalm has preserved a tradition as to its use in the Temple. As the Title of Ps. xxix. showed its use for the last day of Tabernacles so the Hebrew title of Ps. xxx. shews that it was appointed for the next Festival, viz. the "*Dedication of the Temple.*" This is confirmed by *Sofrim*, c. 18, § 2 which refers the Psalm to *Ḥanucca* i.e. to the *Dedication of the Temple* (see Graetz). Now it is an historical blunder to suppose that *Ḥanucca* had its *origin* in the Dedication by Judas Maccabaeus B.C. 165. If the reader will turn to the Introduction to the *Songs of Degrees* he will see that the thought of *Dedication* has its origin in one of Nature's parables. What Judas did was to associate an historical fact, the cleansing of the Temple, with Nature's festival of the Winter Solstice, the season of Light's new birth; a festival which was certainly observed by all nations of antiquity. The new historical significance failed to displace the older associations of the growing light so that the Feast was still sometimes called the "*Feast of Lights*" (Josephus, *Ant.* XII. 7). To all intents and purposes it was a repetition of the Feast of Tabernacles. There was the same carrying of branches (2 Macc. x. 6 f.) the same singing of the *Hallel* each day for eight days; the same symbolism of lights and lamps. It was indeed a transference of the thought of New Year from the Autumnal Equinox (7th month) to the Winter Solstice (10th month). We learn from Maimonides that one observance of *Ḥanucca* (Dedication Feast) was the lighting of candles, one on the first day, two on the second, three on the third, &c. during the eight days of the Feast. Whatever meaning may have been given to this, its *origin* is obvious; from the Winter Solstice begins the *growing light* of the year; it is the 'Birth-day' of the Sun, who, according to Babylonian thought, comes forth then from beneath the waters of death. From this point the motion of the Sun is, for six months, in an ever-widening spiral. Surely this is one of God's parables which His children should interpret? I once saw a Hymn (it was, I think, for S. Thomas' Day, Dec. 21st), in which the thought of the widening spiral from the Winter Solstice was worked out. The writer was probably unconscious of the fact that he was developing an idea which underlay much of the religion of Babylonia.

I shall have occasion, in my Introduction to the Songs of Degrees, to shew the connexion between the Dedication of the Temple, with its 'encompassing' processions, and the Dedication of the Temple of the Universe as typified by the movement of the Sun: suffice it now to state that the latter is the origin of the former and is alluded to in Psalms which may have been written long before the Dedication by Judas Maccabaeus. It is a suggestive fact that Enoch (*Ḥanoc*) and *Ḥanucca* are merely varieties of the same word. Bearing these thoughts in mind we turn to the Psalm itself.

PS. XXX.

The new-born Sun (at Ḥanucca) is a type of Israel's resurrection.

1 I extol Thee, O YHVH, for Thou hast lifted me out^a,   ^a i.e. of a pit
  And not let my foes rejoice over me.
2 O YHVH, my God, I cried unto Thee,
  And Thou hast healed me!
3 O YHVH, from Sheôl Thou hast brought up my soul;
  From being among those that descend to the Pit
  Thou hast made me to live^b!   ^b Ezek. xxxvii. 11—14

Darkness does its work and leads to Light. So God's 'anger' leads to the joy of His Presence.

4 Hymn to YHVH, O ye Saints of His;
  Give thanks to His holy Memorial^c-Name;   ^c Exod. iii. 15
5 For His anger^d is over at once,   ^d Is. liv. 7 ff.; lx. 10; cf. 2 Cor. iv. 17
  While His favour is all life-long^e: ^e or *life itself*
  At evening^f Weeping comes to lodge,   ^f Is. xvii. 14
  But morning^f rings with Song.

v. 1. "*Thou hast lifted me out.*" The verb is an unusual one and would be used for drawing up water in a bucket or drawing a prisoner out of a dungeon such as that in which Jeremiah was plunged (Jer. xxxviii. 7—13).

The speaker feels that he has been brought up from Sheôl (v. 3); that God had given him new life when he had, as we say, one foot in the grave. The Title of the Psalm, which assigns it for the "Dedication of the Temple" (*Ḥanucca*) justifies us in regarding it, not as the experience of an individual but of Israel who having died under the stroke of God's anger (Hos. xiii. 1) has been raised by God to new life (Hos. vi. 2; Ezek. xxxvii. 1—10, quoted by Baethgen).

Thus, at *Ḥanucca*, Israel like another Enoch (*Ḥanoc*) is saved out of death and walks with God. In the Latin use this Psalm is appointed for Easter Eve.

v. 4^b. "*His holy Memorial-Name.*" It is now a recognised fact that this word, which the E.V. translates "*remembrance*" or "*memorial*," really signifies "*Name*." Wherever it is said of God there is, I believe, a reference to the *Eternity of His Mercy*. See Exod. iii. 15; Hos. xii. 5 (6); Ps. xcvii. 12; cii. 12 (13); cxi. 4 (note, p. 43); cxxxv. 13; cxlv. 7 (note, p. 63). It will be seen from these passages, that God's *Memorial-Name* is that Name of Gracious and Merciful, to which His works, in Nature and in History, all point. The word has a special significance here, since the object of the whole Stanza is to shew, from Nature, that God's Mercy exceeds His Anger as far as light exceeds darkness.

v. 5. "*But morning rings with Song.*" Sorrow is only a lodger in God's House. The Parable of the Seasons shews, when truly understood, that God's great end is not sorrow but joy. There is a story quoted from the Talmud (but without reference) in *Psalm Mosaics* as follows:—"When Adam and Eve were driven out of the garden of Eden they wandered over the face of the earth. And the sun began to set, and they looked with fear at the lessening of the light, and felt a horror like death steal over their hearts. And the light of heaven grew paler, and the wretched ones clasped each other in an agony of despair. Then all grew dark, and the luckless ones fell on the earth, silent, and thought that God had withdrawn from them the light for ever; and they spent the night in tears. But a beam of light began to rise over the Eastern hills after many hours of darkness, and the golden sun came back and dried the tears of Adam and Eve, and then they

Israel, like Jonah, had needed the hiding of God's Presence.

6 Methought, when all went well with me, "I shall never never be moved."

cried out with joy and said, 'Heaviness may endure for a night, but joy cometh in the Morning: this is a law that God hath laid upon nature.'"
There is a lovely poem by C. Rossetti on this text which I cannot forbear to quote:

"Nothing is great on this side of the grave,
Nor anything of any stable worth;
Whatso is born from earth returns to earth;
Nothing we grasp proves half the thing we crave;
The tidal wave shrinks to the ebbing wave;
Laughter is folly, madness lurks in mirth;
Mankind sets off a dying from the birth;
Life is a losing game, with what to save?
Thus I sat mourning like a mournful owl,
And like a doleful dragon made ado,
Companion of all monsters of the dark;
When lo! the light cast off its nightly cowl,
And up to heaven flashed a carolling lark,
And all creation sang its hymn anew.

When all creation sang its hymn anew
What could I do but sing a stave in tune?
Spectral on high hung pale the vanishing moon
Where a last gleam of stars hung paling too,
Lark's lay—a cockcrow—with a scattered few
Soft early chirpings—with a tender croon
Of doves—a hundred thousand calls, and soon
A hundred thousand answers sweet and true.
These set me singing too at unawares:
One note for all delights and charities,
One note for hope reviving with the light,
One note for every lovely thing that is;
Till while I sang my heart shook off its cares
And revelled in the land of no more night."

But if light follows darkness it is also true that darkness succeeds to light; we might therefore be tempted to ask which of the two points to God's end? Therefore the Psalmist says "His anger is over at once | While his favour is all life-long." The anger is swift and terrible but it so does its work that the sorrow is turned *into* joy (John xvi. 20). This transmuted sorrow lives on as the soul's brightest possession. It had come in the night as a lodger, but in the morning it is found to be an angel. These transmuted sorrows justify William Blake in saying, "Eternity is in love with the productions of time."

v. 5^b. "*While His favour is all life-long.*" Or "Life (itself) consists in His favour." Eternal life consists in knowing God. It is not measured by duration. There is no doubt an antithesis between "the anger" that "is over at once" and "the favour" that is "for life"; but the former is finite, the latter is infinite.

v. 6. "*Methought when all went well with me.*" Literally "*As for me I said* (or *thought*) *in my tranquillity.*" The word here used for *tranquillity* or *prosperity* does not of itself imply any sin on Israel's part; but the glare of prosperity hides God (Jer. xxii. 21) just as the sun hides the beauty of the stars. In one sense Light is the only revealer; but in another sense Darkness is a revealer as well. Darkness is but a comparative term; it is but the reticence of Light. God teaches

PSALM XXX.

7 Thou, YHVH, through Thy favour, hadst made my hill so
strong.
Thou didst hide Thy Face[a], and I was in dismay[a]!   [a] Ps. civ. 29
8 Then unto Thee, YHVH, I cry;
Unto YHVH[b] I make supplication.   [b] or *Adonai*

But, like Jonah beneath the waters, he had cried to God.

9 "What gain (can there be) in my blood,
In my going to the Pit?
Can dust praise Thee[c],   [c] Cf. Ps. vi.
Can it declare Thy truth?
10 Hear, YHVH, and be gracious unto me
YHVH, be Thou my Helper!"

God had answered him by a resurrection of which Hanucca is a type and pledge.

11 Thou didst turn for me my mourning into dancing,
Thou didst loose my sackcloth and girdle me with gladness,
12 So that my inner-being[d] might hymn Thee without ceasing   [d] *My glory*, see Sept.
YHVH, O my God, for ever will I praise Thee.

---

us this lesson by a thousand voices in the world of Nature; the cold dark Winter nurses the buds of Spring. It seemed to Israel in the full spring-tide of God's favour that Winter could never come— "*I shall never never be moved.*" But Winter came all the same.

v. 7. "*Thou didst hide Thy Face, and I was in dismay!*" This was Israel's Winter. God's "favour" was "life itself" to him (*v.* 5). His soul drooped and shut up like a flower when the Sun of God's Presence was gone. But that Winter was preparing a glorious Spring for Israel: "In a little wrath I hid My face from thee for a moment; but with everlasting kindness will I have mercy on thee, saith the Lord thy Redeemer" (Is. liv. 8).

v. 9. See note on Ps. vi. 5, which is closely parallel.

v. 11. "*Thou didst loose my sackcloth...*" Israel thus interprets the lesson of the Season. With growing Light all Nature casts off her sackcloth and is girdled with gladness. This points to a Divine purpose. This purpose must be fulfilled through Israel; if God so clothe the dumb world with resurrection-life how much more shall He clothe His own Son that serveth Him? We note again in this verse that the joy does not merely *succeed* the sorrow, but is woven out of its very substance; the "mourning is turned into dancing" just as in St John xvi. 20 the "sorrow" is "turned into joy." See also note on *v.* 5.

ADDITIONAL NOTE TO PS. XXX.

This Psalm is well fitted to answer a difficult question in the Spiritual life—*Why does God sometimes hide His Face from us?* To answer this I would suggest the following outline for meditation.

v. 4. God's holy Memorial-Name.... "Gracious and Merciful" (see note 4[b]). All the voices of Nature which point to this are voices of God (read Stanza II.)....

The return of morning-light brings us this message every day from God.... The return of increasing-light (at Winter Solstice) brings us this message in another form every year from God (see note on *v.* 5).

What the Light of the Sun is to Nature, that the Light of God's Countenance is to us. When God looks upon us we are filled with life and joy (*vv.* 1—3 and *vv.* 11, 12). When God looks away from us we are "in dismay" (*v.* 7). Why then does not God always lift up the Light of His Countenance upon us?

Let Nature answer. What would perpetual day be without night?... What would perpetual Summer be without Winter?... Darkness is needed, not merely for rest; it is also a revealer (see note, *v.* 6).

So then the hiding of God's Face may sometimes be for our good—Israel found it so (Read *vv.* 6—8).... He learnt three lessons, (*a*) *his own weakness*, (*b*) *God's strength*, (*c*) *the power of prayer*.

But there must be some other good reason why God's Face should sometimes be hidden; for was it not once hidden from Christ?... Christ did not need to learn the lessons (*a*), (*b*), (*c*) mentioned above.

But Christ *did* need an opportunity for entire devotion to His Father's will—Did not the Darkness give this?... If then there be any servant of God who is in heaviness, because God's Face is not now shining upon him, let him recognise the uses of Darkness. Perhaps God is teaching him the lesson (*a*), or (*b*), or (*c*)? If he has learnt these God may be giving him a precious opportunity for devoted service.

In any case let him remember *v.* 5....

What the morning song of joy will be may be judged from *vv.* 11, 12.

PSALM XXXI.

If we omit a Preface (*vv.* 1—3ᵃ see note) and a Conclusion (*vv.* 23, 24) the Psalm consists of four Stanzas of about equal length, the first three consisting of 5 verses each, and the fourth of 4 verses. At first sight there is a difficulty in passing from the calm trust of Stanza I. (*vv.* 4—8) to the deep depression of Stanza II. (*vv.* 9—13) and then rising again through the growing trust of Stanza III. (*vv.* 14—18) to the exultation of Stanza IV. (*vv.* 19—22). If, however, the reader will verify the references to Jeremiah and to the Lamentations which are given in the margin, he will see that the words are not the words of an individual but of *Israel*, who, being in some peril from enemies, trusts himself in God's hand (Stanza I.), remembering what God had done for him in bringing him back from the Captivity (*vv.* 7, 8): then indeed his case had seemed desperate (see Stanza II.); the Captivity was the death of the Nation (*v.* 22 with note); but even then Israel had trusted God (Stanza III.); and God had brought him up from his grave, and shewn him unlooked-for joy in the Return from Captivity (Stanza IV., see notes). This being so Israel may well trust himself to God in the lesser sorrows of the present. The Key note of the Psalm is struck in *vv.* 15 and 5 "*My times are in Thy hand,*" "*Into Thy hand I commend my spirit.*" Israel, as we have seen, learnt this lesson in the Return from the Captivity. It was not merely that the joys of the Return succeeded to the sorrows of the Captivity but that the joys were woven out of the very substance of the sorrows (see note on *v.* 19). Without that death the resurrection-life of Israel, so fruitful in Revelation, could never have been: 'Ought not the Christ-Nation to have suffered these things and to enter into his Glory?'

The application of the Psalm to Christ Himself needs no development; we may however point out that the Disciples of Christ learnt the lesson in the same way that Israel did. Calvary was to them the death of all their hopes (cf. Stanza II.), but when God had turned for them that sorrow *into* the joy of Easter and of Whitsunday they learned that trust which can say "My times are in Thy hand," "Into Thy hand I commend my spirit." Thus the Psalm has a lesson for all time for the Israel of God (see note *v.* 5).

PS. XXXI.

A moveable Preface which occurs again at the beginning of Ps. lxxi.

1 In Thee, YHVH, I have taken refuge,
Never can I come to shame!
In Thy righteousness deliver me:
2 Incline Thine ear to me,
Make haste to help me:
Be Thou to me a refuge-rock,
A fortress-home, to save me
3 For my rock and my fortress Thou art:

Cf. *Te Deum*

Stanza I.

Israel, looking back on what God had done for him in the Captivity trusts Him for the lesser troubles of the present.

And, for Thine own Name's sake, Thou wilt lead[a] and guide[a] me.
4 Thou wilt free me from this net they have hidden for me,
For Thou art my refuge.
5 Into[b] Thy hand I commend my spirit[b];
Thou hast redeemed me,
YHVH, Thou God of Truth!
6 Thou[c] hatest those that observe[d] vain idols[d]
But as for me I trust in YHVH.
7 I am glad and rejoice in Thy lovingkindness,
Seeing Thou hast looked[e] on mine affliction[e],
Hast known the sorrows of my soul.
8 Thou hast not given me over to the enemy's hand,
But hast set my feet at large.

[a] Ps. xxiii. 2
[b] Luke xxii 46; Acts v 59
[c] So Sept. Sj Targ.
[d] Jonah ii. (9)
[e] Luke i. 4 cf.Gen.xxi 32

vv. 1—3. These verses occur again, with slight verbal changes, in Psalm lxxi., a Psalm which is so similar, in style and subject-matter, to our present Psalm, that I am inclined to think that both were composed for the same Temple-use. These verses, which I have called a moveable Preface, have no very direct connexion with the words which immediately follow; the transition from the 'Rock' and 'Fortress,' of *v.* 3ᵃ, to the 'Guiding Shepherd,' of *v.* 3ᵇ, being very abrupt. It should however be observed that the idea of God as a 'Refuge' is common to *v.* 2ᵃ and *v.* 4ᵇ, and that the words 'I shall never come to shame' (Vulg. "non confundar in aeternum" as in *Te Deum*) are based (*v.* 1) upon the fact that 'I have taken refuge in God' and again (*v.* 17) upon the fact that 'I have called upon Thee.' Again, in *v.* 19ᵃ there seems to be an allusion to *v.* 1ᵃ. Thus we conclude that the Preface is an integral part of Ps. xxxi. though the structure of the Psalm is complete without it.

v. 5. "*Into Thy hand I commend my spirit,*" i.e. 'Into Thy mighty keeping I entrust, as a safe deposit, my very being.' Though, from Calvary onwards, these words have been consecrated to the hour of death, they have a meaning also for the fullest energy of life. When St Peter said, "Let them that suffer according to the will of God commit the keeping of their souls in well-doing unto a faithful Creator" (1 Pet. iv. 19), he did not speak of dying but of living. We need the

PSALM XXXI.

Stanza II.
Israel's sorrow in the Captivity seemed hopeless.

9 Be gracious to me, YHVH, for I am in distress^a;
Mine^b eye is dim through grief^b;—
My soul too and my body;
10 For my life is consumed^c with sorrow,
And my years with sighing;
My strength is enfeebled through mine iniquity^d,
And my bones are languishing:
11 To all my foes I am a scorn;
To my neighbours a burden,
And a terror to my friends;
Those that see me in the street flee away from me;
12 I am forgotten as a dead man out of mind;
I am become like a broken vessel^e.
13 For^f I have heard the slander of the many,
With fear on every side^f,
While they consult together against me,
Planning to take my life.

^a Lam. i. 20
^b Ps. vi. 7

^c Jer. xx. 18

^d or, *my punishment*

^e Jer. xxii. 28

^f Jer. xx. 10

Stanza III.
Yet, even then, Israel trusted in God.

14 But as for me, on Thee I repose O YHVH;
I say, "Thou art my God."
15 My times are in Thy hand^g,
Rescue me from the hand of mine enemies,
And from my pursuers.

^g v. 5

prayer quite as much for life as for death. It is best to read this verse with v. 15 "*My times are in Thy hand.*" Because God is "the God of Truth," (v. 5), the "Faithful Creator," therefore St Paul can look through death to the end of God's great plan and can say, "I know Whom I have believed, and am persuaded that He is able to guard that which I have committed unto Him against that day" (II Tim. i. 12). In this sense, too, Browning has said:

> Grow old along with me!
> The best is yet to be,
> The last of life, for which the first was made:
> Our times are in His hand
> Who saith, "A whole I planned,
> Youth shows but half; trust God: see all, nor be afraid!"

v. 7. "*Seeing Thou hast looked on my affliction.*" The words are almost identical with the play on the name of *Reuben* (Gen. xxix. 32), "She called his name *Reuben* for she said Surely YHVH hath looked on my affliction." The Septuagint, both here and in the Psalm, read τὴν ταπείνωσιν, which is the word used by the Virgin Mary in the Magnificat, "He hath looked upon the *lowly estate* of His handmaiden." This word for "*affliction*" is constantly used of the sorrows of Israel in Captivity, whether in Egypt (Exod. iii. 7, 17; iv. 31; Neh. ix. 9) or in Babylon (Lam. i. 3, 7, 9; iii. 1, 19; Is. xlviii. 10).

The allusion in our Psalm is to God's visiting and redeeming His People by freeing them out of Captivity. This redemption was a type of the great Redemption; consequently the allusion in the Magnificat is not a mere accident.

16 Let the light of Thy countenance shine^a on Thy servant,   ^a Numb. vi.
   Save me in Thy lovingkindness!
17 O YHVH, I cannot come to shame^b,   ^b v. 1
   For I have called upon Thee,
   Let the wicked come to shame^c,   ^c Jer. xvii. 1
   Let them be silent in Sheôl.
18 Let lying lips be stricken dumb,
   Which rail against the righteous,
   With pride and with contempt.

Stanza IV.
The Return from Captivity was to Israel a revelation of the hidden goodness of God.

19 Oh how great is Thy goodness,
   Which Thou hast hidden away for them that fear Thee;—
   Which Thou hast wrought for them that take refuge^d in   ^d v. 1
        Thee;—
   In the very sight^e of the children of men!   ^e Ps. xxiii. 5
20 Thou coverest them in the covert of Thy Presence,
   From the conspiracies of mighty-men!
   Thou hidest^f them, as in a Shrine,   ^f Ps. xxvii. 5
   From the strife of tongues.

v. 16. "*Thy Servant*," i.e. Israel, see Jer. xxx. 10; xlvi. 27 f.; Ezek. xxxvii. 25 (quoted by Baethgen).

v. 19. "*Which Thou hast hidden away..*" God has two ways of hiding. In the time of trouble He hides His people in the Sanctuary of His Presence (see *v.* 20), and He also hides away blessings as a father lays up for his children. To His prodigal sons He may give at once the portion of His "hidden treasure" which falleth to them (see Ps. xvii. 14), but for His faithful children, who are ever with Him, He waits for a convenient time, lest a blessing coming too soon should become a curse. In the life of Israel such a convenient time was the Return from the Captivity. It was a season in which God's goodness was ever coming as a fresh surprise: the joy seemed too great to be true (see Ps. cxxvi. 1—3); Zion saw with wonder (Is. xlix. 21) her sons coming from far; all nations that had despised her now flock to bring to her their choicest tribute (Is. lx. 4 ff.): it was, moreover, a season of Revelation, a season to which we owe the writings of the Second Isaiah and a large number of the Psalms. Well might Israel say, "*Oh how great is Thy goodness which Thou hast hidden away for them that fear Thee; which Thou hast wrought for them that take refuge in Thee;—in the very sight of the children of men!*" These last words denote not merely that God's goodness to Israel is shewn *openly* but that it is shewn in the presence, and in spite of, a hostile world. (See the parallel passage, Ps. xxiii. 5.)

v. 20. The word which we have translated "*conspiracies*" is of doubtful meaning. Aquila seems to identify it with the similar word which the E.V. translates "*the rough places*" (Is. xl. 4). Jerome too translates "*a duritie.*" The primary signification of the root is *to bind*; hence the Targum reads "*from the bands (or troops) of men.*" But though the one word is doubtful the general meaning of the passage is clear:—God's Presence is a Sanctuary (cf. Ps. xxvii. 4, 5) in which perfect rest may be found from all the troubles of earth and from that opposition which the writer of the Epistle to the Hebrews calls "the contradiction of sinners" (Heb. xii. 3). Christ only among men found this perfect rest upon earth. Browning, in his study of Lazarus, has given us a marvellous picture of a man hidden in God's Presence from the strife of tongues.

PSALM XXXI.

21 Blessed be YHVH for He hath distinguished me with His
   lovingkindness,
   As it were in a fenced city.
22 But, as for me, I said[a] in my alarm,   [a] Lam. iii. 18
   I am cut off[b] from the sight of Thine eyes!   [b] Ps. lxxxviii.
   Whereas Thou heardest the voice of my supplication,   5 (6); Jonah
   While I was (yet) crying[c] to Thee.   ii. 4; Lam. iii. 54
                                                  [c] Ps. xxviii. 2;
                                                  Lam. iii. 57

Chorus.
Let all Israel learn   23 Love YHVH, all ye His saints:
the lesson of the past   YHVH that keepeth faithfulness,
(cf. *Stanza I.*).   And plentifully repayeth the proud doer.
                        24 Be strong[d], and let your heart be firm,   [d] Josh. i. 6, 9, 18
                           All ye whose hope is in YHVH.

v. 21. "*He hath distinguished me...fenced city.*" The primary meaning of the verb here used is *to separate* (see Lev. xxvii. 2; Numb. vi. 2, and cf. the kindred word in Ps. xvii. 7), hence *to be wonderful* or *to act wonderously* (Judg. xiii. 19). In the present passage the context decides for the primary sense: as a man is *separated* or *set apart* in the safety of a "fenced city," so Israel feels that God Himself had been to him a strong city (Is. xxvi. 1; xxxiii. 21; Zech. ii. 5). Other nations may have their strongholds but the 'distinguishing' mark of Israel is the Divine 'Presence,' "so shall we be *separated...from* all the people that are upon the face of the earth" (Exod. xxxiii. 16).

v. 22. "*But, as for me, I said in my alarm...*" The season of Israel's panic fear was the season of the Captivity depicted in Stanza II. (*vv.* 9—13). It was then that Israel said, "The waters flowed over my head, I said I am cut off" (Lam. iii. 54; cf. Jonah ii. 4); "I said, My strength and my hope is perished from the Lord" (Lam. iii. 18); "Zion said, The Lord hath forsaken me..." (Is. xlix. 14). Ezekiel expressed the same thought in the vision of dry bones, "Behold, they say, Our bones are dead, and our hope is lost; we are cut off for our parts" (Ezek. xxxvii. 11). The Captivity was the death of the Nation, the Return was a resurrection from the dead.

PSALM XXXII.

This Psalm, which is the second of the penitential Psalms, was used in the Jewish Church for the close of the Day of Atonement. Let us interpret it with this thought only in view. On that one Day the Jewish Church received the most solemn assurance that God had forgiven the guilt of His People and covered all their sin (Ps. lxxxv. 2). God had said "On that Day he (the Priest) shall make Atonement for you to cleanse you; from all your transgressions before the Lord ye shall be clean" (Lev. xvi. 30). This assurance of the forgiveness of the sins of the past year was conveyed to the eyes of the assembled worshippers in three ways, (i) by the scape-goat (Lev. xvi. 21), (ii) by the sacrifices, (iii) by the High

FIRST COLLECTION, 'DAVIDIC' PSALMS.

Priest coming forth from the Holy of Holies (Ecclus. l. 20). If we picture Israel singing Psalm xxxii. at this supreme moment of realized forgiveness we shall best understand the meaning of the Psalm in the Old Testament and its relation to the Atonement of Christ.

In point of structure the Psalm consists of seven Stanzas; the law of formation being $a, b, c, d, c_1, b_1, a_1$; in other words, the first three Stanzas and the last three correspond with one another but in inverted order. Thus the *first* and *last* stanzas (a and a_1) depict the happiness of the sin-forgiven People. The *second* Stanza corresponds with the *sixth* (b with b_1) inasmuch as the Psalmist tells his own brutish silence in the *second* and dissuades from the like folly in the *sixth*. The *third* Stanza is continued and completed by the *fifth*; both tell of the joy of pardon; in the *third* we see the Father falling on the Prodigal's neck and kissing him, while in the *fifth* the Prodigal receives the pledges of restored sonship amid the music and the joy of the Home. The fourth Stanza, which we have marked d, is of course the middle Stanza, and, as such, gives the leading thought "*Now is the acceptable time, Now is the Day of Salvation.*" The Psalm must be studied with its companion, Ps. xxxiii.; it will then be evident that it depicts the experience, not of a private individual but, of Israel.

PS. XXXII.

(*a*) Oh the happiness of the Atonement!

1 Happy[a] is he whose transgression is forgiven,
  Whose sin is covered!
2 Happy is the man to whom YHVH imputes no guilt,
  And in whose spirit there is no guile!

vv. 1, 2. In these verses, sin, that it might appear exceeding sinful, is pictured under four names:—(*a*) *transgression*, (*b*) *sin*, (*c*) *guilt*, (*d*) *guile*. Of these, (*a*) *transgression* consists of acts of disobedience which therefore need pardon; (*b*) *sin* is a missing of the mark, a wrong aim of life, which needs Atonement; (*c*) *guilt* is that sense of sin which creates an obstacle between man and God and which therefore needs a reassurance of favour on God's part; while (*d*), *guile*, is an unwillingness on the sinner's part to face the facts of his own sinfulness; this last therefore needs on God's part a kind severity which shall unsparingly bring the truth home. Now, in the attributes of God (Exod. xxxiv. 7) we find that His Nature is to "*forgive guilt, and transgression, and sin, and by no means spare,*" i.e. we find that, in the very Nature of God, a fourfold provision for the fourfold need of man. Compare Pss. cxxx. 4; lxxxv. 2. In the Attributes of God one word is used for "*forgiveth*" (lit. *beareth*) but in our Psalm we have three: 1st the transgression is *forgiven*, i.e. borne and taken away (cf. Is. liii. 4; Joh. i. 29); 2ndly the sin is *covered*, i.e. it is so expiated that it ceases to exist even for God's eye (Ps. lxxxv. 3; Jer. l. 10; Mic. vii. 19); 3rdly the guilt is *not imputed*, as though God Himself had said "Neither do I condemn thee." In the light of this infinite forgiveness the sinner for the first time sees himself, and then "*in his spirit there is no guile.*"

"When once pardon is realized the believer has courage to be truthful before God: he can afford to have done with "*guile*" in the spirit. Who would not declare all his debts when they are certain to be discharged by another? Who would not declare his malady when he was sure of

PSALM XXXII.

(b) Brutish silence dries up the soul as the rainless season does the earth.

3 When I kept silent, my bones were worn away
Through my moaning all the day long.
4 For day and night Thy hand weighed heavy on me,
My moisture was changed into Summer drought.

(c) Manly confession opens the floodgates of pardon.

5 I acknowledged my sin unto Thee,
And my guilt I did not cover.
I said, I will confess my transgressions to YHVH,
And Thou—Thou didst pardon the guilt of my sin!

a cure? True faith knows not only that "guile" before God is impossible, but also that it is no longer necessary. The believer has nothing to conceal: he sees himself before God, stripped, laid open, and bare; and if he has learned to see himself as he is, so also he has learned to see God as He reveals Himself. There is no guile in the spirit of one who is justified by faith; because in the act of justification truth has been established in his inward parts. There is no guile in the spirit of him who sees the truth of himself in the light of the truth of God. For the truth of God shows him at once that in Christ he is perfectly righteous before God, and in himself he is the chief of sinners. Such a one knows that he is not his own, for he is bought with a price, and therefore he is to glorify God! There is no guile in the spirit of him whose real object is to glorify Christ and not himself. But when a man is not quite true to Christ, and has not quite ceased to magnify self, there may be guile, for he will be more occupied with thoughts about himself than with the honour of Christ. But if the truth, and honour, and glory of Christ be his supreme care, he may leave himself out of the question, and, like Christ, "commit himself to Him that judgeth righteously" [J. W. Reeve, quoted in *Treasury of David*, Vol. ii. p. 100].

v. 1. "*Happy is he,* etc." Literally "*Oh the happiness of,* etc." There are three Psalms in the First Collection, which *begin* with this word, viz. Pss. i., xxxii., and xli. Thus it will be noted that the First Collection opens and closes with a Psalm of Beatitude. Of these P's. i., which is really a Preface to the whole Psalter, dwells on the happiness which comes from feeding, as it were, in meditation, on the Law; P's. xxxii. exults in the happiness of the Atonement; while Ps. xli. passes to the happiness which springs from 'taking thought for the poor and needy.' The happiness of Israel through the Law is characteristic of the time of Deuteronomy: "Happy art thou, O Israel; who is like unto thee, O people saved by the Lord" (Deut. xxxiii. 29). This verse must be interpreted from the 12th verse of Psalm xxxiii.

v. 2. "*Happy is man,* etc." The Hebrew word for *man* here is *Adam*, not *Ish* as in P's. i.; there an *individual* case was supposed, but here *Adam* fixes the thought upon *mankind*, for whom an Atonement has been provided if only they will accept its freely offered pardon. Compare St Paul's argument in Rom. iv. 6—8. This Psalm was used on the Day of Atonement, which was a yearly witness to the fact that mankind was forgiven in God: Verses 1, 2 must have been understood by the Jewish Church in the light of that forgiveness.

v. 3. "*When I kept silent.*" Silence here is not opposed to speech, for he was "moaning all the day long." Kay well quotes Hos. vii. 14; "They *cried not to* ME with their heart, when they *howled* upon their beds." Speech is given to man that he may draw near to God with it. If he use it not to this end he is no better than the brutes. Verses 3, 4 should be compared with the corresponding Stanza, *vv.* 8, 9; in the one Stanza the Psalmist was brutish and ignorant as it were a beast before God, and God was compelled to curb him with a heavy hand (*v.* 4), while, in the other Stanza, the Psalmist, having found the joy of pardon, holds up his own past sorrow as a warning (*v.* 8); if God's children would but come to Him there would be no need for the bit and bridle! Many Commentators regard *vv.* 8, 9 as the words of God, but the parallelism of the Stanzas seems to require the interpretation which I have given.

v. 4. "*My moisture...Summer drought.*" If this Psalm were originally written for the Day of Atonement there would be a special fitness in this image since, in Palestine, the six months of the

FIRST COLLECTION. 'DAVIDIC' PSALMS.

(d) Now is the acceptable time.

6 For this let every saint make his prayer to Thee
In the season of finding^a.
Only in the overflowing of the great waters,
They will not reach unto Him^b.

(e₁) More than pardon—sonship.

7 Thou art a Covert for me,
Thou dost preserve me from trouble.
With ringing songs of deliverance
Thou dost compass me round.

(b₁) Man being not a brute but a son must act as such.

8 I instruct thee, I shew thee the way thou should'st go,
I counsel thee, (keeping) mine eye upon thee.
9 Be not ye like horse and mule which have no understanding,
Whose pride must be curbed with bridle^c and bit,
Or they will not come near unto thee.

(a₁) Oh the happiness of the Atonement!

10 Many are the stripes for the wicked,
But he that trusteth in YHVH,
Lovingkindness will compass him round.
11 Rejoice in YHVH and be glad ye righteous,
Ring out with joy all ye that are upright in heart.

---

rainless season practically end at the Autumnal Equinox, the Day of Atonement being the 10th day after the Equinox.

v. 6. The words translated *great waters* or *many waters* occur twenty-six times in the Old Testament, of which eleven are in the Book of Ezekiel. They follow two very opposite lines of thought thus; (A) they denote the *sea* (Ezek. i. 24; xxvi. 19; xxvii. 26; xliii. 2 etc.). The sea being the home of mystery and terror, the "*great waters*" were used of any overflowing calamity (Ps. xviii. 16 (17); cxliv. 7; Cant. viii. 7 etc.). But (B) they denote also the waters as the *source of fruitfulness* (Ezek. xix. 10; xxxi. 5, 7, 14; xxxii. 13; 2 Chron. xxxii. 4 etc.). This thought seems to be characteristic of Ezekiel, and may possibly be traced to his abode in Babylonia. The question now arises in which of the two senses, (A) or (B), are the words to be interpreted in our Psalm? The context must decide. The word "*overflowing*" would seem at first sight to point to the meaning (A), but on the other hand in Job xxxviii. 25 the "*overflowing* of waters" is evidently used in a beneficent sense of the abundant rain (see context); and the reference to "*Summer drought*" in *v.* 4 inclines us, on the whole, to interpret *v.* 6 as of the season of blessing which man would certainly miss unless he had first made his prayer in the 'season of finding.'

The ten days inclusive between New Year's Day and the Day of Atonement were regarded by the Jews as a critical time of Judgement, during which mercy was extended to the sinner; and to these ten days the words of Is. lv. 6 were applied, viz. "Seek ye YHVH while He may be found .. while He is near." [See my translation of the *Yalkut* on Zechariah, pp. 55, 73.] These days were indeed the Rogation days of the Jewish Church. The seventh month was the time when the rains of Palestine should begin after the long months of "Summer droughts."

PSALM XXXIII.

Though Ps. xxxiii. is not alphabetical it has many of the characteristics of the Alphabetical Psalms. Not only do the 22 verses correspond with the number of the letters in the Hebrew Alphabet but the *ten* stanzas remind us of the way in which the number *ten* enters into the formation of the Alphabetical Psalms (see p. 26). Again, Ps. xxxiii. falls into two distinct Parts, which correspond the one to the other exactly in the way which we have traced in the Alphabetical Psalms (p. 26 etc.). Lastly, it is followed by Ps. xxxiv., which is strictly Alphabetical (see p. 30). It is therefore evident that our present Psalm is a connecting link with Alphabetical Psalms, and should be studied in close connexion with Pss. xxv. and xxxiv. (pp. 26, 30).

We now turn to the Psalm itself. Part I (*vv.* 1—11) refers to *God and the World*; Part II (*vv.* 12—22) refers to *God and Israel*. The five Stanzas of Part I answer, Stanza by Stanza, to the five Stanzas of Part II (see marginal notes). But though these Stanzas answer to one another we note that there is also a relation between the first and last Stanzas, and this is a peculiarity which we have had occasion to note in the Alphabetical Psalms (e.g. Ps. xxv., pp. 28 f.). In Part I God is praised as the Creator of the World; in Part II, as the Redeemer of Israel. Part I fixes our attention on the *Word* of God (*vv.* 4, 6, 9, 11); Part II, upon the *Eye* of God (*vv.* 13—15, 18).

In Part I we see that the *Word*, or purpose, of God in Creation, was (*a*) not arbitrary (*vv.* 4, 5); (*b*) that it was Creative without effort (*vv.* 6, 7); (*c*) that it necessarily demands the homage of all created things; (*d*) that any opposition to the Word or purpose of God must be futile.

In Part II we see that the *Eye*, or choice, of God is, in Israel's case, (*a₁*) not arbitrary (*vv.* 13—15); (*b₁*) that it implies all the power Israel can need (*vv.* 16, 17); (*c₁*) that God's Eye of Providential care responds to the eye of Israel's upward look; (*d₁*) that the great purpose of God for Israel cannot ultimately fail.

The reader will observe the relation of the Stanzas (*a*) (*b*) (*c*) (*d*) to (*a₁*) (*b₁*) (*c₁*) (*d₁*) respectively. For purposes of comparison these Stanzas have been printed on opposite pages as in the Alphabetical Psalms.

FIRST COLLECTION, 'DAVIDIC' PSALMS.

PS. XXXIII (*First half*, God and the World).

Prefate.
Israel's joy in Redemption.

1 Ring out with joy, O ye righteous^a, in YHVH;   ^a v. 12 and Ps. xxxii.
  For to the upright psalms^b are well-seemly^b.   ^b Ps. cxlvii.
2 Give thanks to YHVH with the harp,
  Hymn unto Him to the ten-stringed lute:
3 Sing unto Him a New Song,
  Sweet melody with clashing-trumpet-sound^c.   ^c Ps. xxvii. 6 note

(*a*) God's work of Creation is founded upon right, and therefore is stable.

4 For the Word^d of YHVH is right,   ^d Deut. xxxi 4
  And all His work is faithful.
5 He loveth righteousness and justice,
  The earth is full of the loving-kindness of YHVH.

(*b*) The only power in Creation is the breath of God.

6 By the Word of YHVH the heavens were made,
  And all the host of them by the breath of His mouth;
7 Gathering as in a water-skin^e the waters of the sea,   ^e Sept.
  Storing the deeps (as) in a treasure-house.

(*c*) All created things must pay homage.

8 Let all the earth fear before YHVH,
  Let all the inhabitants of the world stand in awe of Him.
9 For He spake and it became!
  He commanded and it stood fast!

(*d*) His purpose alone will last.

10 YHVH bringeth to nought the counsel^f of the heathen,   ^f v. 11
   He frustrateth the thoughts^g of the nations;   ^g v. 11 Sept. has a double reading of the line
11 The counsel of YHVH ever endureth,
   The thoughts of His heart are from age to age.

vv. 1–3. The best comment on these verses is Ps. cl.: Here, as there, we have every kind of music and every kind of song;—in short a Chorus of Creation.

It is perhaps not altogether fanciful to regard the ten Stanzas of the Psalm as the strings of the "*ten-stringed lute.*"

v. 3. "*Sing...a New Song.*" The other passages in which "the New Song" occurs are Is. xlii. 10; Pss. xl. 3 (4); xcvi. 1; xcviii. 1; cxliv. 9; cxlix. 1; Rev. v. 9; xiv. 3. In all these passages we note two characteristics of the 'New Song,' (1) It is always for new mercies, (ii) It is a Chorus of Creation. The old Song was the Song of Moses at the Red Sea. The next great Redemption was the Redemption from Babylon. All the Old Testament passages in which the "New Song" occurs belong, I believe, to this joyous time. The next great Redemption came about 500 years later, not for one Nation only but for the whole world, through Christ; the New Song of this Redemption is given in Rev. v. 9, and is a Chorus in which the Church, Angels, and all created things unite. The final Redemption is yet to come, but St John had a vision of its New Song (Rev. xiv. 1–3; cf. xv. 2, 3).

PS. XXXIII (*Second half*, God and Israel).

Preface.
Blessed is the Nation of God's free choice (cf. Deut. xxxiii. 29).

12 Happy[a] is the Nation whose God is YHVH!
    The People He chose for Himself as His heritage[b]!

[a] Ps. xxxii. 1
[b] Deut. xxxii. 9

(a_1) God's choice of Israel is founded upon right, and therefore is stable.

13 YHVH looked from heaven,
    He saw all the children of men;
14 He looked forth from the place of His dwelling,
    Upon all the inhabitants of the earth;
15 He it is that formeth all their hearts,
    That taketh note of all their doings.

(b_1) Israel's power is not in horses but in the fact of God's choice (cf. Deut. xxxiii. 29).

16 A king is not saved by the greatness of his host[c],
    Nor a warrior delivered by the greatness of his strength.
17 Vain is the horse[d] for victory;
    By mere greatness of power He[e] doth not deliver.

[c] or *power*
[d] Prov. xxi. 31; Ps. cxlvii. 10
[e] or *he*

(c_1) Israel should pay the homage of an expectant eye.

18 Behold the eye of YHVH is towards them that fear Him,
    Towards them that are expectant[f] of His lovingkindness;
19 To deliver their soul from death,
    And to preserve them in life from famine[g].

[f] v. 22
[g] Ps. xxxvii. 19

Conclusion.
(d_1) Israel's expectation of Redemption to come (cf. vv. 1—3 and vv. 10, 11).

20 Our soul waiteth for YHVH,
    Our Help[h] and our Shield[h] is He!
21 For in Him our heart is glad;
    For we trust in His holy Name.
22 Let Thy lovingkindness, O YHVH, be upon us,
    Even as we wait expectant[i] upon Thee.

[h] Deut. xxxiii. 29
[i] v. 18

v. 6. "*By the Word...by the breath.*" There was no effort in Creation. The Yalkut quotes the legend of God creating all things with the letter *Heh*, i.e. with a mere *breathing*, and adds, "He fainteth not, neither is weary" (Is. xl. 28). Creation came into being and continues to exist simply by the will of God.

v. 7. *Gathering as in a water-skin.* So Sept., Sym., Targum; Jerome, "*quasi in utri.*" The usual rendering, "*in a heap*," though it follows the vowel points, must be rejected because of the parallel passages, Job xxxviii. 8, "or (who) shut up the sea with doors, when it brake forth, (as if) it had issued out of the womb." Also v. 37. "Who can number the clouds by wisdom or who can stay (?) the bottles of heaven?" In our Psalm the thought is centred on the Work of the Third Day of Creation, when God restrained the waters:—"Let the waters be gathered together...and let the dry land appear" (cf. Job xxxviii. 8—11). This work was as easy for God as it would be for a man to fill a water-skin.

(Psalm xxxiv. This Alphabetical Psalm is given pp. 30—33.)

PSALM XXXV.

Before discussing the imprecations in this Psalm we should do well to consider the passages in Jeremiah which are strikingly parallel to Ps. xxxv., and indeed to the whole group of Psalms in which it occurs.

The question between Jeremiah and the false prophets (Jer. v. 31; xiv. 14; xxiii. 14 ff.; xxvii. 14; xxix. 8 f.) was one of life or death for Israel. The false prophets carried the People with them when they spoke smooth words of 'peace': but Jeremiah knew, to his own sorrow, that it was too late for peace. Thus to save his People he suffered as a traitor (ch. xxxvii. 14) and was hated by his own. At such a time indignation against false prophets must have been to Jeremiah loyalty to God and man.

The following passages should be carefully considered:

Jer. xviii. vv. 18—23, R.V. "Then said they, Come, let us devise devices against Jeremiah;...Come, and let us smite him with the tongue (cf. Ps. xxxv. 15), and let us not give heed unto any of his words. Give heed to me, O Lord, and hearken to the voice of them that contend with me (cf. Ps. xxxv. 1, note rare word). Shall evil be recompensed for good? for they have digged a pit for my soul (Ps. xxxv. 7). Remember how I stood before Thee to speak good for them, to turn away Thy fury from them (cf. Ps. xxxv. v. 12 f.). Therefore deliver up their children to the famine, etc., etc.... Yet, Lord, Thou knowest all their counsel against me to slay me (cf. Ps. xxxv. 12); forgive not their iniquity (Ps. xxxv. 4), neither blot out their sin from Thy sight; but let them be overthrown (marg. *made to stumble*, cf. Ps. xxxv. 6) before Thee; deal Thou with them in the time of Thine anger."

Jer. xx. vv. 7—13, "O Lord, Thou hast deceived me, and I was deceived;... I am become a laughing-stock all the day, everyone mocketh me (cf. Ps. xxxv. 16, 21, 25)...because the word of the Lord is made a reproach unto me, and a derision all the day. And if I say, I will not make mention of Him, nor speak any more in His name (cf. Ps. xxxix. 1, 2), then there is in mine heart as it were a burning fire shut up in my bones, and I am weary with forbearing, and I cannot *contain* (cf. Ps. xxxix. 3 with Ps. xxxviii. 13). For I have heard the defaming of many, terror on every side (cf. Ps. xxxi. 13). Denounce, and we will denounce him, say all my familiar friends (Ps. xli. 9), they that watch for my halting (Ps. xxxv. 15 and xxxviii. 17); peradventure he will be enticed, and we shall prevail against him, and we shall take our revenge on him. But the Lord is with me as a mighty one *and* a terrible; therefore my persecutors shall stumble, and they shall not prevail: they shall be greatly ashamed,...even with an everlasting dishonour which shall never be forgotten. But, O Lord of hosts,...let me see Thy vengeance on them; for unto Thee have I revealed my cause. Sing unto the Lord, praise the Lord: for He hath delivered the soul of the needy from the hand of evil-doers" (compare the rapid transitions from imprecation to thanksgiving in Ps. xxxv. *vv.* 9 f., 18, 27 f.).

From Chapter xxiii. (*vv.* 9—end) we learn that the indignation of Jeremiah was directed especially against the Prophets who falsely prophesied peace in the name of God. Thus:

Jer. xxxiii. 11, 12, "For both prophet and priest are profane (cf. note on Ps. xxxv. 16);...wherefore their way shall be unto them as slippery places (note rare word) in the darkness; and they shall be driven on and fall therein" (cf. Ps. xxxv. 6 note).

In this Chapter too there is a remarkable passage in which Jeremiah ridicules the use of the phrase, "*Thus saith* (the Lord)" on the lips of these speakers of smooth words. Thus:

v. 31, "Behold, I am against the prophets, saith the Lord, that use their tongues and say, 'He saith'." These are words of ridicule and translation is not easy—literally "who take their tongues and keep 'saith'-ing 'Thus saith'." The margin of the E.V. has "*that smooth their tongues,*" and I think it probable that Jeremiah chose the unusual expression "*take* their tongues" in order to hint at the meaning of the similar sounding word which signified "*to smooth.*" In any case he ridicules their use of the word "*Thus saith.*" This passage has an important bearing on Ps. xxxvi. 1 (see note). Other close parallels (see notes) of thought and language make it highly probable that our Psalm was written by Jeremiah.

When we read the imprecations of the tender-hearted Jeremiah we must "compare them with the bettering of the times," and do him the justice to remember that those who hated him were hating their own good. Still, for us, the fact remains that the One who alone could say "He that hateth me hateth my Father also" (Joh. xv. 22), was the One who "when he was reviled he reviled not again" (1 Pet. ii. 23). In the wise words of Jer. Taylor, "That zeal only is safe, only acceptable, which increases Charity directly; and because love to our Neighbour and obedience to God are the two great portions of Charity, we must never account our zeal to be good, but as it advances both these, if it be in a matter that relates to both; or, severally, if it relates severally. S. Paul's zeal was expressed in preaching without any offerings or stipend, in travelling, in spending and being spent for his flock, in suffering, in being willing to be accursed for the love of the People of God and his Countrymen. Let our zeal be as great as his was, so it be in affections to others, but not at all in angers against them: In the first there is no danger; in the second there is no safety. In brief, let your zeal (if it must be expressed in anger) be always more severe against thy self than against others." (*Holy Living,* Chap. iv. Sect. 3.)

In point of structure our Psalm falls naturally into three Parts, each of which ends in Thanksgiving.

PS. XXXV.

1 O YHVH strive with them that strive with me,
Fight with them that fight with me.
2 Grasp shield and buckler
And rise to my help!
3 Draw out javelin and dirk to oppose my pursuers,
Say unto my soul: "I am thy salvation."
4 Let them be shamed and disgraced that are seeking my life,
Let them be turned back and dishonoured that are planning my hurt.
5 Let them be as the chaff before the wind, and the Angel of YHVH driving[a];   [a] Ps.
6 Let their way be dark and slippery[b], and the Angel of [b] Jer. YHVH pursuing them.
7 For they have wantonly hidden a net for me,
Wantonly have they dug a pitfall[c] for my life!   [c] Jer. 22
8 May a ruin unforeseen come upon him,
His own net that he hid catch himself,
In a ruin whereby he may fall.

Vow of Thanks-giving.

9 So my soul shall exult in YHVH,
Shall be joyous in His salvation.
10 All my bones shall say;
"YHVH who is like unto Thee,
Delivering the sufferer from his too-strong foe,
Yea the sufferer and the poor from his spoiler?"

11 There rise up wrongful witnesses,
Who question me of what I know nothing[d].   [d] cf. J. 13
12 They reward me evil[e] for good[e].   [e] Jer.
To the very bereavement of life.

---

v. 1. "*them that strive with me.*" A rare word, the only other passage (besides Is. xlix. 25) being the parallel passage in Jeremiah (xviii. 19), "Give heed to me, O YHVH, and hearken to the voice of *them that strive with me*" (see context).

v. 6. "*Let their way be dark and slippery.*" The rare reduplicated word which is here translated "*slippery*" occurs only in the parallel passage of Jeremiah (xxiii. 12), "Wherefore their way shall be unto them as *slippery* (ways) in the darkness." In Daniel xi. 21, 34 it is twice used of *flatteries*, i.e. smooth speeches. These passages are significant; like is punished by like; the false prophets who caused others to fall by their *smooth, slippery* tongues shall themselves be set on *slippery* places and driven into darkness. The verse requires a Dante to illustrate it.

PSALM XXXV.

13 As for me, were they ill?—then my clothing was sackcloth,
   My soul I afflicted with fasting,
   And what my prayer was—may it home^a in my bosom^a!   ^a Matt. x. 13; Lk. x. 6
14 As he were my friend or my brother I walked,
   I went bowed as though it were the mourning of^b a mother.   ^b or *for*
15 But, did I halt^c?—they were glad,   ^c Jer. xx. 10
   And gathered and gathered against me,
   Smiting^d me at unawares   ^d i.e. *with the tongue*; Jer. xviii. 18
   They rent me without ceasing;
16 As dissimulators with mocking scoffs,
   They gnash^e their teeth upon me.   ^e Lam. ii. 16

v. 14. "*As though...of a mother.*" The Hebrew may signify either "as one that mourns for a mother" or "as it were a mother that mourneth." The image in the latter case is far more forcible.

v. 15. "*But did I halt?*"—Literally, *on my halting.* Cf. Jer. xx. 10 "All my familiars watched for my *halting.*" Also Ps. xxxviii. 17 (18). Micah had pictured Israel as a *lame sheep* wandering astray and brought back to the fold by God. This name of the lame one, *her that halteth,* left its mark. (See Mic. iv. 6, 7; Zeph. iii. 19 and cf. Gen. xxxii. 31 (32).)

"*Smiting me...*" This form of the word occurs nowhere else. Some give it a passive sense and translate "*abjects*" i.e. *smitten ones.* But the weight of authority goes the other way, Sym. and Targum agreeing with Jerome's translation *percutientes,* i.e. *smiters.* The parallel passage in Jeremiah xviii. 18 ("Come and let us *smite* him with the tongue") strongly confirms the translation we have given.

"*At unawares.*" Lit. "*and I knew it not.*" Three times in the Psalm this phrase occurs, viz. *vv.* 8, 11, 15. A man could scarcely be said to be smitten and not to know it, but he may be either slandered unawares or slandered about things of which he knows nothing (*v.* 11).

St Jerome, applying the words to Christ, says: "Quid non cognoverit, quaeritur. Quidam putant, dolorem vulnerum quae patiebatur in cruce. Sed melius ad peccata refertur: quod non habuerit conscientiam peccatorum quare crucifixus sit" (*Comment. in Psalmos,* Morin, p. 42).

v. 16. *As dissimulators with mocking scoffs.* The Heb. text reads "*with hypocrites of* (or rather *dissimulators of*) *the scoffers of a cake*"; but the Septuagint, instead of *mgog,* "cake," read *lgog,* "mockery," and translate, "they mocked me with mockery." The letters *l* and *m* are easily mistaken in Hebrew manuscript, and I greatly doubt whether the word *cake* had any place in the original Hebrew text. The English words *hypocrite, hypocrisy* do not at all represent the O.T. use of the corresponding words either in the Hebrew or in the Greek. A *hypocrite* in O.T. was one *who led others into apostasy.* Thus:

Prov. xi. 9 "The *hypocrite* (i.e. *the dissimulator*) with his mouth destroyeth his neighbour."

Is. xxxii. 6 "For the vile person...to practise *hypocrisy* (R.V. *profaneness*), to utter error against the Lord, to make empty the soul of the hungry..."

Jer. xxiii. 11, 15 "For both prophet and priest *are profane,*" "For from the prophets of Jerusalem is *profaneness* (marg. E.V. *hypocrisy*) gone forth into all the land." (See context.)

Compare also Dan. xi. 32 "And such as do wickedly against the Covenant *shall he pervert* (marg. R.V. *make profane*) by flatteries."

The meaning is well seen in 11 Macc. vi. 25 where Eleazar says "and so they, by reason of my *dissimulation* (see Greek) and for the sake of this brief and momentary life, should be led astray because of me..."

I conclude that this verse in the Psalm is to be interpreted from the use of the word in the parallel passage of Jeremiah which refers to the false prophets. (See also p. 143.)

The Yalkut quotes a passage from T. B. *Sanhedrin* 52^a which is interesting from the light it throws on the denunciation of the 'false prophets' in 11 Peter and Jude. The passage is to the

                17 O Lord, how long wilt Thou look on?
                   Bring back my soul from this ruin of theirs,
                   My dear-life[a] from the lions.

Vow of Thanks-   18 I will thank Thee in full Congregation[b],
giving.   Will praise Thee among much people.

                19 Let not my causeless[c] enemies be glad,
                   Nor my wanton foes wink with the eye:
                20 For it is no[d] peace they devise,
                   But slanderous devices against the quiet in the land.
                21 They have made mouths at me,
                   They said "Aha! Aha! our eye hath seen[e]!"
                22 Seen hast Thou, O YHVH—keep not silence;
                   O Lord, be not far from me!
                23 Rouse Thee and wake for my right—
                   O my God and my Lord—for my cause!
                24 Judge me in Thy righteousness, O YHVH, my God,
                   And let them not rejoice over me.
                25 Let them not say in their heart "Aha! we have[f] our wish!"
                   Let them not say, "We have devoured him."
                26 Let them be shamed and dishonoured together
                        That rejoice in my misfortune,
                   Let them be clothed with shame and disgrace
                        That exalt themselves against me.

Vow of Thanks-   27 Let them sing and be glad that delight in my right,
giving.   Let them ever say "YHVH be magnified,"
                   Who delights in His servant's well-being.
                28 And my tongue too shall muse of Thy kindness,
                   Yea, all the day long of Thy praise.

---

following effect. Resh Laqish quotes this verse of our Psalm to explain the fate of Korah, the "*hypocrisy*" of Korah being shewn "in the matter of eating," and thus it was a fitting punishment that "the prince of Gehinnom should *gnash* (with a play upon the name *Korah*) upon them with his teeth." The rare word for "*eating*" occurs again T. B. *Sanhedrin* 103[b], "Great is eating (? hospitality) since it removed two tribes from Israel" (see Buxtorf *s.v.* לינמה); the two tribes being Ammon and Moab, of whom it is said that they are not to enter the Congregation of the Lord, "Because they met you not with bread and with water in the way" (Deut. xxiii. 3 f.).

PSALM XXXVI.

This Psalm consists of two Parts linked together by the three concluding verses (10—12).

Part I (*vv.* 1—4) depicts the downward progress of the unbeliever by four steep steps; *action* (Stanza I.) deepening in each case into its corresponding *character* (Stanza II.). The relation of the four lines of Stanza I. to the four lines of Stanza II. may be indicated as follows (see also marginal notes):

(*a*) Secret pleasure in an act which he knows to be forbidden.
(a^1) Open pleasure in evil for its own sake.

(*b*) God's judgements have no terror for him.
(b^1) He deliberately sets himself to choose the wrong way.

(*c*) He comes to persuade himself that there is no such thing as retribution.
(c^1) He plans evil upon his bed. (Contrast Ps. lxiii. 6 (7).)

(*d*) Transgression which began by being cherished in the heart comes out on the lips—the man has become a scoffer.
(d^1) He loses the spiritual insight whereby good is discerned.

We have here inverted the order of Stanza II. in order to shew the relation between (*a*) and (a^1), (*b*) and (b^1) etc.; the order in the Psalm is, however, the true order by which acts become character—"Pharaoh hardened his heart—and the heart of Pharaoh was hardened."

Part II (*vv.* 5—9) also consists of two Stanzas, the first of which gives four Attributes of God in four consecutive lines, while the second Stanza answers to the first, line by line, shewing the bearing of these four Attributes upon the world of men. The relation of these two Stanzas has been fully treated in the notes.

The Psalm concludes with *vv.* 10—12 which serve to supply a connexion, not otherwise evident, between Parts I and II (see Notes). The juxtaposition of Parts I and II thus brings into sharp contrast the evil of the bad man and the goodness of God and reminds us of Ps. lii. 1, "Why boastest thou thyself in evil, O tyrant? The Lovingkindness of God is for all time." (See context and notes.)

PS. XXXVI (PART I).

The sinner's downward progress in action.	*a* 1 Transgression is pleasant to the wicked in his[a] inmost heart,	[a] Sept. Syr. Vulg.
	b There is no dread of God before his eyes.	cf. Ps. x. xiv. 1
	c 2 For he flatters himself (that there is none) to find[b] and hate his iniquity,	[b] Gen. xliv. 1 Hos. xii. (9)
	d The words of his mouth are mischief and fraud[c].	[c] Ps. x. 7
The sinner's downward progress in *character*.	*d¹* He has ceased to be wise in well-doing;	
	c¹ 4 He devises mischief upon his bed[d],	[d] Mic. ii. 1
	b¹ He takes his stand in a way the reverse of good,	
	a¹ Evil he anything but abhorreth!	

v. 1. The Hebrew text, as it stands, is extremely difficult; we should have to translate "*Thus saith Transgression in the midst of my* (or, following the Versions, *his*) *heart.*" This might be paraphrased, *There is an Oracle of Transgression*, etc., i.e. there is an inner voice which is not the 'Thus saith' of God but the 'Thus saith' of the Devil. We have already seen (p. 143) that, in Jeremiah's time, the cant use of the word "*Thus saith*" (neum) on the lips of the false prophets had moved his indignation: "Behold, I am against the prophets, saith the Lord, that take their tongues and keep saying 'Thus saith'" (Jer. xxxiii. 31). We have also traced the influence of Jeremiah in this group of Psalms. If therefore the present text is to stand we must explain it as a direct allusion to Jeremiah's denunciation of the false prophets in Chapter xxxiii.

I have however ventured, with some hesitation, to adopt the reading suggested by Graetz, i.e. to change the letter א into ע and thus to get the word "*pleasant*" instead of "*Thus saith.*"

This seems to me to be the best solution of the difficulty and it is borne out by the parallelism of the lines which I have marked *a* and *a¹*. If this view be adopted we may compare Prov. ix. 17, where the tempting voice persuades the sinner that secret indulgence is "pleasant."

"*There is no dread of God*..." The word here used for *fear* is quite distinct from that "*fear*" of the Lord which is the beginning of wisdom. The sinner has so put God out of his life that he has lost even the *dread* of judgement.

The nearest parallel to this verse is Ps. x. 5 "Far above, out of sight are Thy judgements." The way in which this self-delusion may come about is depicted in Deut. xxix. 19 f. Tennyson saw that the danger was real for us all "This is a terrible age of unfaith,...One can easily lose all belief, through giving up the continual thought and care for spiritual things" (*A Memoir*, Vol. I. p. 309).

v. 3. "*He has ceased to be wise in well-doing.*" Kay translates "He has ceased to have discernment to do good," i.e. "His *discernment* is only on the side of evil. Cp. Rom. xvi. 19."

v. 4. "*He takes his stand*, etc." i.e. he makes a deliberate choice of the way of death (cf. Ps. i.).

v. 4. "*Evil he anything but abhorreth*," i.e. he dearly loves it. In the corresponding line of *v.* 1 we saw that the single *act* of transgression was pleasant to him: but now the act, by repetition, has become character: he not only does such things but finds his pleasure in evil (cf. Rom. i. 32). This is the lowest stage of the sinner's progress.

PS. XXXVI (PART II, possibly a separate Psalm).

Four Attributes of God.
- (α) 5 YHVH, up to Heaven is Thy LOVINGKINDNESS[a];   [a] Ps. lxxxix. 2 (3)
- (β) Thy FAITHFULNESS[a] to the skies;
- (γ) 6 Thy RIGHTEOUSNESS as the Mountains of God[b],   [b] Ps. civ. 16
- (δ) Thy JUDGEMENTS (are) like the great Deep[c].   [c] Ps. lxxviii. 15

Both man and beast Thou, YHVH, wilt save.

The relation of these four Attributes to men.
- (α¹) 7 How precious[d] is Thy Lovingkindness, O God!   [d] Ps. cxxxix. 17; Is. xxviii. 16
- (β¹) So the sons of men may shelter[e] neath the shadow of Thy wings[e];   [e] Ruth ii. 12
- (γ¹) 8 They are full-fed from the rich-provision[f] of Thy House,   [f] fatness, Jer. xxxi. 14
- (δ¹) And from Thine Eden-stream Thou givest them drink.

9 For with Thee is the Fountain[g] of Life,   [g] Jer. ii. 13; xvii. 13; xviii. 14
And in thy Light we see light.

v. 6. The Yalkut suggests the thought that as the *Mountains* restrain the *Deep* so God's *Righteousness* restrains His *Judgements*. R. Judah says "Except Thy Righteousness had been as the Mountains of God who could abide Thy Judgements, the Great Deep?"

"*Both man and beast.*" Have we any right to place a limit to the power and goodness of God or to assert that in the future man only can share it? (Compare note on Ps. cxlv. 12, p. 66.)

v. 8. "*From Thine Eden-stream Thou givest them drink.*" The reference is to the River of Paradise is quite unmistakeable. This River, with its four streams, was treated by Ezekiel as an allegory. He saw it (Chap. xlvii.) coming forth from the Altar—for the Will of God involves Sacrifice—He saw it encompass the whole Land and carry life wherever it went, making it once more a Paradise—for only when the Will of God is done can man find the joy he was made for. This Will of God which begins in Sacrifice and ends in joy is God's "Eden-stream." There is One who drank of that Cup—"The Cup which my Father hath given me, shall I not drink of it?" —and found the joy,—the Paradise regained. Since then one of His servants saw that Eden-stream coming forth, not from an Altar, but "from the throne of God and of the Lamb" (Rev. xxii. 1). The Cup should remind us of the joy of Christ as well as of the blood of Christ.

vv. 5, 7; (α) with (α¹), "*YHVH, up to Heaven is Thy Lovingkindness,*" "*How precious is Thy Lovingkindness...*" The Lovingkindness of God is that Attribute which expresses His eternal purpose for man, which no ingratitude on man's part can ultimately turn aside (see Exod. xxxiv. 6, 7; Ps. lxxxix. 28 (29), 33 (34), etc.). This *mercy* or *lovingkindness* therefore "endureth for ever." The Psalmist sees this quality of Divine Mercy reaching "up to Heaven" as a safe Refuge (cf. Ps. lxxxix. 2) for the littleness of man, therefore he cries "*How precious,* etc." The word "*precious,*" in Hebrew, signifies that which is *weighty, reliable*; thus the "*precious* corner stone" (Is. xxviii. 16) is that which is a safe foundation (cf. 1 Pet. ii. 4, 6, 7). This last passage shews us the Psalmist's vision fulfilled in Christ; God's Attribute of *lovingkindness* was, in Old Testament times, seen as the Foundation-stone of the Universe, but to us it has been revealed as "a *living Stone.*"

(β) with (β¹), "*Thy Faithfulness to the skies,*" "*So the sons of men may shelter neath the shadow of Thy wings.*" God's *Faithfulness,* which is often coupled with His *Lovingkindness,* represents the same thought from a somewhat sterner point of view; we might illustrate *lovingkindness* by the love of a mother, *faithfulness* by that of a father. The *faithfulness* of God is often used in connexion or with

150   FIRST COLLECTION, 'DAVIDIC' PSALMS.

Conclusion linking Part I with Part II.

10 Continue Thy Lovingkindness to them that know Thee,
And Thy Righteousness to the upright of heart.
11 Let not the foot of pride come upon me,
Nor the hand of the wicked make me an exile.

The Prayer of Ps. xxxv. 5 is suddenly answered.

12 There are they fallen—those workers of wickedness!
They are driven^a—they cannot rise!   ^a Ps.

reference to God's great purpose either in Creation or in the Call of Israel (see Pss. xxxiii. 4; xxxvii. 3; lxxxix. 2, 5, 8, 14, 33; xcviii. 3; c. 5; and cf. 1 Cor. i. 9; 1 Thess. v. 24; etc.). Because of this sure purpose of God, "*the sons of men may shelter neath the shadow of (His) wings.*" Taking shelter under God's wings means such a life-choice as Ruth made (Ruth ii. 12). The verb is used again in connexion with God's wings in Pss. lvii. 1 (2); lxi. 4 (5); xci. 4.

vv. 6, 8; (γ) with (γ¹), "*Thy Righteousness as the mountains of God,*" "*They are full-fed with the rich-provision of Thy House.*" The Mountains of God here signify not merely high mountains but also Nature's Sanctuaries; the mountains both protect and fertilize the valleys; thus in another Psalm (lxxii. 3) it is said, "The mountains shall bring peace to the people and the hills (shall flow down) with righteousness."

The verb we have translated "*they are full-fed*" is specially used of being *full to saturation*; thus, of rain *abundantly watering* the earth (Ps. lxv. 10 (11); Is. lv. 10; lviii. 11, etc.). Hence it is applied to the soul three times in Jer. xxxi. (*vv.* 12, 14, 25), "And their soul shall be as a *watered* garden," "And I will *satiate* the soul of the priests with fatness," "For I have *satiated* the weary soul..." Thus a lovely image from Nature is transferred to the spiritual life; as the streams from the mountains fill the lowlands with plenty, so from God's Sanctuary-Home the hearts of men shall be abundantly satisfied with Righteousness. "Blessed are they that hunger and thirst after Righteousness, for they shall be filled."

(δ) with (δ¹), "*Thy Judgements (are) like the great Deep,*" "*And from Thine Eden-stream Thou givest them drink.*" As, in *v.* 5, God's *Faithfulness* represented the sterner side of His *Lovingkindness*, so here, in *v.* 6, His *Judgements* represent that *Justice* which is the sterner side of His *Righteousness*. They are compared to the *Great Deep*, i.e. the infinite waters out of which all things had their being (Gen. vii. 11; Ps. lxxviii. 15; Is. li. 10; Amos vii. 4).

At first sight it may seem strange that the "Great Deep" of God's "Judgements" should be coupled with the "River of His pleasures," i.e. the stream that waters His own Paradise. But is it not most true that God's own Life and Joy is in *giving forth* life to every creature? "Both man and beast Thou YHVH wilt save," "For with Thee is the Fountain of Life..." If this be so, then this *giving forth* must be 'the River of His Own Paradise.' Of this River He must, if He love men, 'give them to drink.' To us this *giving forth* means *sacrifice*, but some, like James Hinton, have seen that the infinite capacity for sacrifice (the *Great Deep*) is the pledge of the unending ever-springing Joy (the *Eden-stream*) in the Life to come.

Thus (δ) and (δ¹) will ultimately be reconciled, for, as Tennyson once said, (see *Memoir*, Vol. I. p. 466):

"...the great deeps of Eternity
Roar only round the wasting cliffs of Time."

It is a favourite thought with Jeremiah (see marginal references) that God is the "Fountain of the water of Life"; those therefore who forsake God forsake their own life. The ritual of the Water-drawing Festival was intended to perpetuate this thought (see on St John vii. 37 ff.).

vv. 10—12. These verses may very possibly have been added by a later Psalmist. They link together Parts I and II, compare *Lovingkindness* and *Righteousness v.* 10 with Part II, *vv.* 5, 6, 7; also the reference to the wicked, *vv.* 11, 12 with Part I, *vv.* 1—4. The unusual word '*driven*' (i.e. as *outcasts*) certainly has reference to the 5th verse of the preceding Psalm and is the fulfilment of the imprecation there denounced (see note and compare Jer. xxiii. 12). The words "*they cannot rise*" (*v.* 12) carry our thoughts to Ps. i. 5, which Psalm is also recalled by *v.* 4.

(Ps. xxxvii. is among the Alphabetical Psalms. See pp. 34—39.)

PSALM XXXVIII.

The title "*for the Memorial*" or "*to make remembrance*" which occurs here and in Ps. lxx. gives the key to the interpretation. This word was used especially of *calling* sin *to remembrance*. There was a deep sense of conviction among the Hebrews that sin might slumber only to wake up to more terrible retribution, e.g. 1 Kings xvii. 18 "art thou come unto me to *call my sin to remembrance*, and to slay my son": cf. Gen. xli. 9, Ezek. xxi. 24 (29). So the trial of jealousy (Numb. v. 15) was intended to bring home the guilt "it is...an offering *of memorial, bringing iniquity to remembrance*."

For this same end the Day of Atonement was instituted whereby there was "a *remembrance* of sins made every year" (Heb. x. 3); not merely to *remind* man or to *remind* God but to offer to God such recognition as might prevent the accumulated weight of unacknowledged sin from crushing out the life of Israel. Christ's word has changed this "*remembrance of sins*" into the "*remembrance of Me*" (Luke xxii. 19; 1 Cor. xi. 25).

There was another, still more technical, sense of the word *memorial* (*azkara*) in which it was applied to that particular handful of the *meal-offering* which was burnt with frankincense on the altar, i.e. the sample which by its acceptance shewed that the whole offering was accepted by God: this sample was called the "*memorial*" or "*remembrance*" (Lev. ii. 2, 9, 16; v. 12; vi. 15; xxiv. 7; Numb. v. 26).

The Targum actually translates the heading of our Psalm in this sense "*The handful of frankincense, the good memorial for Israel.*" By mentioning frankincense the Targum limits the thought of the *memorial* (*azkara*) by excluding the sin-offering, in which case no frankincense was offered (Lev. v. 12; cf. Numb. v. 26). The Targum would thus imply that Israel was 'a sweet savour, acceptable unto God.'

The Septuagint (εἰς ἀνάμνησιν περὶ σαββάτου) still further limits the thought of the *azkara* or *memorial* by the strange addition relating to the Sabbath. These words must refer to the *memorial of the Shew-bread* which was offered every Sabbath. Thus (Lev. xxiv. 5—8, R. V.) "And thou shalt take fine flour, and bake twelve cakes thereof: two tenth parts of an ephah shall be in one cake. And thou shalt set them in two rows, six on a row, upon the pure table before the Lord. And thou shalt put pure frankincense upon each row that it may be to the bread for a *memorial* (*azkara*, ἀνάμνησιν) even an offering made by fire unto the Lord. Every sabbath day he shall set it in order before the Lord continually; it is on the behalf of the children of Israel, an everlasting covenant."

There is no need to limit the meaning of the *Azkara* either by following the Septuagint or the Targum; the wider meaning of the Hebrew Title is far better.

It will be noticed that the word *azkara* never represents an animal sacrifice but always refers to the *meal-offering*, i.e. the oblation of the fruits of the earth. Was the crushed corn felt to be a type of those sufferings through which alone the true Israel was to become the Bread of the Presence for God and the Bread of Life for the World? If so we not only see the meaning of this Psalm but we also obtain fresh light on the institution of the Holy Communion (Luke xxii. 19) "And He took bread...saying, This is My body which is given for you: this do in *remembrance* of Me (εἰς τὴν ἐμὴν ἀνάμνησιν)."

Though two Psalms only bear this title of *Remembrance*-Psalms there are clearly many others belonging to the same class, and indeed the Chronicler in dividing the Psalms under three heads places these *Remembrance*-Psalms first :—" And he appointed, of the Levites,...to *make remembrance*, and to thank and to praise..." (1 Chron. xvi. 4). [See further on the structure of the *Hodu* and *Hallelujah* Psalms.]

From the above remarks it will follow that the characteristics we should expect to find in the *Remembrance*-Psalms would be (*a*) *a deep sense of the utter unworthiness of the best that man can give: coupled with* (*b*) *an assurance that somehow God has, by sample, accepted of man's gift.*

This Psalm may be divided into *five* Stanzas of *four* verses each followed by a half Stanza of prayer in two verses, the total number of verses being equal to the number of letters in the Alphabet (compare the first 22 verses of Ps. xxii.).

In the first Stanza the Sufferer complains of the deep *inward* sense of guilt.

The second Stanza shews us the *outward* result in "wounds and bruises and festering sores" (Is. i. 6).

In the third Stanza a still lower depth of sorrow is reached; a deep darkness, but a darkness which heralds sunrise; for in it we see that the inward sense of guilt (Stanza I) and the temporal consequences (Stanza II) have taken from the Sufferer all self-trust (*vv.* 9 and 10), all friends (*v.* 11), and left him naked to his enemies (*v.* 12). This is the middle Stanza of the five, and from this point onwards the light, though faint, begins to break.

In the fourth Stanza the Sufferer gives the reason for his silence: he feels that "Merit lives from man to man but not from man, O God, to Thee"—thus he is "silent" even to the injustice of his foes, because he feels that, inasmuch as God permits it, it may, to him, be regarded as "God's doing" (Ps. xxxix. 9). He thus commits himself to Him that judgeth righteously in the full assurance that God would "*answer for him.*"

The fifth Stanza reminds us of the *cruelty* of the foe, as in Ps. xxii., and the Psalm closes with the actual refrain of Ps. xxii. "*Be not far.*"

PS. XXXVIII.

<small>Israel, as a son, accepts chastisement from his Father's hand.</small>

1 "Oh YHVH convict me not in Thine anger,
  Chastise me not in Thy fury"[a];   *Ps. vi. 1
2 For Thine arrows press into me,
  Thy hand presseth upon me.
3 No soundness is there in my flesh because of Thy wrath;
  No health is there in my bones because of my sin:
4 For mine iniquities are gone over my head[b];   [b] Lam. iii. 54;
  As a heavy burden they are too heavy for me to bear.   Ezra ix. 6

<small>The sufferings of Israel depicted as bodily sickness.</small>

5 My stripes[c] are loathsome, are festered, because of my folly: [c] Is. i. 6
6 I am bent[d], am bowed[e] very low,   [d] Lam. iii. 9 (Heb.)
  I go mourning[e] all the day long.   [e] Ps. xxxv. 14
7 For my loins are full of burning,
  And there is no soundness[f] in my flesh: [f] Is. i. 6
8 I am enfeebled and crushed very sore;
  I have roared through my heart's unrest.

v. 1. This Psalm is the third of the 'Penitential' Psalms and is one of the Proper Psalms for Ash-Wednesday. In the Latin Use it is appointed for Good Friday.

The first verse is practically identical with the first verse of Ps. vi. and the Introduction to that Psalm should be read before studying the present Psalm. The standpoint of the Psalm is clearly that of Jeremiah xxx. 11—17. God there promises that the judgement on Israel, though severe, shall be different altogether in kind from that of the Nations of the World "for I will make a full end of all the nations...but I will not make a full end of thee; but I will *chastise* thee with judgement and will in no wise leave thee unpunished (Marg. R.V. *hold thee guiltless*). For thus saith YHVH, Thy hurt is incurable (cf. Mic. i. 9) and thy wound grievous. There is none to plead thy cause: for (thy) wound thou hast no medicines (nor) plaister (cf. Is. i. 6 and *vv.* 3—8 of our Psalm). All thy lovers have forgotten thee (cf. Psalm *v.* 11), they seek thee not for I have wounded thee with the wound of an enemy &c." This passage, which should be studied as a whole, ends as it began, with words of promise. Jeremiah's view of God's *chastisements* may also be gathered from Chaps. x. 24; xxxi. 18; xlvi. 28. This view agrees with Deut. viii. 5 "As a man *chastiseth* his son, so the Lord thy God *chastiseth* thee."

The constant allusions in this Psalm to bodily sufferings, wounds, and even leprosy (*v.* 11) must not lead us to think of an individual sufferer. The references given in the margin will abundantly prove that such language was constantly used of the sufferings of Israel. Lamentations, Chap. III. should especially be studied from this point of view as it is throughout closely parallel with our Psalm and must have been written under similar circumstances if not by the same Author.

v. 8. "*I have roared through my heart's unrest.*" Literally "*I have roared with the roaring of my heart.*" The two words for roaring are from different roots but both are commonly used of the roaring of a lion (see however Ps. xxii. 1 (2); xxxii. 3); this being so, many commentators (Hitzig, Wellhausen, Graetz, Baethgen &c.) change *lbi* "my heart" into *lbia* "a lion." As the next word in the Hebrew begins with the letter *a* no change of the text would be needed. If this be adopted we should have to translate "*I have roared with the roaring of a lion.*"

K.   20

154   FIRST COLLECTION, 'DAVIDIC' PSALMS.

Forsaken like a leper!

9 O Lord, before Thee lies my whole desire,
  My sighing is no secret from Thee.
10 My heart fluttereth, my strength hath left me,
  The light of mine eyes—they are mine no more!
11 My lovers and friends stand aloof from my plague [a],
  And my kinsmen stand afar off.
12 They that seek after my life lay their snares;
  [They that seek my hurt plan destructions] [b]
  And meditate their guile all the day long.

Dumb before his accusers, but not dumb to God (see next Psalm).

13 While I—like the deaf—must hear nothing,
  Like the dumb that cannot open his mouth [c]:
14 I am become as a man without hearing,
  In whose mouth there is no reply,
15 Because to Thee, YHVH, my hope is directed;
  'Tis Thou [d] shalt give the answer O Lord my God.
16 I said, "Let them not rejoice over me";
  When my foot slipped they would magnify themselves against me.

How deeply he feels their cruel ingratitude.

17 For I am ready to fall [e],
  And my grief is ever before me.
18 For my guilt I proclaim,
  And am troubled because of my sin.

---

vv. 17—20. *"For I am ready to fall."* Literally *"I am established for halting."* The paradox is, I think, intentional, and is characteristic of the Book of Job. The word *established* signifies that which is *stable*; fixed as it were on a firm basis (Judg. xvi. 26, 29; 1 Sam. vii. 16, 26; Deut. xiii. 14 (15) &c.). It is as though he said 'the only thing stable in my life is its instability, the only certainty is the certainty of falling.' The parallel passages in Job are the following:—xv. 23 "He knoweth that the day of darkness is *ready* (i.e. an appointed certainty) at his hand"; xviii. 12 "And calamity shall be *ready for his halting.*" Compare also the difficult passage Job xii. 5.

The last word *"to fall"* or *"for halting"* is also strange and only occurs in this sense in the following passages: Job xviii. 12 (quoted above); Ps. xxxv. 15 and Jer. xx. 10 "all my familiar friends, they that watch for my *halting.*" Thus again we are reminded that the present group of Psalms (xxxi.—xli.) has many points of contact, both in thought and language, with the writings of Jeremiah. The problem Jeremiah had to solve was to reconcile the sufferings of Israel with the goodness of God. To us the thought of 'medicinal chastisement' has become a commonplace, at least in theory, but it was not so in the days of Jeremiah and Job.

There is nothing inconsistent between the consciousness of guilt (*vv.* 17, 18) and the assertion of innocence (*vv.* 19, 20). Israel was guilty before God but innocent before the nations of the world. We have already seen how deeply Jeremiah felt the ingratitude of those whom he had striven to help (see p. 142). This went beyond any mere personal feeling: he spoke for God and was hated *because of his following what was good* (*v.* 20). Thus he became the conscious type of the Suffering Servant.

PSALM XXXIX.

19 But my enemies live and are mighty,
And my causeless[a] foes are many.
20 Yea, rendering me evil for good,
They play the adversary because of my following good.

Prayer as in Ps. xxii. "Be not far."
21 Forsake me not O YHVH;
My God, BE NOT FAR from me.
22 Haste Thee to help me
O Lord, my Salvation.

v. 20 f. After our 20th verse a whole line is added in one important MS of the Psalter (Psalterium Graeco-Latinum Veronense) and other ancient authorities, to the following effect " *And they cast out me* (?), *the Beloved, as an abominable corpse.*" It is difficult to see how this line could have originated unless there had been at one time a corresponding line in the Hebrew. The nearest parallel is Is. xiv. 19 "And thou art *cast* out from thy sepulchre like *an abominable branch* (?) (Sept. "*an abominable corpse*")." The Hebrew scholar will do well to read the notes in Field's Hexapla on this verse and also on our Psalm. The original Hebrew for the *Beloved* may have been *Dod* (see Is. v. 1, Heb. and Sept.). I would suggest השליכו אתי דוד כנצר נתעב.

If such a text as this ever existed it would of course lend itself to an obvious Christian interpretation since *Nazareth* is derived from *Nezer* "a branch (?)" and Christians were known by this name of contempt among the Jews. Certainly such a text is in entire harmony with the context, since *v.* 20 (see note) had fixed our thoughts on the cruel ingratitude of these enemies of goodness. Compare also Ps. xxxi. 12.

PSALM XXXIX.

The Title of this Psalm ascribes it both to 'Jeduthun' and to 'David,' the other Psalms bearing Jeduthun's name being Pss. lxii. and lxxvii. which are very similar in tone (see marginal references) treating as they do of the shortness of man's life in the presence of God's Eternity. The meaning of 'Jeduthun' was obscure in quite early times, indeed in the Titles of Pss. lxii., lxxvii. he would seem to have become either a musical instrument or the name of a tune. An earlier tradition however identifies 'Jeduthun' with the sons of 'Asaph' (1 Chron. xvi. 42; xxv. 3; 11 Chron. xxxv. 15; Neh. xi. 17). Now I have already shewn[1] that the '*Asaph*' guild of singers was closely associated with the '*Asiph*' i.e. with the "*Ingathering*" which is called by this name (Exod. xxiii. 16; xxxiv. 22). This Feast was, in later times, identified with *Tabernacles*, but originally it referred to the death of the old year at the Autumnal Equinox and to the "Ingathering" of the fruits of the earth. Thus: Exod. xxiii. 16 "And the

---
[1] See Hulsean Lectures on the '*Asaph*' Psalms.

156   FIRST COLLECTION, 'DAVIDIC' PSALMS.

Feast of *Asiph* at the going out of the year when thou *ingatherest* all thy labours from the field." The other passage fixes the *Asiph* still more precisely at the Equinox, Exod. xxxiv. 22, "And the Feast of *Asiph* at the turning-point of the year" (see Hebrew).

The Present Psalm is fitly used in our Burial Service, but it is even more suitable for a meditation on the death of the old year and on that final *Ingathering* when we shall "ingather all our labours."

> "Time is fled that fleeted so fast:
> All the unmended remains unmended,
> The perfect, perfect: all lots are cast.
>
> Waiting till earth and ocean be rended,
> Waiting for call of the trumpet blast,
> Each soul at goal of the way it wended,
> Man's harvest is past."
>   (C. ROSSETTI.)

Nothing can be more pathetic than the way in which the Psalmist lays the span-long life of man at the feet, as it were, of God's Eternity. The immediate cause of his trouble is the method of God's judgements (see note, *v.* 1 f. and compare the parallel Jeduthun-Psalm, Ps. lxxvii.). He *knows* that God does all things well but the present is terribly hard to bear (cf. *In Memoriam*). He would fain be silent (*vv.* 2, 9), for he fears 'to put in words the grief he feels': but, alas, he is forced to speak (*v.* 3): his plea is the shortness of life, he cannot afford to wait (*vv.* 4—6). "*Mere vanity and nothing more is all man's lot.*" The second part of the Psalm begins with *v.* 7; the Psalmist reminds himself that God is the expectation of Israel; but, even so, he fears lest failing faith should leave him as a byword to the godless (*v.* 8): he prays therefore, in the spirit of Pss. vi. 1; xxxviii. 1, that God would moderate his chastisement (*vv.* 10, 11) and concludes with the same sad refrain with which he had closed the first part of the Psalm, "*Mere vanity and nothing more is all man's lot.*" The third part consists only of two verses (*vv.* 12, 13) of fervent prayer, in which the Psalmist throws the whole burden of his sorrow upon the heart of God and appeals as Time's pilgrim to the hospitality of the Eternal. It is a significant fact that the sad refrain is not repeated after this prayer. The whole Psalm is full of allusions to the Book of Job and I could wish that the reader, before entering upon it, would study the noble Chapter in Dr Fairbairn's "*City of God*" in which he discusses the "*Problem of Job.*"

The Book of Deuteronomy had seemed to promise temporal prosperity as the reward of obedience; but the death of Josiah at Megiddo (B.C. 609), and the Captivity that shortly followed, had created a terrible reaction in the minds of men. The old traditional theology, so well represented by Job's friends, was no longer adequate to meet all the facts of life. A new truth must be reached. The man who shall reach it must, like Job, dare to be true to *all* the facts, even though he should seem to be a blasphemer. This lot, with all its sorrows, fell to Jeremiah and marked him out in in a special way as *the* Prophet of Israel. Is there not a lesson here for our own times?

PS. XXXIX.

I was sore troubled to understand God's judgements and would fain be silent before them,

1 I said I will keep guard on my ways
So as not to sin with my tongue;
I will keep guard on my mouth with a bridle
While the wicked remains before me.

2 I was utterly dumb[a],
Was silent from good
Though my pain moved me greatly:

but silence was impossible.

3 My heart grew hot within me.
As I mused the fire[b] kindled,
So I spake with my tongue.

v. 1 f. The sorrow of the Psalmist arose from beholding the prosperity of the wicked coupled with the afflictions of Israel. This sorrow may best be explained from the words of Jer. xii. 1, "Righteous art thou, O YHVH, when I plead with Thee: yet would I reason the cause with Thee: wherefore doth the way of the wicked prosper? wherefore are all they at ease that deal very treacherously?" (Compare the sorrow of 'Asaph' in Ps. lxxiii. 1—16.) Jeremiah felt this most acutely. How should he vindicate the ways of God to men? The triumph of evil seemed to make his whole message a mockery, "The word of YHVH is made a reproach unto me, and a derision, all the day. And if I say, I will not make mention of Him, nor speak any more in His Name, then He became in mine heart as it were a burning fire shut up in my bones, and I am weary with forbearing and I cannot refrain" (Jer. xx. 8, 9). This sorrow even led him, like Job, to curse the day of his birth (*vv.* 15—18). The Psalmist does not go so far as this, but his words, which are full of allusions to the Book of Job (see note on *v.* 13), shew that the thought of Job is ever present to his mind.

v. 2. "*Was silent from good.*" The words are possibly an abbreviation of the phrase "*from good to ill*" as in Gen. xxxi. 24, "Take heed to thyself that thou speak not with Jacob *good or bad* (lit. 'from good to bad')." It must however be observed that, in the parallel passage which we have just quoted from Jeremiah, the Prophet had declared his resolve "*not to make mention*" of God or "*to speak any more in His name*"; i.e. he had resolved to give up his work for God because of the difficulties of life! This was indeed to be "silent from good"!

v. 3. "*As I mused*" lit. "*in my meditation.*" The word only occurs here and in Ps. v. 1 (2). Graetz suggests an alteration of the text, which he defends from the Peschito, reading "*in my body.*" If this were accepted we should obtain a still more striking parallel to the words of Jer. xx. 9, "then He became in *mine heart* as it were a burning fire shut up in *my bones*," for we should then translate, "*My heart* grew hot within me, The fire kindled in *my body.*" There is, however, no need to make any change in the text, the parallelism is complete without it; "*my heart grew hot*" hints at the conception of a thought and thus corresponds with "*as I mused*" in the second line.

"*So I spake with my tongue.*" Are we to limit this utterance by placing in inverted commas the few words that follow? Shall we not rather say that, as before the Prophet had refused to speak for God, so now, the very discipline of pain had created and compelled new revelation. From one point of view the words which follow are indeed wrung from him by sheer stress of anguish, but from a higher point of view the sorrow is not fruitless. Like Job he suffers and like Job he "beats his music out." When the long-cherished hopes of earthly prosperity were shattered Israel began to understand more of the Life beyond. We catch just a glimpse of this in *v.* 12 and in the fact that the refrain is not repeated at the close of the Psalm. The burning questions of one age become truisms in the next.

Oh God, life is too short to wait!

4 O YHVH, make me know mine end
The measure of my days, what it may be!
Fain would I know how frail I am!
5 Lo! spans-long hast Thou made my days,
And my life-time, in Thy sight^a, is nothing!
6 Merely in a semblance doth man go about,
Merely for a breath are they in turmoil.
He heapeth^b up but knoweth not who shall ingather^c!
₇ MERE^d VANITY AND NOTHING MORE IS ALL MAN'S LOT.

God Himself is my expectation but alas! I am well nigh crushed with His chastisements.

7 And now what is it that I wait^e for, Lord^f?
My hope, it turns to Thee.
8 Deliver me from all my transgressions,
Make me not as a byword to the fool^g.
9 (I am dumb^h and open not my mouth
Because it was Thou that didstⁱ it.)
10 Take Thy plague from off me,
I am consumed by the weight^j of Thy hand^k.
11 With chastisements of sin Thou punishest man,
Thou makest, like the moth, his delights to melt away.
MERE^l VANITY AND NOTHING MORE IS ALL MAN'S LOT.

---

v. 6. "Merely in a semblance...." The best comment is from another 'Asaph' Psalm (Ps. lxxiii. 20) which has many points in common with the present, where the word answers to "*a dream*" in the corresponding member of the verse.

"*He heapeth up but knoweth not who shall ingather.*" If this Psalm were used, as I have suggested, at the *Asiph* or Feast of *Ingathering* there would be a special significance in this allusion. The verb we have translated "*heapeth up*" is used of "*laying up*" corn or "*gathering*" corn (Gen. xli. 35, 49) and the other word, "*ingather*," is the word from which *Asiph* takes its name and which is constantly used of "*gathering in*" the fruits of the earth.

"*Mere vanity and nothing more is all man's lot.*" I have ventured to transpose this refrain from the end of the 5th verse to the end of the 6th. The words *Kol Adam* are not to be translated "*every man*" but "*the whole* (estate or lot) *of man*" just as in Eccles. xii. 13, "for this is the *whole* (duty) *of man*."

v. 7. "And now what is it that I wait for, Lord?" The verb denotes patient *expectation*, e.g. Gen. xlix. 18, "I have waited for Thy salvation." Compare also Ps. xl. 1 (2). It is a favourite thought with Jeremiah that God Himself is the "*expectation*" of Israel. Thus Jer. xiv. 8, "O Thou *expectation* of Israel, the Saviour thereof in the time of trouble," Jer. xvii. 13, "O YHVH, the *expectation* of Israel, all that forsake Thee shall be ashamed," Jer. l. 7, "Even YHVH, the *expectation* of their fathers."

"*My hope*, &c." This word occurs only here and in Job, Proverbs and Lamentations.

v. 11. "With chastisements of sin...." The same word is used in the parallel Psalm lxxiii. 14, "And my *chastisement* every morning." It denotes that *conviction* which brings the sin home.

PSALM XXXIX.

Let my span-long life claim the hospitality of God's Eternal Home.

12 Hear my prayer, O YHVH,
Give ear unto my cry,
Be not silent to my tears!
For I am a stranger-guest with Thee,
A sojourner as all my fathers were.
13 Leave[a] me a space that I may recover[b] my strength
Before I go hence and be no more seen.

[a] Heb. *look away from me*
[b] or *brighten up*

v. 12. "Hear my prayer...my cry...my tears." As in Ps. v. 1, 2 there is a rising order "*my words*," "*my meditation*," "*the voice of my cry*" so here the appeal to God rises in its pathos unto the heart of Him "*cui omnis voluntas loquitur.*" Jerome has well said, "Clamor in scripturis, non vocis, sed cordis est. Denique ad Moysen dicitur 'Quid clamas ad me?' cum Moyses ante non clamasset.......Et apostolus: 'Clamantes in cordibus nostris, abba pater.'......Quando igitur gemitus noster et conscientia deprecatur, istum clamorem intellegit Deus. Unde dicit et Hieremias: 'Non sileat pupilla oculi mei.' Videte quid dicat, Non taceat pupilla oculi mei. Et aliquando pupilla oculi clamat ad Deum. Utique si clamat, lingua clamat, non pupilla oculi. Sed quomodo clamamus in cordibus nostris, quando gemitu Dominum deprecamur; sic quando lacrimas ad Deum fundimus, eo tempore pupilla oculi nostri clamat ad Dominum." (*Tract. de Psalmo* v).

"*For I am a stranger-guest...a sojourner....*" A *stranger* is one without legal rights; a *sojourner* is one who seeks but a temporary rest on his onward journey. But when the weak appeal to the strong the highest claim may lie in having no claim. Thus Abraham appealed to the Hittites, "And Abraham rose up from before his dead, and spake unto the children of Heth, saying, I am a *stranger* and a *sojourner* with you; give me a possession of a burying-place with you..." (Gen. xxiii. 3 f.). We may also compare the remarkable passage (Lev. xxv. 23 f.) in which the words are used to forbid freehold property in Israel, "And the land shall not be sold in perpetuity; for the land is Mine: for ye are *strangers* and *sojourners* with Me" (see context). If God refuse His children a permanent home on earth it must be because "He hath prepared for them a city." The Writer to the Hebrews reminds us that the holy men of old time "all died in faith, not having received (the full meaning—or, as it were, the freehold of) the promises, but that they saw them and greeted them from afar (i.e. they had a Pisgah-view of them) and confessed themselves to be *strangers* and *pilgrims* upon the earth," Heb. xi. 13. No doubt, in our Psalm, the leading thought in the Psalmist's mind is the plea, so often used by Job, that God would remember the shortness of his time on earth. But when God brought home to Israel (or to Job) the fact that one loved by Him might still be a sufferer upon earth the Pisgah-view of the Home beyond began to open before him.

The words of this verse are placed by the Chronicler upon the lips of David (1 Chron. xxix. 15).

v. 13. The whole of this verse is made of quotations from the Book of Job (Kay, Baethgen). Thus Job vii. 19, "How long wilt Thou not *look away from me*, nor let me alone...?" Job xiv. 6, "*Look away from him* that he may rest...." Job x. 20, "Are not my days few? Cease thou, and let me alone, that I may *take comfort* a little (Heb. *recover my strength* or *brighten up*)." The rare word which we translate "*recover my strength*" is only found in Job ix. 27; x. 20; Amos v. 9 and in our Psalm.

Job x. 21. "Before I go whence I shall not return
            Even to the land of darkness and shadow of death."

Job vii. 8. "Thine eyes shall be upon me, but I shall be no more."

Compare also Job vii. 21.

The above passages, if studied with their context, will go far to prove that the writer of our Psalm is actually quoting from the Book of Job. We have also seen that the whole argument of the Psalm finds its best illustration from that Book.

The reader is asked to compare also the following references or allusions.

160   FIRST COLLECTION, 'DAVIDIC' PSALMS.

```
Job ii. 10, "sin with his lips"                    with Psalm xxxix.   v. 1.
 „  iv. 19, " the moth " (see context)                „     „     „    v. 11.
 „  vii. 1, (the general sense)                       „     „     „    v. 4.
 „  vii. 11, " I will not refrain my mouth &c."       „     „     „    vv. 1, 9.
 „  viii. 9, " our days on earth are a shadow "       „     „     „    v. 5.
 „  ix. 34. " Let Him take His rod away from me &c."  „     „     „    v. 10.
 „  xiii. 21, " Withdraw Thine hand far from me "     „     „     „    v. 10
 „  xl. 4 f., " I will lay mine hand upon my mouth…"  „     „     „    v. 9.
```

PSALM XL.

The composite nature of this Psalm has been recognized by many scholars (Cheyne, Graetz etc.). Indeed it could hardly have been otherwise, since the last five verses (13—17) occur again as a separate Psalm (Ps. lxx.) at the close of the Second Book. The whole tone and character of these verses, which we will call Part II, differs entirely from the joyous tone of the first ten verses (Part I) of the Psalm. If we further examine Parts I and II we see that Part I is full of the thoughts and language of Deutero-Isaiah (see notes) and must therefore be assigned to the early years of the Return from Babylon, while Part II belongs distinctly to the group of Jeremiah-Psalms, being closely parallel with Ps. xxxv. (see notes) in which the influence of Jeremiah is most clearly traced.

We have already seen that Part II occurs again as Ps. lxx., where, like Ps. xxxviii., it has the Title "*For the memorial*" or "*To make remembrance.*" These words signified (see p. 152) that though Israel was deeply conscious of unworthiness before God, yet he knew that God accepted his offering just as He accepted the *azkara* or '*memorial*' of frankincense. Now since Part II is identical with Ps. lxx. we are justified in regarding it as a Psalm of the '*memorial*' or '*remembrance.*'

The chief difficulty is in vv. 11, 12 which come between Parts I and II, and which undoubtedly contain allusions to Part I (see notes) while their sorrowful tone agrees rather with Part II.

I would suggest that these verses were added by a later Psalm-writer, who, living in troublous times, wished to hold up the Thanksgiving for deliverance (Part I) as an appeal to God, while, by uniting it with the Psalm of sorrow (Part II), he seems to suggest that the times of Jeremiah have come back. In other words, he appeals to God by holding up, as it were, two pictures, Israel's *ideal* and Israel's *actual*. Israel's *ideal* (Part I) being the loving devotion of a Son in whose heart his Father's pleasure is his own (v. 6 f.): while, alas, Israel's *actual* is a struggle with enemies within and without, lightened only by the thought that though he is "poor and needy" the Lord is "taking thought" for him (v. 17). There have been many periods in Jewish history when such an appeal of hope deferred might have found expression.

We are now in a position to consider the Christian use of the Psalm, which is, in the Western Church, a Proper Psalm for Good Friday.

We may regard Part I, *i.e. vv.* 1—10, as our ideal, or (which amounts to the same) as the words of Christ, offering with joy man's 'reasonable service' of love (Heb. x. 5—9). Then (*vv.* 11, 12) we stand for one moment face to face with our actual selves; so unlike to the Ideal!

This brings us to Part II, the *azkara*, 'memorial' or 'remembrance' (ἀνάμνησις). This is our *sursum corda*; God in accepting Christ has accepted Man; the frankincense burnt on God's Altar is the pledge that the whole of the offering has been accepted by him (Heb. x. 10).

"As for me—poor and needy though I be—
The Lord is taking thought for me" (*v.* 17).

The Writer of the Epistle to the Hebrews shews us how the Divinely appointed "*remembrance*" or recognition of sins led up to, and found its completion in, the perfect obedience of Christ (Chap. x. 3—10).

PS. XL.

PART I. (*Probably belonging to the early days of the Return from Captivity.*)

Israel, like Jonah, has been rescued from the Deep (Babylon) and, like Jonah, will now fulfil his mission to the World.	1 I waited and^a waited for YHVH, And He hath inclined unto me And heard my cry. 2 For He hath brought me up from the pit of tumult^b, From the miry clay;	^a *waiting I waited* ^b Sept. *of misery*

v. 1. "*I waited and waited...*" The rendering of the E.V. "*I waited patiently*," suggests a virtue of patience which is not implied. The words signify the *intent longing* with which Israel had endured the Captivity (cf. Ps. cxxx. 5). This longing for God had now been rewarded (cf. Is. xxv. 9). There is a fine passage in the Yalkut (and Midrash) on this verse, expressing Israel's one duty of hoping against hope, even for ever (cf. Ps. cxxxi. 3).

"*And heard my cry.*" The word here translated *cry* is always used of a *cry of distress* (Exod. ii. 23, of the cry of Israel in Egypt; 1 Sam. v. 12, of a plague-stricken city; Ps. xviii. 6 (7) see notes; Ps. xxxiv. 15 (16); Ps. xxxix. 12 (13) see notes; Ps. cii. 1 (2); Ps. cxlv. 19; Jer. viii. 19, a cry of captivity; Lam. iii. 56).

v. 2. "*For He hath brought me forth from the pit of tumult.*" 'The pit,' 'the mire,' 'the deep waters,' 'the waterflood,' &c. were often used in Hebrew poetry to picture Babylon, that land of waters, which like a great sea-monster had swallowed up Israel. Compare the parallel Psalm, lxix. 1, 14 f., to which this is indeed the answer. Thus the Yalkut on Zech. i. 8 interprets '*the deep*'

FIRST COLLECTION, 'DAVIDIC' PSALMS.

And hath set my feet upon upon a rock,
Giving me firm treading.
3 And hath put a New Song in my mouth,
A Praise-song to our God;

The Nations will be drawn to God as the only true refuge.

Many shall see and shall fear,
And shall put their trust in YHVH.
4 Oh happy is the man[a] that made YHVH his trust[a],   [a] Jer. xvii.
And did not turn to the proud-ones[b],   [b] Sept. *v ties*
Or to apostates[c] with their lies.   [c] doubtful word

God's mercies in the past are numberless, and point to an infinity of Love yet to be revealed.

5 Great things hast Thou done—
    Thou art YHVH, my God!
Thy marvels and Thy purposes to usward—
    There is none that compareth with Thee!—
Would I tell them and speak of them;
They outnumber all recounting.

as Babylon, and quotes Is. xliv. 27. See also Pss. xxx. and xxxi. (pp. 126 ff.), which should be read in connexion with Part I. of the present Psalm, containing as they do the same allusions to the deliverance of Israel from Babylon as of a Jonah from the waters (cf. note on *v.* 4).

"*Giving me firm treading.*" Just as in the parallel Psalm (xxxi. 8), where he says, Thou "*hast set my feet at large.*"

v. 3. "*And He hath put a New Song...*" The "*New Song*" refers to the late deliverance from Babylon. See note on Ps. xxxiii. 3, p. 140.

"*Many shall see and shall fear...*" It is a frequent thought in Deutero-Isaiah that the Gentiles would be drawn to God by witnessing His great work in the redemption of Israel from Babylon (see Isaiah xli. 5; xlv. 22; xlix. 7; lii. 11; lv. 5; lx. 5, &c.).

v. 4. "*Oh happy is the man that made YHVH his trust.*" These words must be explained from the famous passage Jer. xvii. 5—7, which, as we have seen, also underlies Psalm i.

The words of Jeremiah are, "Cursed is the man who trusteth in man......and turneth away his heart from YHVH......Blessed is the man (*geber*, same word as in Psalm) who trusteth in YHVH (cf. *v.* 4 of Psalm) and YHVH becomes his trust (*mibtaḥ*, same word as in Psalm)."

If this passage of Jeremiah was in the writer's mind we can understand why he should have added "*And did not turn to the proud-ones, Or to apostates with their lies.*" Commentators differ as to the exact meaning of these latter words, but the general sense is clear: they indicate a trust in the arm of flesh instead of a trust in God. Such trust is a refuge of lies (Is. xxviii. 15, 17).

The Hebrew is different, but the meaning is identical with Ps. xxxi. 6, "Thou hatest *those that observe vain idols: But as for me...*" It must be noted that these words occur in Jonah ii. 8 f. "*those that observe vain idols* forsake their own mercy (compare Jer. xvii. 5—7 quoted above) *But as for me*, &c." Thus we obtain another link in the chain which binds Pss. xxx., xxxi. and xl. to the Book of Jonah.

The connexion of thought between verses 3 and 4 would seem to be as follows:—'The deliverance from Babylon has not only put a new song in our mouth but it is a vindication of our God before the world: many will see it and be converted to trust in Him, for now they see that the Prophets were right when they said that the only strength and happiness for man is to make God, and not flesh, his trust.'

v. 5. "*Great things*, &c." The word signifies both *great* and *manifold*. In the present passage it directs thought to the *manifold* mercies which God had shewn to Israel in the past (see Neh. ix. 19, 27, 28, 30, 31, 35).

The thought of these manifold deliverances in the past leads naturally to the Covenant Name of

PSALM XL.   163

This Love demands, 6 Sacrifice and oblation Thou didst not delight^a in;—   * v. 7
not sacrifice, but, love   Mine ears hast Thou opened—
in return: I offer my-
self to do His Will,   Burnt-offering and sin-offering Thou didst not ask;
                         7 Then said I, "Lo I come,"
                         With the roll of the Book that is written about me,

God, "*Thou art YHVH* (the Eternal) *my God!*" (cf. Mal. iii. 6). All the mercies that have been shewn in the history of the Nation are but a few utterances of the infinite mercy of the Eternal—*Oh thy marvels and Thy purposes to usward!* Thy "*marvels*" have been shewn, and they seem infinite, "*Would I tell them and speak of them They outnumber all recounting.*" What, then, must Thy "*purposes*" be which still remain to usward? We may compare St Paul's use of the word 'mystery' (Eph. i. 9; iii. 9; Col. i. 26, 27, &c.) as the unfolding of a loving purpose of God.

v. 6. "*Sacrifice and oblation*," &c. The idea that prompted sacrifice was in itself right and good, representing as it did man's tribute of gratitude to God, man's desire to give his best. But what is man's best? The Prophets recognized that sacrifice, as a mere ritual act, was useless, and that, even at the best, it was only a stage in the education of man (see 1 Sam. xv. 22; Amos v. 21—24; Hos. vi. 6; Is. i. 11—13; Mic. vi. 6—8; Jer. vii. 22 f.; Ps. li. 16).

The fact that sacrifice was impossible all through the long years of the Captivity tended, under God's Providence, to create a nobler idea of sacrifice as the gift of self. No doubt there was a reaction in later times, but the thought of the Suffering Servant was never afterwards lost to Israel.

"*Mine ears hast Thou opened.*" Literally, "*Ears Thou hast dug for me.*" Two interpretations are given of these strange words and both seem to me to be unsatisfactory.

(i) They have been explained from Exod. xxi. 1—6, where a slave who loved his master might decline to accept his freedom, in which case "his master *shall bore his ear* with an awl; and he shall serve him for ever." But the language here is entirely different; the word for "*bore*" is from a different root, and surely if the Psalmist had intended an allusion to such a custom he would have said "mine ear" not "mine ears."

(ii) The other interpretation is somewhat better, and has the authority of Cheyne and Delitzsch, viz. 'Thou hast given me the faculty of hearing and obeying Thy Will.' But against this we may argue that the *Hebrew* idiom for an 'open ear' requires a different verb, *galah* (see Job xxxiii. 16; xxxvi. 10, 15; 1 Sam. xx. 12; xxii. 8; 11 Sam. vii. 27; Ruth iv. 4, &c.); or *pathah* (Is. xxxv. 5; xlviii. 8); or *paqah* (Is. xlii. 20); or, better still, the word used in Is. l. 4, when the Suffering Servant says, "morning by morning He *wakeneth for me the ear* so as to hear," &c. Thus both interpretations are attended with difficulty; if however the present text be correct I have no better solution to give; we must however note that the Septuagint had most certainly a different text before them when they translated σῶμα δὲ κατηρτίσω μοι, i.e. "*a body Thou hast prepared* (or *made firm*) *for me.*" Speaking of these words (on Heb. x. 4) Dr Westcott says, "There can be no question that this is the true reading of the Greek. The conjecture that ϹⲰⲘⲀ is an early blunder for ⲰⲦⲒⲀ (the reading of the other Greek versions) cannot be maintained in the face of the evidence." I cannot however believe that the Septuagint used these words as a free paraphrase to express the general meaning of our present Hebrew text: indeed the verb, κατηρτίσω μοι, shews that they read לי כוננת instead of לי כרית (see Heb. and Sept. on Ps. lxviii. 10). If then the Septuagint, which is the oldest translation, had a different Hebrew text before them may it not be that that text represented the true reading? The Septuagint would require some such text as the following אז אמר לי כוננת, i.e. "*Then a body Thou didst prepare* (or *make strong*) *for me.*" The Hebrew word that I have suggested for *body* is twice used of Israel as the Suffering Servant, Is. l. 6, "I gave my *body* to the smiters." Is. li. 23, "Thou hast laid thy *body* to the ground." This part of the Psalm is, as we have seen, full of the thoughts and language of Deutero-Isaiah, such a conception therefore of Israel as offering his body to suffer and fulfil God's will would be quite in accordance with the spirit of the Psalm (compare also Heb. x. 5—10, and especially the argument founded on the word *body* in *v.* 10).

v. 7 f. "*With the roll of the Book,*" &c. If we are right in ascribing this Psalm to the early days of the Return from Babylon then the "*roll of the Book*" would be the Book of Deuteronomy,

21—2

and thus to fulfil Israel's mission to the World.

8 To do Thy will, my God, I do delight^a,
And Thy Law is in my inmost heart.
9 I tell the good-news of Righteousness
In the full assembly;
Lo I withhold not my lips;
Thou, YHVH, Thou knowest it.
10 Thy Righteousness I hide not within my heart;
Thy faithfulness and Thy salvation I tell;
I keep not back Thy mercy and truth
From the full assembly.

which, from the reforms of Josiah, had become essentially the "King's Book" (see Deut. xvii. 14—20; cf. II Kings xxii. 11). This Book was to be the King's *Vade Mecum*, "And it shall be, when he sitteth upon the throne of his kingdom, that he shall write him a copy of this Law in a book, out of that which is before the priests the Levites: and it shall be with him, and he shall read therein all the days of his life...."

Thus when the Psalmist pictures the happy future he sees Israel, represented by the ideal King, with God's Law in his hand as the guide of his life and written also in his heart (v. 8 of Jer. xxxi. 33) as his heart's chief joy. May we not say that the Book of Deuteronomy was in a special way Christ's Book? The way in which He used it to meet His temptations (Matt. iv. 4, 7, 10) and to sum up the whole duty of man (Matt. xxii. 37; Luke x. 27; Mark xii. 29) would seem to shew that He had literally made it a constant study, and though He does not hesitate to go beyond its precepts (Matt. v. 31; xix. 7 f.; cf. Deut. xxiv. 1; Matt. v. 43; cf. Deut. xxiii. 6), yet even so He is only obeying the spirit of Deuteronomy by insisting on a deeper interpretation of the love of God and man.

The rendering of the Sept. and Vulgate, which may be translated "*At the head of the Book*" directed Patristic thought to the protevangelium, some writers (e.g. St Jerome, St Ambrose) referring it to the opening words of the Bible, "In the beginning God created," &c. (Gen. i. 1); others (e.g. Theophylact) to the words, "Let us make man in our Image...," (Gen. i. 26); others again (e.g. St Isidore) find the first promise of the Incarnation in Gen. i. 23, "This is now bone of my bone," &c. (see Neale's Commentary and Suicer *s.v.* κεφαλίς). St Jerome also finds an allusion to the first verse of St John's Gospel, for, in his comment on this Psalm he writes, "propterea laetus in mundum venio. Et de me scribitur: 'In principio erat Verbum, et Verbum erat apud Deum, et Deus erat Verbum'" (*Comment. in Psalmos*, Morin, p. 48).

May it not be that this interpretation influenced the words with which the writer to the Hebrews introduces the quotation of the text in Heb. x. 5 ff.? "Therefore *when He entereth into the world*, He saith, 'Sacrifice and offering.......' Then said I, Lo, I come, in the roll of the Book (or *at the (very) head of the Book*) it is written of Me, to do Thy will, O God."

v. 9. "*I tell the Good-News of Righteousness*." Even if this verse stood alone it would abundantly prove the influence of Deutero-Isaiah. This argument will appeal chiefly to the Hebrew scholar, but the English reader should compare Is. xli. 27; xlii. 6; lxi. 1.

PSALM XL.

Two verses added by a later Editor who wished to adapt the above Psalm to the needs of his own time and to unite it with an earlier Psalm of the time of Jeremiah.

But alas the actual is still far from the ideal!

11 O YHVH do not THOU[a] "withhold[b]" Thy mercy from me, [a] emphatic
Let "Thy mercy and truth[c]" ever preserve me: [b] v. 9
12 For evils have compassed me "beyond number[d],"   [c] v. 10
Mine iniquities[e] overtake me,   [d] v. 5
So that I cannot see,   [e] or punishments
They "outnumber[f]" the hairs of my head,   [f] v. 5
And mine heart hath failed me.

PART II. (*An independent Psalm which occurs again as Ps. lxx. and which probably belongs to the times of Jeremiah.*)

13 "Be pleased, O YHVH, to deliver me;
O YHVH speed to my help.

vv. 11, 12. Just as Isaiah once took an old prophecy of Israel's glory in the latter days (Is. ii. 1—4) and then, in the verses that follow, sharply contrasted this ideal with Israel's sad present, so, I suggest, a later Psalmist, possibly during the troubles of the Persian period, to have taken this Psalm of Israel's ideal, and to have held it up before God as a plea for mercy. I have placed in inverted commas the words in which he alludes to that earlier Psalm. Thus, in that earlier Psalm, Israel had so overflowed with God's "*mercy and truth*" that he could not "*withhold*" his lips" from utterance (*vv.* 9, 10), but now, alas, instead of giving to the heathen he must pray to receive for himself (*v.* 11). In that earlier Psalm God's mercies had been "*beyond number*" (*v.* 5); but now Israel can see nothing but "evils" and sorrows which are "*beyond number*," nay which "*outnumber*" the hairs of his head (*v.* 12).

Another point of connexion, not obvious to the English reader, lies in the emphatic use of *Thou* in *v.* 11; and also in the rare word which we translate "compassed" in *v.* 12. The *locus classicus* for the use of this word is Jonah ii. 5 (6), "The waters *compassed* me," &c.: but we have already seen that Part I. is full of the thought of Jonah (see notes on *vv.* 2, 4).

vv. 13—17. These verses occur again in the Elohistic Psalm lxx. with slight various readings, all of which might be accounted for as mistakes of spelling. If the reader will verify the references to Ps. xxxv. he will see that the standpoint of these verses is exactly that of the former Psalm, which, as we have seen, is so strongly influenced by Jeremiah.

The reader is also asked to notice the close correspondence between the Psalms which form the closing group of Book I. and those which close Book II. We shall return to this point when we come to consider those Psalms in their proper place in the Second Collection.

v. 13. This verse, which is practically identical with the 1st verse of Ps. lxx., is there translated by the Vulgate

"Deus, in adjutorium meum intende:
Domine, ad adjuvandum me festina."

These words were adopted in the Sarum use as the Versicles after the Lord's Prayer at Matins: indeed, as Blunt shews (*Annotated Book of Common Prayer*), "These versicles and responses have been used time immemorial as the opening of the daily service of praise which the Church

14 Let them be shamed^a and confounded together
That are seeking my soul [to destroy it]^b;
Let them be turned backward and disgraced
That find pleasure in my misfortune^c.
15 Let them be dumbfounded^d to their shame
That say [unto me] "Aha, Aha^e!"
16 Let all that seek Thee be joyful and glad in Thee;
Let them that love Thy salvation ever say,
 "YHVH be magnified^f."
17 As for me^g—poor and needy—
The Lord^h taketh thoughtⁱ for me.
My Helper, my Deliverer Thou art:
My God, do not delay!"

---

continually offers to God." Blunt quotes an old exposition of these versicles as follows: "And take heed that all this verse, both that part which is said of one alone, and that which is answered of all together, are said in the singular number: as when ye say 'mine' or 'me' and not 'our' or 'us,' in token that ye begin your praising and prayer in the person of holy Church, which is one, and not many." So in the old English Prymer the singular number was retained,

"God, take heede to myn help:
Lord hie thee to help me";

but in the revision of 1552 the pronouns were changed to the plural,

V. "O God, make speed to save us
R. O Lord, make haste to help us."

Would it not be well for our Public Worship if, having learnt the lesson of individualism, we could once more take up the older thought of the solidarity of the Church?

In passing I may remark that the juxtaposition of these Versicles is most suggestive. First we have a verse whose context points to the unsatisfactory nature of any sacrifice man can offer (Ps. li. 15, see context), and this is followed by the verse we have already quoted from Ps. lxx., the Psalm of the 'Memorial' or 'Remembrance.' Blunt well says that these Versicles "are the *Sursum Corda* of the Daily Service."

PSALM XLI.

Psalm xli., like Ps. xl., is a theodicy. As in Ps. xl. we saw Israel fulfilling his *Duty to God*, yet not finding at once the reward he might have looked for, so in Ps. xli. we find him fulfilling his *Duty to man*, yet without the promised reward of earthly happiness. It consists of three Parts, which are closely related to one another. Part I has 3 verses (a, b, c). Part II has 6 verses, which so correspond with Part I that they may be represented by a_1, b_1, c_1, a_2, b_2, c_2 (see notes). Part III has 3 verses which answer both to Parts I and II, and which may therefore be represented by a_3, b_3, c_3. Part I gives, in a bold sketch, the promise of Deuteronomy, with special reference to the Second[1] Table of the Covenant, the Duty to man. Israel has fulfilled this duty, he has been merciful. How then stands the promise? Surely he should obtain mercy, and should inherit the Land (*vv*. 1—3).

Part II (*vv*. 4—9) contrasts this promise with the sad reality. Israel, the merciful, has found on earth anything but mercy (see notes): Job's experience is repeated in his case.

In Part III (*vv*. 10—12) Israel appeals, like Job, from the cruelty of man to the faithfulness of God.

Such I believe to be, historically, the origin of the Psalm, which, like others of this group, should be studied with constant reference to the Book of Job.

Compared with the Nations of the World Israel represented the virtue of humanity, *man* as contrasted with the *beasts* (Dan. vii., *v*. 3 ff.: *v*. 13), this Psalm therefore, while giving the experience of Israel, is well fitted to depict the reception that the Christ would meet, not from Judas only, but from an ungrateful world.

When once we have realized that the problems which were fought out in the experience of Israel as a Nation were solved in the personal experience of Christ we shall obtain that light on social and national duties which our own age is feeling after.

[1] The reader will observe that Ps. xl., on the contrary, deals rather with the Duty to God, i.e. with the First Table of the Covenant.

PS. XLI.

The merciful man (Israel) should find mercy and happiness on earth.

(*a*) 1 Happy is he who is considerate for the afflicted;
YHVH will deliver him in the evil day:
(*b*) 2 YHVH will guard him and give him life,
That he may be happy in the Land;
Nor wilt Thou give him up to his foes' desire:
(*c*) 3 YHVH will support him on the couch of languishing;
Thou turnest all his bed for him in sickness.

But I (Israel) have found just the reverse!

(*a*₁) 4 But I say, YHVH be gracious unto me!
Heal my soul, for I have sinned against Thee.

v. 1. "*Happy is...*" It is unfortunate for the English reader that this word which occurs twenty-five times in the Psalter should have been translated in the E.V. by the word "*blessed*" nineteen times, and six times by the word "*happy*," which is the true meaning. The Hebrew has two distinct words for "*happy*" and "*blessed*," and though in the Jewish mind the two thoughts were more nearly related than they were with us, still the distinction should always be observed; indeed if in the present passage we were to translate "*Blessed is...*" we should lose the whole point of the passage, which is to indicate that *earthly prosperity* and *happiness* is the natural result which Israel had been led to expect in return for acts of kindness to the afflicted.

If we omit the Preface (Pss. i., ii.) which begins and ends with this word (Ps. i. 1; ii. 12), we note that it occurs six times in the First Collection, and that these six instances are in, what we may call, the present group of Psalms (xxxii. 1, 2; xxxiii. 12; xxxiv. 8 (9); xl. 4 (5); xli. 1 (2)). The key-note to all these passages is Deut. xxxiii. 29, "Happy art thou, O Israel... O people saved by VHVH." Thus in Ps. xxxii. 1, 2 we have the happiness of the Nation for whom God has found Atonement; in Ps. xxxiii. 12 the happiness of the People He has chosen for His own heritage: in Ps. xxxiv. 8 (see p. 32) the whole experience of life is used to point the moral that the Covenant-keeping People will "never lack one good thing"; in Ps. xl. 4 (see note) we come to the happiness of Israel, rewarded because he "made VHVH his trust." We note that this passage, like Ps. i., is founded upon Jer. xvii. 5—7 (where, however, Jeremiah does not say "*Happy* is the man..." but "*Blessed* is the man..." Perhaps his own experience had taught him the distinction?) We also saw that in Ps. xl. (Part I.) Israel was filled with the spirit of philanthropy, the spirit indeed of Deutero-Isaiah. If, before the Captivity, he had been a Jonah in his exclusiveness, now, after his deliverance, he is a Jonah in his missionary zeal. He has then been "*considerate for the afflicted*," and now at length may expect in return the favour of God and the gratitude of man. This is the subject of Ps. xli. 1—3. The best comment is Job xxix. 12 ff., where the same problem is discussed, "I delivered the poor that cried, The fatherless also, that had none to help him ...... Then I said I shall die in my nest, And I shall multiply my days as the sand: My root is spread out to the waters (cf. Jer. xvii. 5—7) &c.,... but now" &c. (see Chap. xxx.).

v. 2. "*That he may be happy in the Land.*"—The Second Table of the Covenant relates to the Duty to man. The reward of this Second Table is to inherit the Land. Israel has fulfilled this Duty and has reason to expect the promise of Deuteronomy.

v. 4. "*But I say...*" The thought is exactly similar to that of Job xxx. 1, quoted above (note *v*. 1). There is a relation between the verses 1—3 and 4—9 which may be indicated thus:—

PSALM XLI.

(b_1) 5 My foes bespeak evil for me;
"When will he die and his name perish?"
(c_1) 6 If he visit me he speaketh falsehood,
His heart gathereth to itself slander;
When he goeth forth he utters it.
(a_2) 7 They all whisper together—these haters of mine;
Against me, they think that the evil is mine^a: ^a Job xi. 6;
                                                               xxii. 5 ff.;
(b_2) 8 "Some heavy crime is cleaving to him,   Is. liii. 4
And now he is down he will never again rise."
(c_2) 9 Even my familiar friend whom I trusted—
He that eateth my bread—hath lifted the heel against
me.

But, in spite of all, (a_3) 10 But Thou, YHVH, be gracious and raise me up
my hope is in God.   So that I may reward^b them.   ^b Contrast Ps.
                                                                       xxxv. 12;
                                                                       xxxviii. 20
                                                                       (21)

vv. 1—3. I had reasonably expected.   *vv. 6—9. I have found, on the contrary.*
(a) v. 1. Forgiveness of sins (cf. *the evil day*).   (a_1, a_2) v. 4 with v. 7. The sense of sin op-
                                                      presses me, and is burdened by the unkind
                                                      judgments of men.
(b) v. 2. Protection from foes and long, happy life   (b_1, b_2) v. 5 with v. 8. Foes count on my speedy
in the Land of Promise.   death and think it the fit reward of some
                                                      great crime!
(c) v. 3. Comfort and support on the bed of   (c_1, c_2) v. 6 with v. 9. Sick-bed visitors indeed!
sickness.   Job's comforters!
                                                      Even my own trusted friend!

v. 9. "*Even my familiar friend...*" Literally "*the man of my peace,*" a phrase found in
Jeremiah (xx. 10; xxxviii. 22). The reader will again notice the famous passage Jer. xx. to which
we have had occasion to refer so frequently in this group of Psalms. The only other passage in
which this phrase is found is in the Prophecy of Obadiah against Edom, a prophecy which occurs
also in Jer. xlix. 7—22. The words (Obad. v. 7) are as follows:—"All the men of thy covenant
have deceived thee; thy familiar friends (*men of thy peace*) have prevailed against thee; thy very
bread(eaters) have put a wound on thee." Edom has been faithless to his 'brother' Israel and will
himself experience the ingratitude that he has shewn. We are not to think of an individual traitor
like Ahithophel, but rather of an Edom who in the hour of Israel's humiliation was false to the ties
of blood (cf. Ps. cxxxvii. 7; Lam. iv. 22). This desertion, which was so keenly felt by Israel, was
experienced in all its fulness by our Lord, who quotes this verse (St John xiii. 18).

v. 10. The Midrash on this verse is worth translating. It is as follows:—"'*And Thou YHVH
be gracious unto me and raise me up again, that I may requite them.*' He said to him, 'David, what
wouldst thou requite them? evil?' He answered, 'God forbid! *for as for me, when they were sick
my clothing was sackcloth* (Ps. xxxv. 13), but when I am sick they pray for me that I may die;
yet when they are sick I pray for them and cover myself with sackcloth, *I afflict my soul with
fasting.*' They said to him, 'David, who knows what that sackcloth meant, and what it was that
thou didst pray for them?' He answered, 'If so let it come upon myself, *and let my prayer return
into mine own bosom* (Ps. xxxv. 13), therefore (I say), *Thou, YHVH, be gracious unto me.*' Then
the Holy One, blessed be He, said, 'Seeing that thou hast done this I know indeed that thou hast
pleasure in Me.'"

K.

170   FIRST COLLECTION, 'DAVIDIC' PSALMS.

(b_2) 11 Hereby shall I know that Thou hast pleasure in me,
In that my foe does not triumph over me.
(c_2) 12 As for me, in mine integrity Thou upholdest me,
And settest me before Thy Face for ever.

Ascription of praise,   13 Blessed be YHVH, the God of Israel,
to close Book I.   From Aeon to Aeon!
                         Amen and Amen!

---

vv. 10—12. The general relation of these verses, which we have called Part III., to the expectation of Israel (Part I.) as contrasted with the actual experience of Israel (Part II.), may be shewn in a paraphrase as follows:—

v. 10 with *vv.* 1, 4 and 7, 'I, the merciful, looked indeed for mercy (*a*). But, on earth, men did their utmost to shut out the mercy of heaven (a_1 with a_2). But, in spite of this I can still say, "*be gracious unto me*" (cf. *v.* 10 with *v.* 4). I know that Thou wilt raise me up, even though it be from the gates of death, and I, the merciful, shall reward them.' [N.B. It is quite possible that on the lips of the Psalmist these last words denoted vengeance: but if so he fell short of his own ideal of the merciful man. The Christian will best interpret the spirit of the words by reading them in the spirit of Christ.]

v. 11 with *vv.* 2, 5 and 8, 'I, the merciful, looked for long and happy days in the Land, shielded from enemies (*b*). But, on earth, enemies were all round me, not only gloating over my troubles, but, hardest of all, claiming them to spring from the anger of my God against some horrible sin of mine (b_1 with b_2). But, in spite of this, I commit my cause to God: He will shew openly before the world that *He does take pleasure in me*' (*v.* 11).

v. 12 with *vv.* 3, 6 and 9. 'I, having shewn mercy to others, looked for comfort and support in my own sickness (*c*). But, on earth, my sick-bed visitors merely watched me for evil (c_1), and those that should have been bound to me by every sacred tie were ready to spurn me with the heel (c_2). But, in spite of all this, God *is* my support (cf. *v.* 12 with *v.* 3). He upholds me, so that I am not alone; He sets me before His Face for ever, so that the old promise finds in my case a deeper meaning, "Thou turnest all his bed for him in sickness."'

CAMBRIDGE: PRINTED BY J. AND C. F. CLAY, AT THE UNIVERSITY PRESS.

www.ingramcontent.com/pod-product-compliance
Lightning Source LLC
Chambersburg PA
CBHW020249170426
43202CB00008B/291